Second Workshop on Natural Language Processing and Computational Social Science 2017

Held at ACL 2017

Vancouver, Canada
3 August 2017

ISBN: 978-1-5108-4579-4

ACL 2017

The 55th Annual Meeting of the
Association for Computational Linguistics

Proceedings of the Second Workshop on Natural Language
Processing and Computational Social Science

August 3, 2017
Vancouver, Canada

Introduction

Welcome to the Second Workshop on NLP and Computational Social Science!
After a successful installation last year, we again received a large number of high-quality submission this year, an indication that interest in the topic is growing. We received 31 submissions, and due to a rigorous review process by our committee, we accepted 18. The program this year includes 4 papers presented as spotlight talks, and 14 posters.

We are especially excited to see so many submissions from outside of NLP, and hope to continue the tradition to foster a dialogue between NLP researchers and users of NLP technology in the social sciences.

We are also glad to present a fantastic selection of invited speakers from various aspects of computational social science.

We would like to thank all authors of the accepted papers, our invited speakers, and the fantastic organizing committee that made this workshop possible, and, last but not least, all attendees!
The NLP and CSS workshop organizing team

Organizers:

Dirk Hovy (University of Copenhagen), Svitlana Volkova (PNNL), David Bamman (UC Berkeley), David Jurgens (Stanford), Brendan O'Connor (UMass Amherst), Oren Tsur (Harvard/Northeastern) and A. Seza Doğruöz (independent researcher)

Program Committee:

Natalie Ahn
Nikolaos Aletras
Kristen M. Altenburger
Tim Althoff
Timothy Baldwin
John Beieler
Eric Bell
Reihane Boghrati
Kalina Bontcheva
Ryan Boyd
Kaiping Chen
Munmun De Choudhury
Matthew Denny
Valery Dzutsati
Jacob Eisenstein
Jesse Freitas
Justin Garten
Dan Goldwasser
William L. Hamilton
Oul Han
Abram Handler
Marti A. Hearst
Graeme Hirst
Eduard Hovy
Loring Ingraham
Kristen Johnson
Kenneth Joseph
Sunghwan Mac Kim
Vivek Kulkarni
Vasileios Lampos
Corey Lester
Kate Loveys
Peter Makarov
Rada Mihalcea
Slava Mikhaylov
Dong Nguyen
Alice Oh
Cecile Paris
Michael J. Paul
Thierry Poibeau
Christopher Potts

Adam Poulston
Vinodkumar Prabhakaran
Daniel Preoţiuc-Pietro
Sravana Reddy
Rebecca Resnik
Ludovic Rheault
Molly Roberts
Pedro Rodriguez
Carolyn Rose
Sara Rosenthal
Derek Ruths
Fiona Shen-Bayh
Mark Stevenson
Brandon Stewart
Ian Stewart
Anders Søgaard
Rachael Tatman
Rob Voigt
Stephen Wan
Alex Wang
Zeerak Waseem
Swede White
Steven Wilson

Invited Speaker:

Lyle Ungar, University of Pennsylvania
Gideon Mann, Bloomberg
Brandon Stewart, Princeton

Table of Contents

Workshop Program

Aug-3-2017

9:00–10:30   **Session 1**

9:00–9:15   *Welcome*
Organizers

9:15–10:00   *Invited Talk 1*

10:00–10:30   **Spotlight Paper Session**

10:00–10:15   *Language-independent Gender Prediction on Twitter*
Nikola Ljubešić, Darja Fišer and Tomaž Erjavec

10:15–10:30   *When does a compliment become sexist? Analysis and classification of ambivalent sexism using twitter data*
Akshita Jha and Radhika Mamidi

10:30–11:00   *Morning coffee break*

11:00–12:15   **Session 2**

11:00–11:45   *Invited Talk: Measuring Psychological Traits using Social Media*
Lyle Ungar

11:45–12:15   Spotlight Paper Session

11:45–12:00   *Personality Driven Differences in Paraphrase Preference*
Daniel Preoţiuc-Pietro, Jordan Carpenter and Lyle Ungar

12:00–12:15   *Never Tell Me the Odds: How Belief Dynamics Shape Audience Experience (non-archival)*
Shengli Hu

12:15–14:00   *Lunch break*

14:00–15:30   Session 3

14:00–14:45   *Invited Talk: The War on Facts*
Gideon Mann

14:45–15:30   One-minute-madness paper presentation

14:45–14:48   *community2vec: Vector representations of online communities encode semantic relationships*
Trevor Martin

14:48–14:51   *Telling Apart Tweets Associated with Controversial versus Non-Controversial Topics*
Aseel Addawood, Rezvaneh Rezapour, Omid Abdar and Jana Diesner

14:51–14:54   *Cross-Lingual Classification of Topics in Political Texts*
Goran Glavaš, Federico Nanni and Simone Paolo Ponzetto

14:54–14:57   *The Role of Network Structure for Gender Prediction (non-archival)*
Kristen M. Altenburger and Johan Ugander

14:57–15:00   *The Role of Party and Incumbency in Identification of Argumentation Strategies in Political Debate (non-archival)*
Justin Garten, Kenji Sagae, Zahra Kamel, Nitika Awasthi and Morteza Dehghani

15:00–15:03   *Mining Social Science Publications for Survey Variables*
Andrea Zielinski and Peter Mutschke

15:03–15:06   *Linguistic Markers of Influence in Informal Interactions*
Shrimai Prabhumoye, Samridhi Choudhary, Evangelia Spiliopoulou, Christopher Bogart, Carolyn Rose and Alan W Black

15:06–15:09   *Non-lexical Features Encode Political Affiliation on Twitter*
Rachael Tatman, Leo Stewart, Amandalynne Paullada and Emma Spiro

15:09–15:12   *Syntactic Alignment in Power Relations (non-archival)*
Reihane Boghrati, Justin Garten and Morteza Dehghani

15:12–15:15   *Modelling Participation in Small Group Social Sequences with Markov Rewards Analysis*
Gabriel Murray

15:15–15:18   *Code-Switching as a Social Act: The Case of Arabic Wikipedia Talk Pages*
Michael Yoder, Shruti Rijhwani, Carolyn Rosé and Lori Levin

15:18–15:21   *How Does Twitter User Behavior Vary Across Demographic Groups?*
Zach Wood-Doughty, Michael Smith, David Broniatowski and Mark Dredze

15:21–15:24   *Ideological Phrase Indicators for Classification of Political Discourse Framing on Twitter*
Kristen Johnson, I-Ta Lee and Dan Goldwasser

15:24–15:27   *Market Evolution of Sharing Economy vs. Traditional Platforms: A Natural Language Processing Approach*
Mohsen Mosleh and Babak Heydari

15:30–16:45   *Coffee break and posters*

16:45–17:45   Session 4

16:45–17:30   *Invited Talk*
Brandon Stewart

17:30–17:45   *Closing remarks and wrap-up*
Organizers

Language-independent Gender Prediction on Twitter

Nikola Ljubešić
Dept. of Knowledge Technologies
Jožef Stefan Institute
Jamova cesta 39
1000 Ljubljana, Slovenia
nikola.ljubesic@ijs.si

Darja Fišer
Faculty of Arts
University of Ljubljana
Aškerčeva cesta 2
1000 Ljubljana, Slovenia
darja.fiser@ff.uni-lj.si

Tomaž Erjavec
Dept. of Knowledge Technologies
Jožef Stefan Institute
Jamova cesta 39
1000 Ljubljana, Slovenia
tomaz.erjavec@ijs.si

Abstract

In this paper we present a set of experiments and analyses on predicting the gender of Twitter users based on language-independent features extracted either from the text or the metadata of users' tweets. We perform our experiments on the TwiSty dataset containing manual gender annotations for users speaking six different languages. Our classification results show that, while the prediction model based on language-independent features performs worse than the bag-of-words model when training and testing on the same language, it regularly outperforms the bag-of-words model when applied to different languages, showing very stable results across various languages. Finally we perform a comparative analysis of feature effect sizes across the six languages and show that differences in our features correspond to cultural distances.

1 Introduction

Gender prediction is a well-established task in author profiling, useful for a series of downstream analyses (Schler et al., 2006; Schwartz et al., 2013; Bamman et al., 2014) as well as predictive model improvements (Hovy, 2015). Most existing work on predicting gender focuses on exploiting the linguistic production of the users (Koppel et al., 2003; Schler et al., 2006; Kucukyilmaz et al., 2006; Burger et al., 2011; Miller et al., 2012; Rangel et al., 2016), just rarely using non-linguistic information such as metadata (Plank and Hovy, 2015) or visual information (Alowibdi et al., 2013).

In this paper we investigate the possibility of predicting gender of a Twitter user regardless of the language used in his or her tweets. We perform our experiments on an existing dataset of Twitter users speaking six different languages that were manually annotated for their gender. Our language-independent gender predictor relies on general linguistic features, such as the usage of punctuation, and non-linguistic features calculated from Twitter metadata, such as the user interaction in the form of replying, retweeting and favoriting, time of posting, color choices, client usage etc.

The potential of a language-independent procedure for gender prediction is substantial both for the field of natural language processing where using extra-linguistic variables is currently gaining momentum, as well as disciplines from social sciences and the humanities working with user-generated content, where such factors have a long tradition. We believe that building such language-independent procedures is the only tractable way of moving forward given the number of different languages used in social media and the existence of training data only for a few high-density languages.

In the next section we briefly describe the dataset we performed our experiments on, in Section 3 we describe our language-independent features, in Section 4 we give the experimental setup of our gender prediction experiments, while in Section 5 we present the gender prediction results, as well as a series of analyses of the feature spaces across languages. In Section 6 we give some conclusions and directions for further research.

1

Proceedings of the Second Workshop on Natural Language Processing and Computational Social Science, pages 1–6,
Vancouver, Canada, August 3, 2017. ©2017 Association for Computational Linguistics

2   The Dataset

In our experiments we fully rely on the TwiSty corpus (Verhoeven et al., 2016) which was developed for research in author profiling. It contains personality (MBTI) and gender annotations for a total of 18,168 authors posting in German, Italian, Dutch, French, Portuguese or Spanish. The manual gender annotations in the TwiSty corpus are based on the user's name, handle, description and profile picture and follow the performative view of gender, i.e., that gender is discriminated by performances that respond to societal norms or conventions (Larson, 2017). The corpus is distributed in the form of Twitter user IDs and specific tweet IDs of that user.

In this work we use only the user IDs and their gender and language annotations to collect timelines of users through the Twitter API. For each user we collect up to 3,200 tweets (API restriction) and discard users with less than 100 tweets. By doing so we collected 45 million tweets for 16,156 users across the six languages.

3   The Features

In this section we present the 51 user-level features which we consider to be good feature candidates for language-independent gender prediction. These features follow one of the four following feature types:

- `perc` - percentage of user tweets satisfying a condition (like the percentage of tweets containing emojis)

- `mean` - mean of a continuous tweet-level variable (like the mean of the posting hour)

- `med` - median of a continuous tweet-level variable

- `var` - variance of a continuous tweet-level variable

- `user` - variables derived from user-level metadata (such as the average number of tweets published daily)

Following the `perc` type, we define the following features: usage of various clients for posting the tweets (Android, iOS, web), presence of specific textual elements (emojis, emoticons, URLs, hashtags, mentions, commas, ellipses, question-marks, exclamation marks) and criteria depending on tweets' metadata (replies, posting during working hours, posting during weekends, truncated tweets, favorited tweets, quotes, retweeted tweets).

By following the three types, `mean`, `med` and `var`, we encode the following distributions in our feature space: retweet count, favorite count, posting hour, day of week the tweet was posted and tweet length.

The last feature type, `user`, is used to encode the following information: average daily number of tweets, overall number of tweets, number of tweets the user has favorited, number of followers, number of friends, the ratio of follower to friend numbers, number of lists the user is on, whether the user has a background image defined, whether the user has the default profile image, whether the user has a profile description, whether the user has a location defined, and red, green and blue color component intensity (two-digit hexadecimal code from the RGB color definition) of the user's text and background color.

4   Experimental Setup

In this section we outline the setup of our gender classification experiments, whose results we report in Section 5.1.

We train models based on standardized (zero mean, unit variance) language-independent features described in the previous section with support vector machines (SVMs) using a radial basis function (RBF) kernel and optimizing the γ and C hyperparameters via 5-fold cross-validation.

To have a reasonable point of comparison for our language-independent models, we built bag-of-words (BoW) models on a concatenation of all tweets of a user by using lowercased character 5-grams as features and an SVM with a linear kernel.

We use character 5-grams as they have proven in our initial experiments to yield better results than words or character n-grams of different length. We use a linear kernel and not the RBF one in these experiments as the number of features is much higher than the number of instances. We do not perform any input processing except lowercasing as we expect useful signal for the task to be present in non-alphabetic characters, URLs, hashtags, mentions etc.

The number of features in our BoW models ranges from 6.2 million for German to 51.2 million for Spanish.

We discriminate between in-language and

Lang	Inst. #	MFC	ILBoW	CLBoW	DE	IT	NL	FR	PT	ES
DE	376	36.63	77.91	61.26	69.37	**63.30**	**67.26**	**68.35**	65.59	**69.92**
IT	429	50.96	62.46	58.66	**66.98**	63.91	**66.76**	**63.73**	**63.47**	**66.12**
NL	933	34.59	80.68	61.55	62.10	**61.15**	68.02	**57.87**	59.64	**64.68**
FR	1207	41.78	78.70	56.61	**69.70**	**65.12**	62.68	67.47	**65.60**	**66.35**
PT	3572	43.97	85.26	53.18	**61.94**	**57.31**	57.23	**62.65**	69.51	68.12
ES	9639	41.13	83.04	57.99	**62.89**	55.80	**64.85**	**66.82**	67.27	71.47

Table 1: Gender classification results on the six languages (rows), columns encoding the testing language (Lang), number of instances (Inst. #) and the weighted F1 results on most-frequent class baseline (MFC), in-language bag-of-words (ILBoW), average cross-language bag-of-words (CLBoW) and the six language-independent models. Bold results outperform the corresponding BoW baseline.

cross-language experiments. In all in-language experiments we perform 5-fold cross-validation, while in cross-language experiments we simply apply the model from the training language on the test language dataset.

We use weighted F1 as our evaluation metric and the most-frequent class baseline as our weak baseline.

5 Results

In the first part of this section we report on the gender classification results while in the second part we perform a series of feature analyses.

5.1 Gender Classification

We report results on gender classification in Table 1. Each of the rows represents the evaluation on a specific language encoded in the first column. The second column contains the number of instances, i.e., users available per language. The next column encodes the most-frequent class baseline (MFC) while the two columns that follow contain the bag-of-words results, either in the in-language setting (ILBoW) or the cross-language setting (CLBoW) for which, due to space constraints, we report only the average results over the five different languages.

In the remaining six columns we report the results obtained with models based on the language-independent features trained on specific language datasets. If the training language is the same as the testing language, we report the 5-fold cross-validation results. The results given in bold are of those systems that perform better than the BoW model with the same training and testing language.

The first observation we make is that all the models outperform the MFC baseline significantly. In-language BoW models perform, as ex-

pected, in all cases better than the average cross-language BoW model. They also perform better than most language-independent models, the Italian one being an exception. In cases where the training and testing language differ, in most cases the models based on language-independent features outperform the BoW models. We can observe a positive effect of the training data size on most of the BoW models since in the three languages with less training data (first three rows) CLBoW models outperform the language-independent ones only in three (20%) settings, while for the last three languages this is the case in five (33%) settings.

Finally, the language-independent models show much more consistent results than BoW models in the cross-lingual setting with an average per-language variance of the cross-lingual experiments of 0.001 for language-independent models and 0.01 for BoW models.

5.2 Feature Analysis

To obtain a better understanding of the informativeness of specific features for the task at hand, we performed a univariate analysis of each feature in each language. On a scaled (zero mean, unit variance) dataset of each language, we ranked the features by the p-value of the Mann Whitney U test.[1] In Table 2 we present features ranked by the average rank throughout our six languages. Due to space constraints we present only the 30 highest ranked features.

Each feature in each language is quantified by the effect size of the gender-conditioned distributions which we simply calculate as the difference

---

[1] The p-value quantifies the probability that we falsely reject the null hypothesis that the two gender-conditioned samples were selected from populations having the same distribution.

Feature	Avg rank	DE	IT	NL	FR	PT	ES
perc_emoji	1.17	0.63	0.21	0.45	0.49	0.41	0.5
mean_retweet_count	11.5	0.09	0.03	0.09	0.38	0.27	0.22
red_back	12.0	0.24	0.09	0.13	0.23	0.38	0.42
perc_http	13.5	-0.21	-0.24	-0.25	-0.15	-0.27	-0.17
perc_ios	14.0	-0.23	-0.22	-0.09	-0.19	-0.09	-0.13
var_retweet_count	15.17	-0.1	0.05	0.1	0.11	0.03	0.04
perc_retweeted	15.33	-0.01	0.2	-0.2	0.2	0.26	0.17
perc_question	16.0	-0.35	-0.13	-0.1	-0.29	-0.14	-0.11
user_tweet_per_day	17.0	0.08	0.19	0.01	0.31	0.15	0.12
perc_emoticon	18.17	-0.23	-0.25	-0.17	-0.18	-0.24	-0.1
user_location	18.67	-0.17	-0.2	-0.21	-0.11	-0.17	-0.12
mean_hour	19.33	0.08	0.23	0.18	0.22	-0.1	-0.02
var_len_text	20.0	0.25	0.24	0.2	0.24	0.01	0.08
user_favour_count	20.33	0.06	0.09	0.02	0.1	0.02	0.06
user_tweet_count	20.33	0.03	0.2	-0.01	0.23	0.13	0.09
user_follow_friend_rat	21.5	-0.13	0.12	-0.05	-0.08	-0.04	-0.03
mean_favorite_count	21.5	0.16	0.09	0.02	-0.07	-0.02	-0.03
med_hour	22.0	0.13	0.23	0.17	0.2	-0.01	-0.07
green_back	22.17	0.2	0.04	-0.04	0.12	0.26	0.25
blue_back	22.33	0.27	0.06	-0.01	0.11	0.29	0.33
perc_is_quote	22.83	-0.04	0.17	-0.21	0.18	0.17	0.03
perc_favorited	23.33	0.31	0.16	-0.02	0.14	0.05	0.01
med_retweet_count	24.17	-0.08	-0.06	-0.09	0.16	0.06	0.04
var_favorite_count	24.17	-0.09	0.07	0.07	-0.12	-0.02	-0.03
var_hour	25.17	-0.11	-0.01	-0.1	-0.14	0.21	0.05
user_red_text	25.83	0.15	0.05	0.09	0.22	0.13	0.16
user_listed_count	28.33	-0.12	-0.09	-0.09	-0.17	-0.0	-0.07
perc_exclamation	28.83	0.26	0.09	0.49	-0.04	-0.04	0.14
var_day	29.17	0.09	0.1	-0.0	0.14	0.12	0.12
perc_hash	29.67	-0.11	-0.05	-0.03	-0.16	-0.09	-0.11

Table 2: Representation of 30 (out of 51) features with the highest average rank across languages. Each feature in each language is represented through the difference between feature means of the female and male subsets in a standardized dataset. Red encodes higher female mean, blue male.

in the mean of the female and the male subsample. A positive value therefore means that female users have a higher average value of that feature than male users, and vice versa. Let us repeat that these calculations were performed on scaled data, therefore these quantifications are comparable across variables. To simplify the reception of the data, we color the background of each cell either with red (female) or blue (male) with the color intensity corresponding to the effect size.

Such a feature representation enables a comparison of various features, as well as identical features across languages. Given the good results of the classification task presented in the previous subsection, we hypothesize that the effect sizes, and especially their signs, should correspond between languages.

This hypothesis is largely confirmed, especially on the highest ranked features. The three highest ranked features – percentage of emoji usage, mean retweet count and intensity of the red component in the background color – signal that the user is female across all the six languages. The two features that follow – percentage of tweets containing URLs and percentage of tweets sent from an iOS device – are indicative of the male gender, again, across all the languages. Among the top 20 features, 5.3 out of 6 features on average have an identical sign, while among the top 30 features this is the case for 5.1 features.

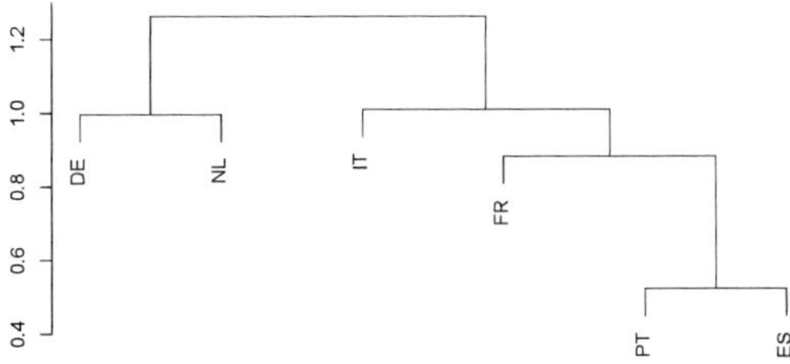

Figure 1: Dendrogram of the hierarchical language clustering. Each language is represented with feature effect sizes of all 51 language-independent features.

Regarding the use of emojis and emoticons, is it quite interesting that emojis are in all six languages preferred by the female gender while emoticons are preferred, again in all six languages, by the male gender. Male users tend to use more questionmarks, hashtags and share their location across all languages, while female users tend to produce more tweets per day, tweets of varying length, favorite more tweets and use more of the red color component in the tweet text, again, across all the languages.

Finally, given that there still is variation in our feature effect sizes across languages, we investigated whether this variation follows cultural differences between the speakers of the six languages. To investigate this matter we represented each of the six languages as a vector of the 51 effect sizes from Table 2 and performed agglomerative clustering of the six languages by using the Euclidean distance and the complete agglomeration method. The resulting dendrogram is presented in Figure 1.

The dendrogram shows that the difference between the features across languages corresponds to the linguistic as well as cultural distance of the cultures the languages are dominant in. We argue that the measured differences are mostly due to cultural differences as just the small number of punctuation-based variables, more precisely 4 out of 51, have any linguistic merit while the rest of the variables encodes other behavioral differences.

The two languages with the most similar feature effect sizes are Portuguese and Spanish, this cluster being expanded with French and then Italian. At a similar distance threshold point, German and Dutch are merged into one cluster.

Some of the variables that support such a clustering outcome are (1) the percentage of tweets that are retweeted which tends to be higher for male users in German and Dutch and for female users in the remaining languages, (2) the average posting hour that is higher for male Portuguese and Spanish users and female users in the remaining languages, (3) the average number of favorites per tweet which is higher for male users in French, Portuguese and Spanish and female users in the remaining languages (4) the percentage of tweets that are quotes which is higher among male users in German and Dutch and among female users in the remaining languages and (5) the variance of posting hour which is higher for female users in Portuguese and Spanish and for male users in the remaining languages.

6 Conclusion

In this paper we have presented a first run at the problem of language-independent gender identification among Twitter users. We have shown that with 51 language-independent features in the cross-lingual setting we regularly beat the bag-of-words baseline, and, furthermore, that the language-independent models have a ten times smaller F1 variance, which proves for our models to be more robust than the bag-of-words models, and therefore more reliably applicable to new languages.

We have analyzed the effect sizes of specific features among languages and have shown that our features regularly correspond across languages which also explains why the models work reliably across languages. By performing hierarchical clustering over languages represented through feature effect sizes we have shown that the difference in feature values across languages corresponds to the cultural distances of the speakers of those languages.

While the results presented in this paper are promising, there is a series of open questions that have to be explored. The most pressing one is the representativeness of users in the TwiSty corpus as they are Twitter users that have self-reported their personality test results. A way of measuring this representativeness is to apply these models to another gender prediction dataset. Further features should also be explored (network-based, image content etc.), as well as the potential of building additional language-independent author profiling models, such as age or educational level predictors.

Acknowledgments

The work described in this paper was funded by the Slovenian Research Agency within the national basic research project "Resources, methods and tools for the understanding, identification and classification of various forms of socially unacceptable discourse in the information society" (J7-8280, 2017-2020).

References

Jalal S. Alowibdi, Ugo A. Buy, and Philip Yu. 2013. Language independent gender classification on twitter. In *Proceedings of the 2013 IEEE/ACM International Conference on Advances in Social Networks Analysis and Mining*. ACM, New York, NY, USA, ASONAM '13, pages 739–743.

David Bamman, Jacob Eisenstein, and Tyler Schnoebelen. 2014. Gender identity and lexical variation in social media. *Journal of Sociolinguistics* 18(2):135–160.

John D. Burger, John Henderson, George Kim, and Guido Zarrella. 2011. Discriminating Gender on Twitter. In *Proceedings of the 2011 Conference on Empirical Methods in Natural Language Processing*. Association for Computational Linguistics, Edinburgh, Scotland, UK., pages 1301–1309. http://www.aclweb.org/anthology/D11-1120.

Dirk Hovy. 2015. Demographic Factors Improve Classification Performance. In *Proceedings of the 53rd Annual Meeting of the Association for Computational Linguistics and the 7th International Joint Conference on Natural Language Processing (Volume 1: Long Papers)*. Association for Computational Linguistics, Beijing, China, pages 752–762. http://www.aclweb.org/anthology/P15-1073.

Moshe Koppel, Shlomo Argamon, and Anat Rachel Shimoni. 2003. Automatically categorizing written texts by author gender. *Literary and Linguistic Computing* 17:401–412.

Tayfun Kucukyilmaz, Berkant Barla Cambazoglu, Cevdet Aykanat, and Fazli Can. 2006. Chat Mining for Gender Prediction. In *ADVIS*. Springer, volume 4243 of *Lecture Notes in Computer Science*, pages 274–283.

Brian Larson. 2017. Gender as a variable in natural-language processing: Ethical considerations. In *Proceedings of the First ACL Workshop on Ethics in Natural Language Processing*. Association for Computational Linguistics, Valencia, Spain, pages 30–40. http://www.aclweb.org/anthology/W/W17/W17-1604.

Z. Miller, B. Dickinson, and W. Hu. 2012. Gender Prediction on Twitter Using Stream Algorithms with N-Gram Character Features. *International Journal of Intelligence Science* 2(24).

Barbara Plank and Dirk Hovy. 2015. Personality Traits on Twitter or How to Get 1,500 Personality Tests in a Week. In *Proceedings of the 6th Workshop on Computational Approaches to Subjectivity, Sentiment and Social Media Analysis*. Association for Computational Linguistics, Lisboa, Portugal, pages 92–98. http://aclweb.org/anthology/W15-2913.

Francisco Rangel, Paolo Rosso, Ben Verhoeven, Walter Daelemans, Martin Potthast, and Benno Stein. 2016. Overview of the 4th Author Profiling Task at PAN 2016: Cross-genre Evaluations. In *Working Notes Papers of the CLEF 2016 Evaluation Labs. CEUR Workshop Proceedings*. CLEF and CEUR-WS.org.

Jonathan Schler, Moshe Koppel, Shlomo Argamon, and James W. Pennebaker. 2006. Effects of Age and Gender on Blogging. In *AAAI Spring Symposium: Computational Approaches to Analyzing Weblogs*. AAAI, pages 199–205.

H A Schwartz, J C Eichstaedt, M L Kern, L Dziurzynski, S M Ramones, M Agrawal, A Shah, M Kosinski, D Stillwell, M E Seligman, and L H Ungar. 2013. Personality, gender, and age in the language of social media: the open-vocabulary approach. *PLoS One* 8(9).

Ben Verhoeven, Walter Daelemans, and Barbara Plank. 2016. Twisty: a multilingual twitter stylometry corpus for gender and personality profiling. In *Proceedings of the 10th Annual Conference on Language Resources and Evaluation (LREC 2016)*. ELRA, ELRA, Portorož, Slovenia.

When does a Compliment become Sexist? Analysis and Classification of Ambivalent Sexism using Twitter Data

Akshita Jha   **Radhika Mamidi**

Kohli Center on Intelligent Systems (KCIS),
International Institute of Information Technology, Hyderabad (IIIT Hyderabad)
akshita.jha@research.iiit.ac.in, radhika.mamidi@iiit.ac.in

Abstract

Sexism is prevalent in today's society, both offline and online, and poses a credible threat to social equality with respect to gender. According to ambivalent sexism theory (Glick and Fiske, 1996), it comes in two forms: Hostile and Benevolent. While hostile sexism is characterized by an explicitly negative attitude, benevolent sexism is more subtle. Previous works on computationally detecting sexism present online are restricted to identifying the hostile form. Our objective is to investigate the less pronounced form of sexism demonstrated online. We achieved this by creating and analyzing a dataset of tweets that exhibit benevolent sexism. We classified tweets into 'Hostile', 'Benevolent' or 'Others' class depending on the kind of sexism they exhibit, by using Support Vector Machines (SVM), sequence-to-sequence models and FastText classifier. We achieved the best F1-score using FastText classifier. Our work aims to analyze and understand the much prevalent ambivalent sexism in social media.

1 Introduction

Sexism, as given by the Oxford dictionary, is the *'prejudice, stereotyping, or discrimination, typically against women, on the basis of sex'*. Sexism is rife in the society's belief system and its manifestation online is not uncommon (Eadicicco, 2014). For example, Australian game show, *My Kitchen Rules* often prompts sexist tweets against its female participants. E.g.: *'Trying to find something pretty about these blonde idiots. #MKR'*. However, evidence suggests that sexist remarks may not always express negative emotion (Becker and Wright, 2011). For instance,

Rio Olympics shed light on the blatant as well as seemingly innocuous sexism that female athletes face, when, after the victory of 3-time Olympian Corey Cogdell-Unrein in women's trap shooting, Chicago Tribune tweeted, *'Wife of a Bears' lineman wins a bronze medal today in Rio Olympics'*[1]. Katie Ledecky's record breaking win in 400-meter freestyle race was applauded by a lot of people while simultaneously commenting that *'she swims like a man'*[2]. These are excellent examples of benign form of sexism prevailing in these times.

In their seminal paper, Glick and Fiske (1997) proposed ambivalent sexism theory that talked about two related but opposite orientations towards a particular gender: (i) Hostile Sexism (HS), *i.e.*, sexist antipathy and (ii) Benevolent Sexism (BS), *i.e.*, a subjectively positive view towards men or women. Hostile sexism is angry, harsh and expresses an explicitly negative viewpoint. E.g.: *'Jus gonna say it...again....DUMB BITCH! #MKR'*. Benevolent Sexism, on the other hand, is often disguised as a compliment. E.g.: *'They're probably surprised at how smart you are, for a girl'*. Moreover, there is a reverence for the stereotypical role of women as mothers, daughters and wives. BS puts women on a pedestal, but reinforces their sub-ordination. E.g.: *'No man succeeds without a good woman besides him. Wife or mother. If it is both, he is twice as blessed'*. Despite the positive feelings of BS, it's underpinnings lie in masculine dominance and stereotyping both men and women. It shares the common assumption that women inhabit restricted domestic roles and are the 'weaker sex'. Although, it may not be immediately apparent, this also implicitly stereotypes men.

Sexism has far-reaching consequences for women as well as men. It has been seen that despite it's seemingly positive and inoffensive tone,

---

[1]https://twitter.com/chicagotribune/status/762401317050605568
[2]https://tinyurl.com/y7zgsuyr

Proceedings of the Second Workshop on Natural Language Processing and Computational Social Science, pages 7–16,
Vancouver, Canada, August 3, 2017. ©2017 Association for Computational Linguistics

benevolent sexism has worse effects than hostile sexism on women's cognitive performance (Dardenne et al., 2007). Furthermore, the experiments conducted by Russo et al. (2014) demonstrate how social justification (Jost et al., 2004; Jost and Kay, 2005) and benevolent sexism are positively correlated. Additionally, they conclude that gender inequality is promoted not only by hostile sexism but also by the subtle and more deceptive, benevolent sexism.

Recently, efforts have been made for detection of sexist content from the internet. Some of the tweets in Waseem and Hovy's (2016) publicly available hate speech dataset of 16k tweets are sexist. But as expected in a hate speech corpus, these sexist tweets express only hostile sexism. It is evident that the approaches that detect sexism online have overlooked benevolent sexism.

In order to address the above shortcoming, we propose computational models to automatically classify a tweet into one of the three classes:

- *Benevolent*: if tweet exhibits subjectively positive sentiment but is sexist

- *Hostile*: if the tweet exhibits explicitly negative emotion and is sexist

- *Others*: if the tweet is not sexist

To the best of our knowledge, there has not been any previous study in computationally identifying benevolent sexism and classifying sexist content into two different classes depending on the nature of sexism.

The rest of the paper is organized as follows. Section 2 presents existing literature in related areas like hate speech detection, sentiment analysis and identification of sexist content from social psychology point of view. Section 3 illustrates the process of dataset creation and annotation for BS tweets. Additionally, it describes the available dataset of HS tweets that we used for our experiments. Section 4 and 5 describe the technical aspects of the experiments conducted for the classification of tweets. We discuss the results of the experiments in Section 6 before concluding the paper in Section 7.

2   Related Work

A considerable amount of work has been done in social psychology for identification of sexist content and its impact. Research has provided evidence that not only men but also women endorse sexist beliefs (Barreto and Ellemers, 2005; Glick et al., 2000; Jackman, 1994; Kilianski and Rudman, 1998; Swim et al., 2005). Becker and Wagner (2008) introduce Gender Identity Model (GIM) using social identity theory (SIT) (Hogg, 2016) and social role theory (SRT) (Eagly et al., 2000) to explain women's endorsement of sexist beliefs. They conclude that women reject benevolent and hostile sexism when they highly identify themselves with the category 'women' and have a progressive outlook. In contrast, gender role preference has weaker or no effect on sexist beliefs when women do not strongly identify themselves with their gender in-group.

The work by Bolukbasi et al. (2016) revealed the hidden gender bias in Word2Vec. They showed how Word2Vec word embeddings were sexist because of the bias in news articles that made up the Word2Vec corpus. For a relation like, *'father : doctor :: mother : x'*, Word2Vec gives *x = nurse*. And the query *'man : computer programmer :: woman : x'*, returns *x = homemaker*. In order to address this warping, they transformed the vector space using a method called 'hard de-biasing' and removed the bias.

Hate speech detection, that includes identification of sexist content, has garnered a lot of attention in recent times. Djuric et al. (2015) try to address this problem in online user comments. Using neural networks, they learn distributed low-dimensional text representations, where semantically similar comments and words reside in the similar part of vector space. They, then, feed this to a linear classifier to identify hateful and clean comments. Davidson et al. (2017) use hate speech lexicon to collect tweets containing hate speech keywords. They train a multi-class classifier to separate these tweets into one of the three classes: those containing hate speech, only offensive language, and those with neither. Hate speech dataset, containing sexist tweets, has been made publicly available by Waseem and Hovy (2016). This dataset contains 16k tweets that fall into one of the three classes: sexist, racist or neither. They list a set of criteria based on critical race theory to annotate the data and then use Support Vector Machines (SVM) with handcrafted features to classify tweets. However, one of the major drawbacks of the decsribed approaches and dataset is that it takes into account only hostile sexist tweets.

To better understand the nature of sexism, sentiment analysis can be done. In recent times, sentiment analysis of Twitter data has received a lot of attention (Pak and Paroubek, 2010). Some of the early works by Go et al. (2009) and Bermingham and Smeaton (2010) use distant learning to acquire sentiment data. They show that using unigrams, bigrams and part-of-speech (POS) tags as features, SVM outperforms other classifiers like Naive Bayes and MaxEnt. To remove the need for feature engineering, Agarwal et al. (2011) use POS-specific prior polarity features and tree kernel for sentiment analysis. To detect contextual polarity using phrase-level sentiment analysis, Wilson et al. (2005) identify whether a phrase is neutral or polar. If the phrase is polar, they then disambiguate the polarity of the polar expression. State-of-the-art sentiment analyzers use deep learning techniques like Convolutional Neural Network (CNN) (Dos Santos and Gatti, 2014) and Recursive Neural Network (Tang et al., 2015) based approach to learn features automatically from the input text.

3 Dataset

For the purpose of classification of tweets on the basis of the type of sexism, we required a dataset that displayed benevolent sexism (BS). Hence, we created our own corpus of tweets belonging to 'Benevolent' class. In addition to this, we used the publicly available hate speech corpus (Waseem and Hovy, 2016) to collect tweets belonging to 'Hostile' and 'Others' classes. Tweets labelled as 'sexist' and 'neither' in the hate-speech dataset make up the 'Hostile' and 'Others' class in our corpus respectively. Distribution of tweets in the combined corpus has been shown in Table 1.

	Total Tweets	**Unique Tweets**
Benevolent	7,205	712
Hostile	3,378	2,254
Others	11,559	7,129
Total	22,142	10,095

Table 1: Distribution of tweets in the combined corpus.

For creation of the Benevolent Sexist dataset, we collected a total of 95,292 tweets. Out of these, we manually identified 7,205 BS tweets (including retweets). This dataset is publicly available[3].

[3]Dataset: https://github.com/AkshitaJha/NLP_CSS_2017/

However, the total number of unique tweets identified, after removing retweets, were only 712 in number. The total number of tokens in the created dataset is 74,874. The mean length of BS tweets is 80.95, with a standard deviation of 25.75. The dataset also contains the metadata of each tweet, like username, time of creation of the tweet, it's geographic location, number of retweets and number of likes.

3.1 Data Collection

We collected data using the public Twitter Search API. The terms queried were common phrases and hashtags that are generally used when exhibiting benevolent sexism. Some of them were: *'as good as a man'*, *'like a man'*, *'for a girl'*, *'smart for a girl'*, *'love of a woman'*, *'#adaywithoutwomen'*, *'#womensday'*, *'#everydaysexism'* and *'#weareequal'*. These lead to a dataset of tweets that were sexist in nature, both towards women and men. E.g.: *'He is a man who can't act like a man'* is sexist towards men. We extracted tweets that were in English. After we had manually identified benevolent tweets (explained is Section 3.2), we asked three 23-year old non-activist feminists to cross-validate the collected unique tweets to remove any kind of annotator bias. Fleiss' kappa score was calculated to assess the reliability of the agreement between the validators. It was found to be 0.74 which corresponds to 'substantial agreement' between the annotators (Fleiss et al., 1969).

3.2 Identification

To identify and annotate BS, we made use of the ambivalent sexism theory proposed by Glick and Fiske (1997) in social psychology. Sexism is hypothesized to encompass three sources of male ambivalence: *Paternalism, Gender Differentiation and Heterosexuality*. Each of these three components have two types, one of them results in hostile sexism and the other gives rise to benevolent sexism.

- *Paternalism*: Paternalism encompasses *dominative paternalism* and *protective paternalism*. Supporters of the former hold the view of women not being fully competent adults (Brehm, 1992; Peplau et al., 1983); whereas those who support the latter, view women as the weaker sex who need to be loved, cherished and protected (Peplau et al., 1983; Tavris et al., 1984). Protective paternalism

Paternalism	HS (Dominative)	: Women should stay at home.
	BS (Protective)	: Women are like flowers who need to be cherished!
Gender Differentiation	HS (Competitive)	: Women are incompetent at work.
	BS (Complementary)	: It's so good that I thought your brother wrote it!
Heterosexuality	HS (Hostility)	: I would like to fuck Kat, stupid slut!
	BS (Intimacy)	: What is man without the love of a woman!

Table 2: Examples tweets showing ambivalent sexism.

results in benevolent sexism whereas dominative paternalism results in hostile.

- *Gender Differentiation*: Akin to dominative paternalism, *competitive gender differentiation* justifies patriarchy in the society by viewing men as ones having governing capabilities in the society (Tajfel, 2010). This gives rise to hostile sexism. On the other hand, *complementary gender differentiation* results in benevolent sexism as it shows women having favourable traits that men stereotypically lack (Eagly and Mladinic, 1994).

- *Heterosexuality*: Similarly, *heterosexual intimacy* gives rise to benevolent sexism by viewing women as romantic objects with a genuine desire for psychological closeness (Berscheid et al., 1989); and *heterosexual hostility* is shown in cases where, for some men sexual attraction towards women may not be separate from the desire to dominate them (Bargh and Raymond, 1995; Pryor et al., 1995). This results in hostile sexism.

Table 2 shows some example tweets that highlight the ambivalent sexist attitude towards women. In order to clearly identify benevolent sexism, we studied the tweets and analyzed if it showed any one the three behaviors: *protective paternalism, complementary gender differentiation,* and *heterosexual intimacy*. If the tweet exhibited any one of the above, we annotated it as benevolently sexist.

3.3 Comparison of Hostile and Benevolent Sexist Tweets

The statistical difference in the distribution of hostile and benevolent sexist tweets in the combined dataset can be determined from Table 2. It is interesting to note that despite the total number of BS tweets (7,205) being almost double the total number of HS tweets (3,378), the number of unique BS

tweets (712) is just one-third that of the unique HS tweets (2,254). Since benevolent sexism seems harmless, noble, and even romantic at times, it is retweeted more number of times as compared with tweets that exhibit hostile sexism.

Hostile	Benevolent
not	man
sexist	woman
#mkr	women
women	like
kat	#womensday
girls	love
like	good
call	girl
#notsexist	#adaywithoutwomen
female	without

Table 3: Most frequent content words in HS and BS tweets.

Table 3 shows the most common content words used in hostile and benevolent tweets. Apart from the words, 'girl(s)' and 'women', which are frequent in both kinds of tweets (as sexism is commonly expressed against females), we see that content words with high frequency differ significantly.

Hostile	Benevolent
kat and andre	think like man
sexist don't like	act like man
call sexist whatever	act like lady
sexist can't stand	last love man
blondes pretty faces	first love woman
dumb blondes pretty	love like woman
sexist hate female	without love woman
don't like female	lady think like
comedians aren't funny	man love like

Table 4: Most frequent tri-grams in HS and BS tweets.

Most frequent trigrams in hostile and benevolent tweets are shown in Table 4. As hypothesized, benevolent tweets have trigrams that express positive attitudes while trigrams of hostile tweets express explicit negative attitude.

Table 5 illustrates the most frequent adjectives used for both hostile and benevolent tweets. We observe that frequent adjectives in HS tweets display a negative sentiment whereas adjectives in BS tweets display positive sentiment.

Hostile	Benevolent
dumb	real
hot	strong
bad	beautiful
stupid	better
awful	great

Table 5: Most frequent adjectives in HS and BS tweets.

All the above illustrations are in line with our hypothesis which states that sexism in the benevolent form is camouflaged as a compliment and is hence difficult to pinpoint; whereas, hostile sexism is evidently negative and can be easily identified as sexist.

3.4 Pre-processing

Pre-processing of tweets involved removal of usernames, punctuations, emoticons, hyperlinks/URLs and RT tag. Stop words were intentionally retained. The reason for this was that each tweet can contain a maximum of only 140 characters and removal of stop words would only lead to loss of information. For example in the tweet, *'Every guy should admit that #adaywithoutwomen is not a day worth living'*, stop word removal would remove *'not'* which as a result, would change a BS tweet to an HS tweet.

4 Methodology

For classification of tweets into one of the three classes: 'Benevolent', 'Hostile' and 'Others', we made use of machine learning techniques described below.

4.1 SVM

Support Vector Machines (SVM) (Cortes and Vapnik, 1995) are supervised learning models used for classification. To classify tweets in our dataset, we used term frequency-inverse document frequency (TF-IDF) (Salton and Buckley, 1988) as a feature, as it captures the importance of the given word in a document. TF-IDF is calculated as:

$$tfidf(t, d, D) = f(t, d) \times log\frac{N}{|\{d \epsilon D : t \epsilon d\}|}$$

where $f(t, d)$ indicates the number of times term, t appears in context, d and N is the total number of documents; $|\{d \epsilon D : t \epsilon d\}|$ represents the total number of documents where t occurs.

We ensure that SVM uses TF-IDF, to construct a separating hyperplane for given labelled training data and classify new tweets into one of the three classes: 'Benevolent', 'Hostile', or 'Others'. To find the optimal hyperplane, SVM tries to find a decision boundary that maximizes the margin by minimizing $||\mathbf{w}||$:

$$min f : \frac{1}{2}||\mathbf{w}||^2,$$

$$s.t. \quad y^{(i)}(\mathbf{w}^T\mathbf{x}^{(i)} + b) \geq 1, \quad i = 1, ..., m$$

where $\mathbf{w}$ is the weight vector, $\mathbf{x}$ is the input vector and b is the bias.

4.2 Sequence to Sequence model

A basic sequence-to-sequence model consists of an encoder and a decoder (Sutskever et al., 2014; Cho et al., 2014). For our experiment, we made use of a bi-directional RNN encoder-decoder (Schuster and Paliwal, 1997) with attention mechanism (Bahdanau et al., 2014) that employs Long Short Term Memory (LSTM) cells (Hochreiter and Schmidhuber, 1997) to modulate the flow of information. The encoder reads the input sequence and generates an intermediate hidden representation of fixed length, $\mathbf{c_o}$ given by:

$$\mathbf{c_o} = \sum_t \alpha_{ot}\mathbf{h_t}$$

where $\mathbf{h_t}$ denotes the hidden representation of $\mathbf{x_t}$, $\alpha_{ot} \epsilon [0, 1]$ and $\sum_t \alpha_{ot} = 1$. A learned alignment model computes the weight, $\alpha_o t$, for each $\mathbf{c_o}$ such that:

$$\alpha_{ot} = \frac{exp(e_o t)}{\sum_{t'} exp(e_o t')}$$

$$e_o t = a(\mathbf{s_{o-1}}\mathbf{h_t})$$

where $\mathbf{s_o}$ is the output of a recurrent hidden layer and $a(.)$ is a feed-forward neural network that computes $\mathbf{h_t}$. The decoder then maps the intermediate representation into either one of the 'Benevolent', 'Hostile' or 'Others' class by computing:

$$P(y_1, .., y_O | \mathbf{x_1}, .., \mathbf{x_T}) = \prod_{o=1}^{O} P(y_o | y_1, .., y_{o-1}, \mathbf{c_o})$$

where lengths of the output and the input are O and T respectively. The posterior probability, y_o is calculated as:

$$P(y_o | y_1, .., y_{o-1}, \mathbf{c_o}) = g(\mathbf{y_o}, \mathbf{s_o}, \mathbf{c_o})$$

where $\mathbf{y_o}$ is the vector representation of y_o, i.e., a one-hot vector followed by neural projection layer for dimension reduction and $g(.)$ is a softmax function.

4.3 FastText

FastText classifier, made available by Facebook AI Research has proven to be efficient for text classification (Joulin et al., 2016). It is often at par with deep learning classifiers in terms of accuracy, and much faster for training and evaluation. FastText uses bag of words and bag of n-grams as features for text classification. Bag of n-grams feature captures partial information about the local word order. FastText allows update of word vectors through back-propagation during training allowing the model to fine-tune word representations according to the task at hand (Bojanowski et al., 2016). The model is trained using stochastic gradient descent and a linearly decaying learning rate.

5 Experiments and Results

Experiments conducted for classification of tweets have been described below. We trained and tested our algorithm only on unique tweets to avoid learning any kind of bias from retweets. For evaluating the experiments, we use precision, recall and f-measure.

5.1 Polarity Detection

To detect the polarity of each tweet, we experimented with rule-based sentiment analysis techniques using linguistic features. First, using the Penn Treebank tagset (Marcus et al., 1993), all tweets were tagged for part-of-speech (POS). After this, we used the Stanford Shallow Parser (Pradhan et al., 2004) to chunk tweets and get all the phrases. We calculated the positive score and the negative score for each phrase in the tweet, using SentiWordNet (Baccianella et al., 2010) and subjectivity lexicon (Taboada et al., 2011). The overall sentiment score of a tweet was calculated by summing up the individual score of the phrases in the tweet. If this overall sentiment score of the tweet was greater than 0, then the tweet was marked as positive; if the overall sentiment score was less than 0, it was marked as negative; else the tweet was marked as neutral. Table 6 shows the results of the basic sentiment analysis of tweets.

	Hostile	Benevolent	Others
Positive	3.07%	83.06%	7.34%
Negative	86.48%	2.77%	15.72%
Neutral	10.45%	14.17%	76.94%

Table 6: Sentiment Analysis of tweets in the dataset.

5.2 SVM

For the purpose of our experiment, we used TF-IDF as a feature for SVM to classify previously unseen tweets into one the three classes. We implemented SVM using scikit (Pedregosa et al., 2011) library. Table 7 shows the precision, recall and F1-score after performing 10-fold cross validation.

5.3 Sequence to Sequence model

The implementation of the described Sequence to Sequence model has been done using tf-seq2seq framework (Britz et al., 2017) for Tensorflow (Abadi et al., 2016). The experiment was conducted after splitting the training set and the test set in the ratio $7 : 3$. For 1000 epochs, with a batch-size of 32, the precision, recall and F1-score have been shown in Table 7.

5.4 FastText

The training set and the test set were split in $7 : 3$ ratio for FastText. Table 8 reports precision at 1 of running FastText, using 100 dimension word vectors, for 5, 8, 10 and 15 epochs with a learning rate of 0.1 and the size of context window as 5. It is observed that there is no improvement in the F1-score after 10 epochs.

	SVM			Seq2Seq		
	P	**R**	**F1**	**P**	**R**	**F1**
Benevolent	0.97	0.69	**0.80**	0.69	0.77	0.73
Hostile	0.89	0.33	0.48	0.57	0.65	**0.61**
Others	0.80	0.99	**0.89**	0.91	0.87	0.88

Table 7: Comparision of Precision (P), Recall (R) and F1 score (F1) of classification of tweets into HS, BS and Others class using SVM and Seq2seq models.

Epochs	Precision	Recall	F1-Score
5	0.81	0.81	0.81
8	0.84	0.84	0.84
10	0.87	0.87	0.87
15	0.87	0.87	0.87

Table 8: FastText Prec@1 for different epochs.

6 Discussion

Using basic linguistic features, rule-based polarity detection of tweets show that benevolent sexism have positive polarity whereas the tweets exhibiting hostile sexism have a negative polarity. This is in accordance with our hypothesis which states that benevolent sexism expresses a positive outlook, in contrast to hostile sexism that displays negative emotion.

For the purpose of classification of tweets into 'Benevolent', 'Hostile' or 'Others' class, Support Vector Machines (SVM) and Sequence to Sequence (Seq2Seq) classifier were implemented for baseline experiments. In SVM, the precision for the 'Benevolent' and 'Hostile' class is unusually high whereas the recall, specifically for the 'Hostile' class, is quite low. This implies that only 69% of BS tweets and 33% of HS tweets of the previously unseen test set have been labelled correctly. On comparing this with the results of Seq2Seq model, we observe that although the precision for classification of tweets into 'Benevolent' and 'Hostile' is not as high as that of SVM, the recall is 77% and 65% respectively for the two classes, which is better than the recall achieved using SVM. Seq2Seq takes into account the structure of the tweet, unlike the TF-IDF feature used in SVM, which is invariant to word order. This results in better recall.

The number of tweets in 'Others' class is significantly more than the number of tweets in 'Hostile' and 'Benevolent' classes combined. The performance of SVM and Sequence to Sequence models is known to improve, as the size of varied training data increases. This is further reflected in the high precision, recall and the comparable F1-score achieved for the 'Others' class using the two models.

Overall, SVM gives a slightly better F1-score for 'Benevolent' and 'Others' class, whereas Sequence to Sequence classifier performs better for 'Hostile' class. FastText outperforms both the above classifiers, with an F1-score of 0.87 for Prec@1. Since, a tweet has limited number of characters and may not exhibit long range dependencies, the word order of a tweet is successfully captured by FastText, by using it's bag of n-gram feature. This, combined with the fact that FastText has lesser number of parameters to tune, results in it's better performance than the proposed Seq2Seq model.

7 Conclusion and Future Work

We presented a detailed analysis for detection and classification of sexism in twitter data by building a combined corpus of benevolent and hostile sexist tweets. Using ambivalent sexism theory, we annotated tweets that showed sexism in the benevolent form. A limitation of our approach was that the method of gathering benevolently sexist tweets was biased towards the initial search terms and likely missed many forms of benevolent sexism. In future, we aim to address this concern by increasing the size of the dataset, using the aforementioned ambivalent sexism theory, while additionally solving the issue of the comparatively lesser number of unique benevolently sexist tweets. We also plan to take into consideration the gender of the user, the geographic location of a tweet and its length as features for future experiments.

Apart from understanding and identifying various kinds of sexism, the created dataset can additionally be used to recognize and analyze the events that trigger sexism online. The methods described can also be used in contexts outside of social media, such as within workplace communications as means for automated assessment and eventual intervention. While the problem is far from solved, our experiments can be treated as a baseline for future work.

Our work is a step towards building a gender-neutral society. The insights derived from the analysis and experiments presented in this paper may prove beneficial in understanding the prevalence of ambivalent sexism in social-media data and serve as a starting point for more work in this field.

Acknowledgments

We thank the annotators and the three anonymous reviewers for their useful comments.

References

Martín Abadi, Ashish Agarwal, Paul Barham, Eugene Brevdo, Zhifeng Chen, Craig Citro, Greg S Corrado, Andy Davis, Jeffrey Dean, Matthieu Devin, et al. 2016. Tensorflow: Large-scale machine learning on heterogeneous distributed systems. *arXiv preprint arXiv:1603.04467* .

Apoorv Agarwal, Boyi Xie, Ilia Vovsha, Owen Rambow, and Rebecca Passonneau. 2011. Sentiment analysis of twitter data. In *Proceedings of the workshop on languages in social media*. Association for Computational Linguistics, pages 30–38.

Stefano Baccianella, Andrea Esuli, and Fabrizio Sebastiani. 2010. Sentiwordnet 3.0: An enhanced lexical resource for sentiment analysis and opinion mining. In *LREC*. volume 10, pages 2200–2204.

Dzmitry Bahdanau, Kyunghyun Cho, and Yoshua Bengio. 2014. Neural machine translation by jointly learning to align and translate. *arXiv preprint arXiv:1409.0473* .

John A Bargh and Paula Raymond. 1995. The naive misuse of power: Nonconscious sources of sexual harassment. *Journal of Social Issues* 51(1):85–96.

Manuela Barreto and Naomi Ellemers. 2005. The perils of political correctness: Men's and women's responses to old-fashioned and modern sexist views. *Social Psychology Quarterly* 68(1):75–88.

Julia C Becker and Ulrich Wagner. 2008. Doing gender differently–. *Womens Internalization of Sexism: Predictors and Antidotes* page 51.

Julia C Becker and Stephen C Wright. 2011. Yet another dark side of chivalry: Benevolent sexism undermines and hostile sexism motivates collective action for social change. *Journal of personality and social psychology* 101(1):62.

Adam Bermingham and Alan F Smeaton. 2010. Classifying sentiment in microblogs: is brevity an advantage? In *Proceedings of the 19th ACM international conference on Information and knowledge management*. ACM, pages 1833–1836.

Ellen Berscheid, Mark Snyder, and Allen M Omoto. 1989. The relationship closeness inventory: Assessing the closeness of interpersonal relationships. *Journal of personality and Social Psychology* 57(5):792.

Piotr Bojanowski, Edouard Grave, Armand Joulin, and Tomas Mikolov. 2016. Enriching word vectors with subword information. *arXiv preprint arXiv:1607.04606* .

Tolga Bolukbasi, Kai-Wei Chang, James Y Zou, Venkatesh Saligrama, and Adam T Kalai. 2016. Man is to computer programmer as woman is to homemaker? debiasing word embeddings. In *Advances in Neural Information Processing Systems*. pages 4349–4357.

Sharon S Brehm. 1992. *Intimate relationships*. Mcgraw-Hill Book Company.

D. Britz, A. Goldie, T. Luong, and Q. Le. 2017. Massive Exploration of Neural Machine Translation Architectures. *ArXiv e-prints* .

Kyunghyun Cho, Bart Van Merriënboer, Caglar Gulcehre, Dzmitry Bahdanau, Fethi Bougares, Holger Schwenk, and Yoshua Bengio. 2014. Learning phrase representations using rnn encoder-decoder for statistical machine translation. *arXiv preprint arXiv:1406.1078* .

Corinna Cortes and Vladimir Vapnik. 1995. Support-vector networks. *Machine learning* 20(3):273–297.

Benoit Dardenne, Muriel Dumont, and Thierry Bollier. 2007. Insidious dangers of benevolent sexism: consequences for women's performance. *Journal of personality and social psychology* 93(5):764.

Thomas Davidson, Dana Warmsley, Michael Macy, and Ingmar Weber. 2017. Automated hate speech detection and the problem of offensive language. *arXiv preprint arXiv:1703.04009* .

Nemanja Djuric, Jing Zhou, Robin Morris, Mihajlo Grbovic, Vladan Radosavljevic, and Narayan Bhamidipati. 2015. Hate speech detection with comment embeddings. In *Proceedings of the 24th International Conference on World Wide Web*. ACM, pages 29–30.

Cícero Nogueira Dos Santos and Maira Gatti. 2014. Deep convolutional neural networks for sentiment analysis of short texts. In *COLING*. pages 69–78.

Lisa Eadicicco. 2014. This female game developer was harassed so severely on twitter she had to leave her home. *http://www.businessinsider.com/brianna-wu-harassed-twitter-2014-10?IR=T, Oct.* .

Alice H Eagly and Antonio Mladinic. 1994. Are people prejudiced against women? some answers from research on attitudes, gender stereotypes, and judgments of competence. *European review of social psychology* 5(1):1–35.

Alice H Eagly, Wendy Wood, and Amanda B Diekman. 2000. Social role theory of sex differences and similarities: A current appraisal. *The developmental social psychology of gender* pages 123–174.

Joseph L Fleiss, Jacob Cohen, and BS Everitt. 1969. Large sample standard errors of kappa and weighted kappa. *Psychological Bulletin* 72(5):323.

Peter Glick and Susan T Fiske. 1996. The ambivalent sexism inventory: Differentiating hostile and benevolent sexism. *Journal of personality and social psychology* 70(3):491.

Peter Glick and Susan T Fiske. 1997. Hostile and benevolent sexism: Measuring ambivalent sexist attitudes toward women. *Psychology of women quarterly* 21(1):119–135.

Peter Glick, Susan T Fiske, Antonio Mladinic, José L Saiz, Dominic Abrams, Barbara Masser, Bolanle Adetoun, Johnstone E Osagie, Adebowale Akande, Amos Alao, et al. 2000. Beyond prejudice as simple antipathy: hostile and benevolent sexism across cultures. *Journal of personality and social psychology* 79(5):763.

Alec Go, Richa Bhayani, and Lei Huang. 2009. Twitter sentiment classification using distant supervision. *CS224N Project Report, Stanford* 1(12).

Sepp Hochreiter and Jürgen Schmidhuber. 1997. Long short-term memory. *Neural computation* 9(8):1735–1780.

Michael A Hogg. 2016. Social identity theory. In *Understanding Peace and Conflict Through Social Identity Theory*, Springer, pages 3–17.

Mary R Jackman. 1994. *The velvet glove: Paternalism and conflict in gender, class, and race relations.* Univ of California Press.

John T Jost, Mahzarin R Banaji, and Brian A Nosek. 2004. A decade of system justification theory: Accumulated evidence of conscious and unconscious bolstering of the status quo. *Political psychology* 25(6):881–919.

John T Jost and Aaron C Kay. 2005. Exposure to benevolent sexism and complementary gender stereotypes: consequences for specific and diffuse forms of system justification. *Journal of personality and social psychology* 88(3):498.

Armand Joulin, Edouard Grave, Piotr Bojanowski, and Tomas Mikolov. 2016. Bag of tricks for efficient text classification. *arXiv preprint arXiv:1607.01759* .

Stephen E Kilianski and Laurie A Rudman. 1998. Wanting it both ways: Do women approve of benevolent sexism? *Sex roles* 39(5):333–352.

Mitchell P Marcus, Mary Ann Marcinkiewicz, and Beatrice Santorini. 1993. Building a large annotated corpus of english: The penn treebank. *Computational linguistics* 19(2):313–330.

Alexander Pak and Patrick Paroubek. 2010. Twitter as a corpus for sentiment analysis and opinion mining. In *LREc*. volume 10.

Fabian Pedregosa, Gaël Varoquaux, Alexandre Gramfort, Vincent Michel, Bertrand Thirion, Olivier Grisel, Mathieu Blondel, Peter Prettenhofer, Ron Weiss, Vincent Dubourg, et al. 2011. Scikit-learn: Machine learning in python. *Journal of Machine Learning Research* 12(Oct):2825–2830.

Letitia Anne Peplau et al. 1983. Roles and gender. *Close relationships* pages 220–264.

Sameer S Pradhan, Wayne H Ward, Kadri Hacioglu, James H Martin, and Daniel Jurafsky. 2004. Shallow semantic parsing using support vector machines. In *HLT-NAACL*. pages 233–240.

John B Pryor, Janet L Giedd, and Karen B Williams. 1995. A social psychological model for predicting sexual harassment. *Journal of Social Issues* 51(1):69–84.

Silvia Russo, Filippo Rutto, and Cristina Mosso. 2014. Benevolent sexism toward men: Its social legitimation and preference for male candidates. *Group Processes & Intergroup Relations* 17(4):465–473.

Gerard Salton and Christopher Buckley. 1988. Term-weighting approaches in automatic text retrieval. *Information processing & management* 24(5):513–523.

Mike Schuster and Kuldip K Paliwal. 1997. Bidirectional recurrent neural networks. *IEEE Transactions on Signal Processing* 45(11):2673–2681.

Ilya Sutskever, Oriol Vinyals, and Quoc V Le. 2014. Sequence to sequence learning with neural networks. In *Advances in neural information processing systems*. pages 3104–3112.

Janet K Swim, Robyn Mallett, Yvonne Russo-Devosa, and Charles Stangor. 2005. Judgments of sexism: A comparison of the subtlety of sexism measures and sources of variability in judgments of sexism. *Psychology of Women Quarterly* 29(4):406–411.

Maite Taboada, Julian Brooke, Milan Tofiloski, Kimberly Voll, and Manfred Stede. 2011. Lexicon-based methods for sentiment analysis. *Computational linguistics* 37(2):267–307.

Henri Tajfel. 2010. *Social identity and intergroup relations.* Cambridge University Press.

Duyu Tang, Bing Qin, and Ting Liu. 2015. Document modeling with gated recurrent neural network for sentiment classification. In *EMNLP*. pages 1422–1432.

Carol Tavris, Carole Wade, and Carole Offir. 1984. *The longest war: Sex differences in perspective*. Harcourt.

Zeerak Waseem and Dirk Hovy. 2016. Hateful symbols or hateful people? predictive features for hate speech detection on twitter. In *Proceedings of NAACL-HLT*. pages 88–93.

Theresa Wilson, Janyce Wiebe, and Paul Hoffmann. 2005. Recognizing contextual polarity in phrase-level sentiment analysis. In *Proceedings of the conference on human language technology and empirical methods in natural language processing*. Association for Computational Linguistics, pages 347–354.

Personality Driven Differences in Paraphrase Preference

Daniel Preoţiuc-Pietro
Positive Psychology Center
University of Pennsylvania
danielpr@sas.upenn.edu

Jordan Carpenter
Kenan Institute for Ethics
Duke University
jmc51@duke.edu

Lyle Ungar
Computer and Information Science
University of Pennsylvania
ungar@cis.upenn.edu

Abstract

Personality plays a decisive role in how people behave in different scenarios, including online social media. Researchers have used such data to study how personality can be predicted from language use. In this paper, we study phrase choice as a particular stylistic linguistic difference, as opposed to the mostly topical differences identified previously. Building on previous work on demographic preferences, we quantify differences in paraphrase choice from a massive Facebook data set with posts from over 115,000 users. We quantify the predictive power of phrase choice in user profiling and use phrase choice to study psycholinguistic hypotheses. This work is relevant to future applications that aim to personalize text generation to specific personality types.

1 Introduction

The task of user trait prediction from text has increased in popularity and importance with the availability of user generated content which encodes various information about the author of the text. Using machine learning techniques and large data sets, past research managed to predict with varying degrees of accuracy a series of both demographic traits such as age (Rao et al., 2010; Sap et al., 2014), gender (Burger et al., 2011; Rangel et al., 2015; Flekova et al., 2016a), location (Eisenstein et al., 2010), political affiliation (Volkova et al., 2014; Preoţiuc-Pietro et al., 2017), popularity (Lampos et al., 2014), occupation (Preoţiuc-Pietro et al., 2015b; Liu et al., 2016), income (Preoţiuc-Pietro et al., 2015c; Flekova et al., 2016b) and psychological traits such as personality dimensions (Schwartz et al., 2013; Preoţiuc-Pietro et al., 2016a) or mental states (De Choudhury et al., 2013; Coppersmith et al., 2014; Preoţiuc-Pietro et al., 2015a).

For psychological traits of users, a key set of traits is represented by personality, with the Five Factor Model or the 'Big Five' being the most widely used model for representing personality. This posits the existence of five traits in which people vary: openness to experience, conscientiousness, extraversion, agreeableness and neuroticism (McCrae and John, 1992). Methods for user trait prediction can uncover sociological insight into user behaviour or implicit biases and also improve a range of applications in recommender systems, targeted marketing or in natural language processing where they can lead to improvements in tasks such as text classification (Hovy, 2015) or sentiment analysis (Volkova et al., 2013). While these methods achieve good predictive performance, they pose significant challenges to the anonymization of identity online.

Most differences in language use across traits are topical. For example, users high in extraversion post more about social activities ('party', 'cant wait', 'weekend'), while introverts prefer to post more about computer related activities ('Internet', 'computer', 'anime'). Users high in neuroticism post about their negative feelings ('depressed', 'sick of', 'lonely'), while users low in neuroticism post more about religion ('blessings', 'praise') or sports ('basketball', 'soccer', 'success') (Park et al., 2015).

However, stylistic rather than topical differences are needed in some applications. For example, (Mirkin et al., 2015) propose that the output text of machine translation systems should reproduce the traits of the author of the source text. In this case, topical information is fixed, and the trait information can be transmitted only using stylistic cues. Following the work of (Preoţiuc-Pietro et al., 2016b) who studied demographic traits, we

Proceedings of the Second Workshop on Natural Language Processing and Computational Social Science, pages 17–26,
Vancouver, Canada, August 3, 2017. ©2017 Association for Computational Linguistics

study in this paper user personality differences in paraphrase choice – a specific type of stylistic difference. Paraphrases represent alternative ways to convey the same information (Barzilay, 2003), using either single words or short phrases. Table 1 presents a couple of motivating examples of two group of words and phrases which are all paraphrases of each other ordered by the frequency of use for each personality trait.

In this study, we measure for the first time the differences in paraphrase usage between personality types from a large social media data set in an attempt to obtain language differences isolated from topical influence. Our analysis measures similarities between personality traits, the predictive power of stylistic words and a number of psycholinguistic theories about word choice. The paraphrase scores for each of the five personality traits are available online.[1]

2 Data

Our complete data set consists of approximately 15 million Facebook status updates posted by 115,312 users, representing the full MyPersonality data set (Kosinski et al., 2013). Participants volunteered to share their status updates as part of the MyPersonality application, providing informed consent for data collection. In the MyPersonality application they took a variety of questionnaires, including the International Personality Item Pool proxy for the NEO Personality Inventory Revised (NEO-PI-R) (McCrae and John, 1992; Costa and McCrae, 2008), based on which the five personality trait scores are computed for each user (ranging from 1 to 5).

We split our users into binary groups for each personality trait. In order to have non-overlapping groups, we selected the top 20% users as being high in one trait and the bottom 20% as low in that trait. Data set statistics are presented in Table 2. Our methodology requires a split of users into dichotomous groups in order to compute paraphrase preference. We acknowledge that this split represents a simplification of personality traits and of the subsequent personality prediction task, although this was also used in some previous research (Mairesse et al., 2007; Celli et al., 2014) and, due to the ordinal nature of the personality scores, is highly unlikely to qualitatively affect our results.

---

[1] http://www.preotiuc.ro

Personality Trait	Low	High
Openness	≤ 3.25 (25,211 users)	≥ 4.5 (24,700 users)
Conscientiousness	≤ 2.75 (23,221 users)	≥ 4.049 (23,639 users)
Extroversion	≤ 2.75 (23,802 users)	≥ 4.25 (26,310 users)
Agreeableness	≤ 3 (27,723 users)	≥ 4.25 (23,750 users)
Neuroticism	≤ 2 (25,798 users)	≥ 3.5 (23,339 users)

Table 2: Personality score thresholds and number of users in each personality trait group for the analysis.

3 Quantifying Personality Differences

We use the Paraphrase Database (PPDB) (Ganitkevitch et al., 2013) as our source of paraphrases, owing to its very large size and quality. PPDB 2.0 (Pavlick et al., 2015b) contains 23.820.422 paraphrases derived from a large collection of bilingual texts by pivoting methods. The phrases part of paraphrases are up to three tokens in length (1–3 grams). In PPDB 2.0, each paraphrase pair comes with predicted scores for the relation type between the two phrases ('Equivalence', 'Entailment', 'Exclusion', 'Other relation', 'Unrelated') obtained using a supervised regression model using lexical, distributional and other features (Pavlick et al., 2015a). While there is no inarguable definition of the paraphrase term (Androutsopoulos and Malakasiotis, 2010; Bhagat and Hovy, 2013), in this work we are most interested in the most restrictive type of relationship ('Equivalence') as described in (Pavlick et al., 2015a). We thus use paraphrase pairs that have an equivalence score of at least 0.2 (chosen based upon the inspection of the pairs), leaving us with 6.157.570 paraphrase pairs.

Given a paraphrase pair, we use phrase occurrence statistics computed over our data set to measure the phrase choice difference over user attributes. For the rest of this paragraph, we exemplify with the trait of extraversion, but the computation is analogous for the other four traits.

To score how much a user group favors a phrase w, we compute the scores Extravert(w) and Introvert(w). These are computed by counting the number of times phrase w was used by a user divided by the total number of words of that used, then averaging across all users high or low extraversion respectively. For each phrase we then compute a score:

$$\text{Extraversion}(w) = \log\left(\frac{\text{Extravert}(w)}{\text{Introvert}(w)}\right) \quad (1)$$

Within a paraphrase pair (w_1, w_2), the difference Extraversion(w_1)−Extraversion(w_2) measures the

Low	Openness	Conscientiousness	Extraversion	Agreeableness	Neuroticism
	firstly (-1.24)	firstly (-0.62)	above all (-0.30)	first of all (-0.20)	foremost (-0.24)
	first (-1.03)	foremost (-0.23)	firstly (-0.13)	first (-0.09)	most importantly (-0.21)
	foremost (-0.47)	first of all (-0.20)	first (-0.11)	foremost (-0.07)	above all (-0.08)
	first of all (0.49)	first (0.00)	foremost (-0.07)	above all (0.03)	first (0.01)
	most of all (0.59)	above all (0.14)	most of all (0.10)	firstly (0.14)	most of all (0.02)
	most importantly (0.79)	most importantly (0.16)	first of all (0.26)	most importantly (0.19)	first of all (0.03)
	above all (0.86)	most of all (0.42)	most importantly (0.48)	most of all (0.21)	firstly (0.40)
High	Openness	Conscientiousness	Extraversion	Agreeableness	Neuroticism

Low	Openness	Conscientiousness	Extraversion	Agreeableness	Neuroticism
	Stunning (-.45)	Magnificent (-1.12)	Excellent (-.42)	Marvelous (-.85)	Tremendous (-.57)
	Great (-.34)	Awesome (-.40)	Splendid (-.37)	Unbelievable (-.51)	Remarkable (-.28)
	Wonderful (-.20)	Super (-.36)	Marvelous (-.31)	Remarkable (-.25)	Terrific (-.22)
	Magnificent (-.18)	Splendid (-.30)	Awesome (-.26)	Stunning (-.17)	Marvelous (-.17)
	Super (-.18)	Amazing (-.21)	Exciting (-.14)	Excellent (-.16)	Unbelievable (-.09)
	Gorgeous (-.12)	Excellent (-.12)	Fantastic (-.10)	Super (-.10)	Incredible (-.08)
	Exciting (-.10)	Stunning (-.08)	Great (-.07)	Gorgeous (-.09)	Fabulous (-.07)
	Fabulous (-.09)	Gorgeous (-.08)	Wonderful (-.07)	Awesome (.00)	Awesome (-.03)
	Amazing (-.07)	Incredible (-.04)	Super (-.04)	Fabulous (.02)	Excellent (-.03)
	Tremendous (-.04)	Exciting (.00)	Incredible (-.02)	Amazing (.05)	Great (-.02)
	Awesome (-.02)	Unbelievable (.03)	Unbelievable (-.02)	Great (.07)	Wonderful (-.02)
	Unbelievable (.00)	Fantastic (.07)	Remarkable (-.01)	Fantastic (.10)	Exciting (.01)
	Fantastic (.03)	Great (.18)	Amazing (.07)	Incredible (.18)	Fantastic (.02)
	Marvelous (.13)	Fabulous (.23)	Terrific (.07)	Exciting (.19)	Splendid (.05)
	Terrific (.22)	Wonderful (.38)	Gorgeous (.12)	Terrific (.27)	Super (.06)
	Incredible (.22)	Terrific (.39)	Stunning (.19)	Tremendous (.31)	Amazing (.09)
	Splendid (.29)	Marvelous (.50)	Magnificent (.31)	Wonderful (.35)	Gorgeous (.29)
	Excellent (.36)	Remarkable (.55)	Fabulous (.37)	Splendid (.39)	Magnificent (.44)
	Remarkable (.61)	Tremendous (.70)	Tremendous(.72)	Magnificent (.51)	Stunning (.57)
High	Openness	Conscientiousness	Extraversion	Agreeableness	Neuroticism

Table 1: Two example groups of phrases that are all paraphrases of each other. Words and phrases are ordered by frequency of use. The top words are more frequently used by users low in each personality trait, with words further down the list being more specific of users high in the respective personality trait. The number in brackets represents the score with which the word is related to each trait (described in Section 3).

stylistic distance between users high in extraversion compared to users low in extraversion. This method of computing stylistic distance is similar to the work of Pavlick and Nenkova (2015) who studied paraphrasing in the context of formality and complexity and to that of Preoţiuc-Pietro et al. (2016b) who looked at differences between gender, age and occupational class groups.

In a few experiments, we also use paraphrase clusters which are created by using the transitive closure of pairwise paraphrases, as the supervised model for scoring equivalence combined with our threshold leads to transitivity not holding in our list of pairs. Within these clusters, we subtract the mean phrase score to adjusts for topic prevalence and to lead to a score of 0 representing a point of alignment across all clusters. In total, we derive 785.226 paraphrase clusters (mean = 7.43 words, median = 4 words, st.dev = 11.06 words). Out of these, on average 171.788 clusters (mean = 5.20 words) across the five personality traits contain at least two words scored for phrase choice, as we remove words with low frequency in our data (a relative frequency of under 10^{-5} in our data set).

4   Predicting Personality

We first test the predictive power of paraphrases in the prediction task of whether a user is high or low in each personality trait. We randomly select 90% of the users to build the scores for all phrases and keep 10% of users for evaluating prediction accuracy. We use the Naïve Bayes classifier to assign a score to each user. We use this classifier as this computes for each word the log probability of the word belonging to one class (similar to the measure we previously defined) and computes the dot product between this distribution and the user phrase frequency vector. We chose this algorithm over others to directly tests the viability of our metric. The prior class distribution is estimated based on the training data and we use Laplace smoothing.

To measure the influence of paraphrase choice, we compare the performance of the model using only phrases appearing in at least one paraphrase pair (a proxy for stylistic choice, 62.919 phrases), the rest of the phrases separately (a proxy for topical information, 54.197 phrses) as well as the combined set of phrases. The vocabulary consists of 117.117 phrases (1–3 grams) which have a relative frequency of over 10^{-5} in our data set. Results on predicting personality for unseen users measured in accuracy are shown in Table 3.

	Ope	Con	Ext	Agr	Neu
Random Baseline	.500	.500	.500	.500	.500
Only Paraphrases	.603	.551	.519	.551	.549
Phrases w/o Paraphrases	.573	.589	.578	.553	.590
All Phrases	**.623**	**.639**	**.597**	**.593**	**.631**

Table 3: User attribute prediction results evaluated in accuracy. Using only paraphrases that capture more stylistic rather than topical differences between different personality trait groups, our method still shows good predictive power comparing to using all phrase (1–3 grams) features.

We notice that overall personality can be predicted with significant margins even when using a simple Naive Bayes approach without any feature selection. Both phrases part of paraphrase pairs and not part of paraphrase pairs significantly improve on the random baseline with one exception (Extraversion and paraphrases). However, the numbers are lower than in the case of user demographics (Preoţiuc-Pietro et al., 2016b), which is to be expected when predicting psychological traits (Schwartz et al., 2013; Rangel et al., 2015).

We highlight that in the case of openness to experience, the phrases that are part of paraphrase pairs obtain better prediction performance in accuracy than the other set of phrases. The latter perform better when predicting conscientiousness, extraversion and neuroticism and comparable in case of agreeableness. Combining all phrases consistently obtains the best results.

5   Trait Differences

A very revealing aspect of paraphrase choice for each trait is the order of preference within a para-

phrase cluster, as exemplified in Table 1. To quantify this preference across all clusters, we compute the cluster rank similarity between all pairs of user traits. The average Kendall τ rank correlation coefficient across all clusters is presented in Table 4. As certain personality trait scores are correlated and some users might be part of multiple groups, we also show the correlations between the trait scores in Table 5. As the number of users is very large (>100.000), all correlations in Tables 4 and 5 are significant.

The results on paraphrase choice show a few distinctive patterns. In both paraphrase choice and actual personality scores, neuroticism is anti-correlated with all other four traits, albeit more strongly in case of personality scores. Openness to experience is weakly negatively correlated with all four traits in paraphrase choice, while it is overall weakly positively correlated with the other traits in personality scores. Paraphrase choice is positively correlated across the other three traits (conscientiousness, extraversion, agreeableness), similarly to actual personality scores and with comparable correlations numbers.

Overall, this analysis demonstrates that overall, stylistic paraphrase choice largely reflects user level differences with some variation in case of openness to experience.

	Ope	Con	Ext	Agr	Neu
Ope	–	-.071	-.018	-.040	-.028
Con	-.071	–	.134	.174	-.211
Ext	-.028	.134	–	.107	-.180
Agr	-.040	.174	.107	–	-.174
Neu	-.028	-.211	-.180	-.174	–

Table 4: Average Kendall τ rank correlation between paraphrase cluster usage compared across different user traits. Spearman rank correlation and Pearson correlation reveal similar patterns.

	Ope	Con	Ext	Agr	Neu
Ope	–	.031	.129	.039	-.047
Con	.031	–	.192	.177	-.303
Ext	.129	.192	–	.169	-.337
Agr	.039	.177	.169	–	-.326
Neu	-.047	-.303	-.337	-.326	–

Table 5: Correlation between personality traits in our data set.

6 Linguistic Hypotheses

We investigate a number of psycholinguistic hypotheses about language choice and style by using our paraphrase based method. We argue that word choice within a paraphrase pair excludes the topical influence that confounds studies using all words (Sarawgi et al., 2011)

6.1 Word Properties

Using unigram paraphrases, we study if any user group is more likely to use a word based on the following properties:

Word Length We compute the difference in word length in a paraphrase pair as a simple proxy for word complexity.

Number of Syllables We compute the difference in the number of syllables in a paraphrase pair as another simple proxy for word complexity.

Word Rareness To measure word frequency, we use a reference corpus retrieved from the 10% sample of the Twitter stream between 2 January – 28 February 2011 (~ 400 million tweets), filtered for English using the Trendminer pipeline (Preoţiuc-Pietro et al., 2012). We measure which word from a pair is more frequently used overall by computing a ratio between the frequencies of the two words within a pair.

Perceived Happiness We use the Hedonometer (Dodds et al., 2011, 2015) to obtain happiness ratings for single words. The Hedonometer consists of crowdsourced happiness ratings for 10,221 of the most frequent English words. The ratings range between 8.5 and 1.3 ($\mu = 5.37$, $\sigma = 1.08$). Note these do not only infer the emotional polarity of words (e.g., 'happiness' is more positive than 'terror'), but also how words are perceived by the reader individually without text context (e.g., 'mommy' is perceived happier than 'mom'). We compare the user group preference with the difference in happiness ratings.

Affective Norms To compliment the happiness ratings, we use information about the affective norms of words. In the dimensional model of emotions, any particular emotion can be defined as a set of values on a number of different dimensions. One of the most popular models consists of three dimensions (Mehrabian and Russell, 1974): **Valence** – pleasant vs. unpleasant; **Arousal** – excited vs. calm; **Dominance** – controlled vs. in-control.

We use a list of $\sim$14,000 words rated in all three affective norms introduced in (Warriner et al., 2013). For words rated in both perceived happiness and valence, the correlation is very high ($r = .918$).

Concreteness Concreteness evaluates the degree to which the concept denoted by a word refers to a perceptible entity (Brysbaert et al., 2014). Although the paraphrase pairs refer to the same entity, some words are perceived as more concrete (or conversely more abstract) than others. The dual-coding theory posits that humans process and represent verbal and non-verbal information in separate, related systems. According to this, both concrete and abstract words are represented in the verbal system, but only concrete words are represented in the non-verbal system. Thus, concrete words are more easily learned, remembered and processed than abstract words (Paivio, 2013). We use a list of 37,058 English words with ratings of concreteness on a scale from 5 (e.g., 'tiger' – 5) to 1 (e.g., 'spirituality' – 1.07) introduced in (Brysbaert et al., 2014).

Imageability The construct of imageability represents how easily a particular word elicits a mental picture of the word's referent (Toglia and Battig, 1978). Imagery is thought to be an important aspect of the non-verbal system in the dual-coding theory and is correlated with concreteness ($r = .78$) (Gilhooly and Logie, 1980). We use 6,000 ratings on the ease or difficulty with which words arouse mental images for mono- and disyllabic words (Cortese and Fugett, 2004; Schock et al., 2012), ranging from e.g., 1.2 – 'an' to 7 – 'blizzard'.

Sensory Experience Sensory experience ratings reflect the extent to which a word evokes a sensory and/or perceptual experience in the mind of the reader (Juhasz and Yap, 2013). In contrast to imageability which explicitly refers to visual and sound images and asks raters to attempt to build a mental image of the concept, the sensory experience ratings measures the ability for a word to evoke an actual sensation (taste, touch, sight, sound, or smell) that occurs when reading the word. Although sensory experience and imageability are correlated ($r = .586$) (Juhasz and Yap, 2013), the two variables independently predict unique variance in lexical-decision latencies (Juhasz et al., 2011). We use the ratings from (Juhasz and Yap, 2013) which consist of 5,000 word ratings (e.g., 1 – 'those'; 3 –

Feature	Ope	Con	Ext	Agr	Neu
Word length	.182**	.097**	.080**	.010	−.065**
#Syllables	.067**	.045**	.047**	.016*	−.020*
Word rareness	−.022**	.005	.013*	.007	−.004
Happiness	−.027*	.039**	.034*	.040**	.004
Valence	−.041**	.050**	.050**	.054**	.006
Arousal	−.012	−.001	.028*	.005	−.024*
Dominance	−.043**	.036**	.031*	.030*	.000
Concreteness	−.068**	−.014	.010	−.007	.023*
Imageability	−.061*	−.010	.026	.027	.016
Sensory Experience	−.010	−.018	.023	.001	.064**
Age-of-Acquisition	.163**	−.002	−.060**	−.032*	−.014

Table 6: Correlation coefficients between word property differences and word preference by users high in each personality trait across all paraphrase pairs – $p < 0.05$, two tailed t-test, significant after false discovery rate multi-comparison corrections: Benjamini-Hochberg (*), Bonferroni (**).

'relief'; 6 – 'music').

Age-of-Acquisition   Age-of-Acquisition is a psycholinguistic variable referring to the age at which a word is typically learned (Kuperman et al., 2012). Words with higher age-of-acquisition are anti-correlated to sensory experience ($r = −.586$), imageability ($r = −.440$) (Juhasz and Yap, 2013) and correlated with length in letters ($r = .549$), syllables ($r = .528$) and, to a lesser extent, to abstractness ($r = .166$) (Kuperman et al., 2012). We use the age-of-acquisition ratings for 30,000 words rated with the year in which the words are acquired (e.g., 'momma' – 1.58; 'foot' – 3.44; 'bipartisan' – 16.2) introduced in (Kuperman et al., 2012).

6.2   Paraphrase Entropy

Additionally, we are interesting in identifying which personality groups prefer using a more diverse set of alternative phrases, rather than using a few idiosyncratic phrases. Using all paraphrase clusters (1–3 grams), we compute the average entropy over paraphrase cluster distributions. A higher entropy means the distribution is less peaked towards a specific word, thus showing higher variety in choice.

6.3   Results

We establish if a group of users prefers words within paraphrase pairs with one of the characteristics presented in the previous section using the following method. For each trait and paraphrase pair, we compute the stylistic difference between the words within a pair (see Section 3). Then, for each trait, we run a Pearson correlation between

the vector of stylistic difference scores for each pair and the vector containing the differences in word characteristics (e.g. the difference between the number of syllables of the two words). For each word property, we only retain the paraphrase pairs where we can measure both words, which leads to different numbers of pairs (and hence difference significance thresholds) for each test. The Pearson correlation results are shown in Table 6. We observe there are several statistically significant differences in paraphrase choice between the user groups. Paraphrase entropy by personality trait groups are presented in Table 7.

Personality Trait	Low	High
Openness [(**)]	.838	.924
Conscientiousness	.893	.894
Extroversion [(**)]	.901	.891
Agreeableness [(*)]	.899	.894
Neuroticism [(**)]	.900	.892

Table 7: Average paraphrase cluster entropies for each personality trait. The higher the entropy, the more diverse is the paraphrase choice of the specific group of users. Mean differences are tested for significance using the Mann-Whitney Test: $p \leq .05^{(*)}, p \leq .001^{(**)}$.

The trait that leads to the largest number of significant correlations with phrase choice is openness to experience. Users high in openness prefer words which are longer and with more syllables. These patterns are consistent with the theory that open people are intellectually attuned, creative, and curious (McCrae and Costa Jr, 1997). Simultaneously, openness to experience was negatively related to concreteness, dominance, valence and happiness. This indicates that users who are high in openness are more likely to express themselves in indirect and abstract ways, and they are less likely to prefer explicitly happier words. Again, these are consistent with a more cerebral or artistic mode of communication. Word rareness is anti-correlated with high in openness. However, we noticed that word rareness captures in a large extent also misspellings and alternative spellings. In terms of entropy however, openness to experience generates by far the largest difference in group means for entropy. Those interested in novelty and new experiences may especially dislike phrasing the same concept in the same way over time when other options are available, prefer idiosyncratic words and may have larger vocabularies.

Conscientiousness, extraversion and agreeableness have similar correlations across all phrase choice traits. Users high in these three traits prefer words that are longer and have more syllables. However, for extraversion and agreeableness, age-of-acquisition results show that these groups tend not to choose words acquired later and entropy results show a more limited breadth in usage, both indicative of less complex word choice. Especially, introverts score higher in these choices, perhaps because introverts prefer solitary activities such as reading and may therefore have larger and more sophisticated vocabularies (Furnham, 1981).

All three traits prefer happier and more dominant words, which, at least for extraversion, is unsurprising as these qualities are part of the definition of the trait (Watson and Clark, 1997). Users high in agreeableness are also known to express higher positive valence and conscientious users tend to be more dominant.

Despite the opposite patterns in language use associated with these three traits and openness, these are positively correlated in the user population. Therefore, the two sets of correlations are not simply the same effect explained in two different ways.

Neuroticism exhibits the fewest correlations with phrase choice. Users high in this trait prefer words that are shorter, have fewer syllables and have a slightly lower entropy, which indicates a mild tendency for simpler, idiosyncratic words. Finally, users high the neuroticism prefer words that are higher in sensory experience, and to a lesser degree, that are more concrete. This underlines the preference of this group of users to use social media as a means of communicating about the immediate context.

7 Conclusions

We have studied phrase choice, a particular type of stylistic language difference, across the Big Five personality traits for the first time. We used a large data-driven paraphrase dictionary as our source of paraphrases in combination with statistics computed over large volumes of Facebook status updates. We have shown paraphrase words are, with one exception, predictive of the personality traits and that differences exist in phrase choices. Our analysis of several psycholinguistic word characteristics showed that personality correlates with many systematic word choices and these are intuitive and correspond to theories of personality.

Differences in paraphrase choice are likely to be useful in text-to-text generation and dialogues systems. Tailoring automatically generated text based on personality traits might be desirable in multiple scenarios, such as for tutoring or customer support. However, in most of these cases, the topic is fixed and personalization can be achieved only at a stylistic level. To this end, we make our scored paraphrase choices across personality traits publicly available.

Acknowledgments

The authors acknowledge the support of the Templeton Religion Trust, grant TRT-0048.

References

Ion Androutsopoulos and Prodromos Malakasiotis. 2010. A Survey of Paraphrasing and Textual Entailment Methods. *Journal of Artificial Intelligence Research* 38:135–187.

Regina Barzilay. 2003. *Information Fusion for Multi-document Summarization: Paraphrasing and Generation*. Ph.D. thesis, Columbia University.

Rahul Bhagat and Eduard Hovy. 2013. What is a paraphrase? *Computational Linguistics* 39(3):463–472.

Marc Brysbaert, Amy Beth Warriner, and Victor Kuperman. 2014. Concreteness Ratings for 40 Thousand Generally known English Word Lemmas. *Behavior Research Methods* 46(3):904–911.

D. John Burger, John Henderson, George Kim, and Guido Zarrella. 2011. Discriminating Gender on

Twitter. In *Proceedings of the 2011 Conference on Empirical Methods in Natural Language Processing.* EMNLP, pages 1301–1309.

Fabio Celli, Elia Bruni, and Bruno Lepri. 2014. Automatic Personality and Interaction Style Recognition from Facebook Profile Pictures. In *Proceedings of the 22nd ACM International Conference on Multimedia.* MM, pages 1101–1104.

Glen Coppersmith, Mark Dredze, and Craig Harman. 2014. Quantifying Mental Health Signals in Twitter. In *Workshop on Computational Linguistics and Clinical Psychology: From Linguistic Signal to Clinical Reality (CLPsych).* ACL, pages 51–60.

Michael J Cortese and April Fugett. 2004. Imageability Ratings for 3,000 Monosyllabic Words. *Behavior Research Methods, Instruments, & Computers* 36(3):384–387.

Paul T Costa and Robert R McCrae. 2008. The Revised NEO Personality Inventory (NEO-PI-R). *The SAGE Handbook of Personality Theory and Assessment* 2:179–198.

Munmun De Choudhury, Michael Gamon, Scott Counts, and Eric Horvitz. 2013. Predicting Depression via Social Media. In *Proceedings of the Seventh International AAAI Conference on Weblogs and Social Media.* ICWSM, pages 128–137.

Peter Sheridan Dodds, Eric M. Clark, Suma Desu, Morgan R. Frank, Andrew J. Reagan, Jake Ryland Williams, Lewis Mitchell, Kameron Decker Harris, Isabel M. Kloumann, James P. Bagrow, Karine Megerdoomian, Matthew T. McMahon, Brian F. Tivnan, and Christopher M. Danforth. 2015. Human Language Reveals a Universal Positivity Bias. *Proceedings of the National Academy of Sciences of the United States of America (PNAS)* 112(8):2389–2394.

Peter Sheridan Dodds, Kameron Decker Harris, Isabel M Kloumann, Catherine A Bliss, and Christopher M Danforth. 2011. Temporal Patterns of Happiness and Information in a Global Social Network: Hedonometrics and Twitter. *PloS ONE* 6(12):e26752.

Jacob Eisenstein, Brendan O'Connor, Noah A. Smith, and Eric P. Xing. 2010. A latent variable model for geographic lexical variation. In *Proceedings of the Conference on Empirical Methods in Natural Language Processing.* EMNLP, pages 1277–1287.

Lucie Flekova, Jordan Carpenter, Salvatore Giorgi, Lyle Ungar, and Daniel Preoţiuc-Pietro. 2016a. Analyzing Biases in Human Perception of User Age and Gender from Text. In *Proceedings of the 54th Annual Meeting of the Association for Computational Linguistics.* ACL, pages 843–854.

Lucie Flekova, Lyle Ungar, and Daniel Preoctiuc-Pietro. 2016b. Exploring Stylistic Variation with Age and Income on Twitter. In *Proceedings of the 54th Annual Meeting of the Association for Computational Linguistics.* ACL, pages 313–319.

Adrian Furnham. 1981. Personality and Activity Preference. *British Journal of Social Psychology* 20(1):57–68.

Juri Ganitkevitch, Benjamin Van Durme, and Chris Callison-Burch. 2013. PPDB: The Paraphrase Database. In *Proceedings of the 2013 Annual Conference of the North American Chapter of the Association for Computational Linguistics.* NAACL, pages 758–764.

Ken J Gilhooly and Robert H Logie. 1980. Age-of-acquisition, Imagery, Concreteness, Familiarity, and Ambiguity Measures for 1,944 Words. *Behavior Research Methods & Instrumentation* 12(4):395–427.

Dirk Hovy. 2015. Demographic Factors Improve Classification Performance. In *Proceedings of the 53rd Annual Meeting of the Association for Computational Linguistics.* ACL, pages 752–762.

Barbara J Juhasz and Melvin J Yap. 2013. Sensory Experience Ratings for over 5,000 mono-and Disyllabic Words. *Behavior Research Methods* 45(1):160–168.

Barbara J Juhasz, Melvin J Yap, Joanna Dicke, Sarah C Taylor, and Margaret M Gullick. 2011. Tangible Words are Recognized Faster: The Grounding of Meaning in Sensory and Perceptual Systems. *The Quarterly Journal of Experimental Psychology* 64(9):1683–1691.

Michal Kosinski, David Stillwell, and Thore Graepel. 2013. Private Traits and Attributes are Predictable from Digital Records of Human Behavior. *Proceedings of the National Academy of Sciences of the United States of America (PNAS)* 110(15):5802–5805.

Victor Kuperman, Hans Stadthagen-Gonzalez, and Marc Brysbaert. 2012. Age-of-acquisition Ratings for 30,000 English Words. *Behavior Research Methods* 44(4):978–990.

Vasileios Lampos, Nikolaos Aletras, Daniel Preoţiuc-Pietro, and Trevor Cohn. 2014. Predicting and Characterising User Impact on Twitter. In *Proceedings of the 14th Conference of the European Chapter of the Association for Computational Linguistics.* EACL, pages 405–413.

Ye Liu, Luming Zhang, Liqiang Nie, Yan Yan, and David S Rosenblum. 2016. Fortune Teller: Predicting your Career Path. In *Proceedings of the AAAI Conference on Artificial Intelligence.* AAAI, pages 201–207.

François Mairesse, Marilyn A Walker, Matthias R Mehl, and Roger K Moore. 2007. Using Linguistic Cues for the Automatic Recognition of Personality in Conversation and Text. *Journal of Artificial Intelligence Research* 30:457–500.

Robert R McCrae and Paul T Costa Jr. 1997. Conceptions and Correlates of Openness to Experience. *Handbook of Personality Psychology* pages 825–847.

Robert R McCrae and Oliver P John. 1992. An Introduction to the Five-Factor Model and its Applications. *Journal of Personality* 60(2):175–215.

Albert Mehrabian and James A Russell. 1974. *An Approach to Environmental Psychology*. MIT Press.

Shachar Mirkin, Scott Nowson, Caroline Brun, and Julien Perez. 2015. Motivating Personality-aware Machine Translation. In *Proceedings of the 2015 Conference on Empirical Methods in Natural Language Processing*. EMNLP, pages 1102–1108.

Allan Paivio. 2013. *Imagery and Verbal Processes*. Psychology Press.

Gregory Park, H.Andrew Schwartz, Johannes Eichstaedt, Margaret Kern, Michal Kosinski, David Stillwell, Lyle Ungar, and Martin Seligman. 2015. Automatic Personality Assessment through Social Media Language. *JPSP* 108:934–952.

Ellie Pavlick, Johan Bos, Malvina Nissim, Charley Beller, Benjamin Van Durme, and Chris Callison-Burch. 2015a. Adding Semantics to Data-driven Paraphrasing. In *Proceedings of the 53rd Annual Meeting of the Association for Computational Linguistics*. ACL, pages 1511–1522.

Ellie Pavlick, Juri Ganitkevitch, Pushpendre Rastogi, Benjamin Van Durme, and Chris Callison-Burch. 2015b. PPDB 2.0: Better Paraphrase Ranking, Fine-grained Entailment Relations, Word Embeddings, and Style Classification. In *Proceedings of the 53rd Annual Meeting of the Association for Computational Linguistics*. ACL, pages 425–430.

Ellie Pavlick and Ani Nenkova. 2015. Inducing Lexical Style Properties for Paraphrase and Genre Differentiation. In *Proceedings of the 2015 Annual Conference of the North American Chapter of the Association for Computational Linguistics*. NAACL, pages 218–224.

Daniel Preoţiuc-Pietro, Jordan Carpenter, Salvatore Giorgi, and Lyle Ungar. 2016a. Studying the Dark Triad of Personality using Twitter Behavior. In *Proceedings of the 25th ACM Conference on Information and Knowledge Management*. CIKM, pages 761–770.

Daniel Preoţiuc-Pietro, Johannes Eichstaedt, Gregory Park, Maarten Sap, Laura Smith, Victoria Tobolsky, H Andrew Schwartz, and Lyle H Ungar. 2015a. The Role of Personality, Age and Gender in Tweeting about Mental Illnesses. In *Proceedings of the Workshop on Computational Linguistics and Clinical Psychology: From Linguistic Signal to Clinical Reality*. NAACL.

Daniel Preoţiuc-Pietro, Vasileios Lampos, and Nikolaos Aletras. 2015b. An Analysis of the User Occupational Class through Twitter Content. In *Proceedings of the 53rd Annual Meeting of the Association for Computational Linguistics*. ACL, pages 1754–1764.

Daniel Preoţiuc-Pietro, Ye Liu, Daniel J. Hopkins, and Lyle Ungar. 2017. Beyond Binary Labels: Political Ideology Prediction of Twitter Users. In *Proceedings of the 55th Conference of the Association for Computational Linguistics*. ACL.

Daniel Preoţiuc-Pietro, Sina Samangooei, Trevor Cohn, Nicholas Gibbins, and Mahesan Niranjan. 2012. Trendminer: An Architecture for Real Time Analysis of Social Media Text. In *Workshop on Real-Time Analysis and Mining of Social Streams (RAMSS)*. ICWSM.

Daniel Preoţiuc-Pietro, Svitlana Volkova, Vasileios Lampos, Yoram Bachrach, and Nikolaos Aletras. 2015c. Studying User Income through Language, Behaviour and Affect in Social Media. *PLoS ONE* .

Daniel Preoţiuc-Pietro, Wei Xu, and Lyle Ungar. 2016b. Discovering User Attribute Stylistic Differences via Paraphrasing. In *Proceedings of the Thirtieth AAAI Conference on Artificial Intelligence*. AAAI, pages 3030–3037.

Francisco Rangel, Fabio Celli, Paolo Rosso, Martin Potthast, Benno Stein, and Walter Daelemans. 2015. Overview of the 3rd Author Profiling Task at PAN 2015. In *CLEF*.

Delip Rao, David Yarowsky, Abhishek Shreevats, and Manaswi Gupta. 2010. Classifying Latent User Attributes in Twitter. In *Proceedings of the 2nd International Workshop on Search and Mining User-generated Contents*. SMUC, pages 37–44.

Maarten Sap, Gregory Park, Johannes Eichstaedt, Margaret Kern, Lyle Ungar, and H Andrew Schwartz. 2014. Developing Age and Gender Predictive Lexica over Social Media. In *Proceedings of the 2014 Conference on Empirical Methods in Natural Language Processing*. EMNLP, pages 1146–1151.

Ruchita Sarawgi, Kailash Gajulapalli, and Yejin Choi. 2011. Gender Attribution: Tracing Stylometric Evidence beyond Topic and Genre. In *Proceedings of the Fifteenth Conference on Computational Natural Language Learning*. CONNL, pages 78–86.

Jocelyn Schock, Michael J Cortese, and Maya M Khanna. 2012. Imageability Estimates for 3,000 Disyllabic Words. *Behavior Research Methods* 44(2):374–379.

H Andrew Schwartz, Johannes C Eichstaedt, Margaret L Kern, Lukasz Dziurzynski, Stephanie M Ramones, Megha Agrawal, Achal Shah, Michal Kosinski, David Stillwell, Martin EP Seligman, and Lyle H Ungar. 2013. Personality, Gender, and Age in the Language of Social Media: The Open-vocabulary Approach. *PLoS One* 8.

Michael P Toglia and William F Battig. 1978. *Handbook of Semantic Word Norms*. Lawrence Erlbaum.

Svitlana Volkova, Glen Coppersmith, and Benjamin Van Durme. 2014. Inferring User Political Preferences from Streaming Communications. In *Proceedings of the 52nd Annual Meeting of the Association for Computational Linguistics*. ACL, pages 186–196.

Svitlana Volkova, Theresa Wilson, and David Yarowsky. 2013. Exploring Demographic Language Variations to Improve Multilingual Sentiment Analysis in Social Media. In *Proceedings of the 2013 Conference on Empirical Methods in Natural Language Processing*. EMNLP, pages 1815–1827.

Amy Beth Warriner, Victor Kuperman, and Marc Brysbaert. 2013. Norms of Valence, Arousal, and Dominance for 13,915 English Lemmas. *Behavior Research Methods* 45(4):1191–1207.

David Watson and Lee Anna Clark. 1997. Extraversion and its Positive Emotional Core. *Handbook of Personality Psychology* pages 767–793.

community2vec: Vector representations of online communities encode semantic relationships

Trevor Martin

Department of Biology, Stanford University
Stanford, CA 94035
trevorm@stanford.edu

Abstract

Vector embeddings of words have been shown to encode meaningful semantic relationships that enable solving of complex analogies. This vector embedding concept has been extended successfully to many different domains and in this paper we both create and visualize vector representations of an unstructured collection of online communities based on user participation. Further, we quantitatively and qualitatively show that these representations allow solving of semantically meaningful community analogies and also other more general types of relationships. These results could help improve community recommendation engines and also serve as a tool for sociological studies of community relatedness.

1 Introduction

Social media usage and participation in online communities has grown steadily over the last decade (Perrin, 2015). As we increasingly live our lives online, it is important to characterize the online communities we inhabit and understand the relationships between them. Our expanding reliance on online communities also represents an exciting opportunity to understand the links between different interests and hobbies, as candid participation across online communities is more immediately and scalably measurable compared to offline communities.

Recent work has shown that vector representations and embeddings of entities are a powerful tool across a range of applications from words (Mikolov et al., 2013a) to DNA sequences (Asgari and Mofrad, 2015). In particular, the co-occurrence based embeddings of words in a cor-

pus has been demonstrated to encode meaningful semantic relationships between them (Mikolov et al., 2013b). In this paper we extend the concept of vector embeddings to represent an unstructured collection of online communities and show that the co-occurrence of users across online communities also embeds the semantic relations between them. Further downstream applications of these results could include improved community recommendation engines and advertisement targeting.

We focus our analysis on the social sharing site Reddit, the 4th most popular website in the US (Alexa, 2017), which has user created and managed communities called subreddits.[1] Subreddits are communities centered around particular topics and interests where users can post articles and comments while also voting content up or down to make it more or less visible. To our knowledge this paper represents the first use of vector based representations of such communities to solve analogies and perform semantically meaningful calculations of relationships.

2 Related Work

Reddit is relatively understudied compared to other social networks such as Facebook, but an increasing body of work has used its data to look at topics ranging from online user behavior (Hamilton et al., 2017) to user migration across social media platforms (Newell et al., 2016). A map of Reddit using commenter co-occurrences has also been previously created using a much smaller sample of comment data (Olsen and Neal, 2015) by treating the co-occurrence matrix as a weighted graph and extracting the network backbone. Relatedly, there has been interest in developing vector representations of graph structures as shown by techniques

---

[1] Subreddits are typically denoted with a leading /r/, for example /r/dataisbeautiful is the "dataisbeautiful" subreddit.

Proceedings of the Second Workshop on Natural Language Processing and Computational Social Science, pages 27–31,
Vancouver, Canada, August 3, 2017. ©2017 Association for Computational Linguistics

like DeepWalk (Perozzi et al., 2014) and node2vec (Grover and Leskovec, 2016), which we could potentially use to create additional vector representations to test below. Reddit communities do not have a built-in explicit graph structure though, as there are not defined links between communities in the same manner as users can be linked by friendship requests on sites like Facebook. In this paper we show that semantically meaningful maps of communities can be created using the NLP toolbox originally created for mapping the semantic similarity of words, without a need for defining an explicit graph.

3   Method

Our method for uncovering semantic relationships between online communities begins by creating vector representations of each community based on how often users comment across communities using one of the three methods outlined below. Broadly, we follow the general framework of Levy et al. (2015), where in our modified framework communities take on the role of words and user co-occurrence the role of word co-occurrence. We then simply add and subtract these community vectors to evaluate semantic correctness. Here, we use a publicly available corpus of all Reddit comments from January 1st, 2015 through April 30th, 2017 as the input to each technique. This data set consists of roughly 1.8 billion comments across 60,978 subreddit communities.[2]

3.1   Subreddit Vectors

We first create a symmetric matrix of community-community user co-occurrences $\mathbf{X}$, whose entries $\mathbf{X_{ij}}$ indicate the number of unique users who commented 10 times or more in each subreddit.

Explicit: Our explicit subreddit representation first simply subsets the co-occurrence matrix $\mathbf{X}$ to include only the subreddits with unique author ranks between 200 and 2,201 as context subreddits (columns of $\mathbf{X}$). The choice of rank cutoff here is arbitrary but based on the idea that performance can be increased by adjusting the number of context tokens (Bullinaria and Levy, 2007). We choose the subreddits with the most unique authors because these are likely to encode the most useful information and drop the top 200 subred-

dits because many of these are "default" subreddits that all Reddit users are subscribed to and thus are unlikely to have as rich co-occurrence information. Then we transform this new matrix $\mathbf{X_{:,201:2200}}$ using the positive pointwise mutual information metric to weigh each count by its informativeness, where $p(i,j)$ is the joint probability of seeing authors in both subreddits i and j and $p(i)$ and $p(j)$ are the probabilities of seeing an author in each subreddit respectively:

$$PMI(i,j) \equiv \log \frac{p(i,j)}{p(i)p(j)}$$

$$PPMI(i,j) = \begin{cases} 0, & \text{if } PMI(i,j) < 0 \\ PMI(i,j), & \text{otherwise} \end{cases}$$

The subreddit vectors (rows) of the resulting $PPMI$ matrix are then scaled to unit length.

PCA: We also create a dense vector representation of subreddits by calculating the principal components of the $PPMI$ transformation above applied to the matrix $\mathbf{X_{:,1:5000}}$, which is $\mathbf{X}$ subset to the top 5,000 context subreddits by unique author ranks. We extract the top 100 principal components and scale each subreddit vector to unit length.

GloVe: Finally, we create a second dense vector representation of subreddits by running the GloVe algorithm (Pennington et al., 2014), originally developed to create embeddings for word-word co-occurrence matrices, on the raw co-occurrence matrix $\mathbf{X}$. The resulting size 100 GloVe subreddit vectors are again scaled to unit length.

3.2   Subreddit Algebra

Combinations of subreddit representations (subreddit algebra) are performed through standard vector addition and subtraction. The similarity between two subreddits is defined here as the *cosine similarity*, given by:

$$\text{cosine similarity}(\vec{A}, \vec{B}) = \frac{\vec{A} \cdot \vec{B}}{\|\vec{A}\|\|\vec{B}\|}$$

Where $\vec{A}$ and $\vec{B}$ are the vector representations of subreddit A and B respectively. Subreddits are ranked in similarity by ordering from largest cosine similarity to smallest.

---

[2]Reddit data available at: `https://bigquery.cloud.google.com/table/fh-bigquery:reddit_comments.all_starting_201501`

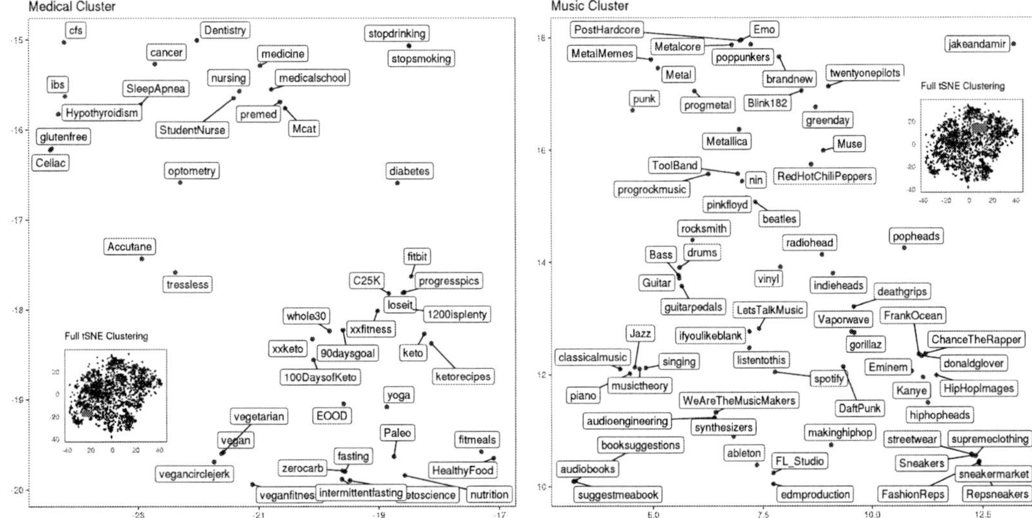

(a) View of subreddits representing medical interests and health conscious lifestyles.

(b) View of subreddits representing music genres and performing groups.

Figure 1: Examples of semantically meaningful clusters in t-SNE visualization of GloVe subreddit vectors. Zoomed-in region of t-SNE visualization indicated in red on figure insets.

4 Evaluation

We quantitatively evaluate the efficacy of subreddit algebra by assessing its ability to identify local sports team subreddits from combinations of league and geography subreddits. Additionally, we qualitatively evaluate our the results by identifying specific interesting subreddit relationships and visualizing the subreddit vector space as a whole.

4.1 tSNE Clustering

To check that our vector representations of subreddit communities are reasonable, we used t-SNE (Maaten and Hinton, 2008) to project the high-dimensional vector representations of each subreddit into two dimensions for visualization. Examples of typical semantically meaningful clusters that we can observe in these t-SNE projections are given in Figure 1. Figure 1a shows that medical and health related subreddits cluster together and Figure 1b shows the dense clustering of music and band related subreddits and clustering within this larger group by music genre.[3] These natural groupings suggest that our vector representations are reasonable and are encoding semantically relevant information about each subreddit.

4.2 Automated Semantic Relationship Test

In order to quantitatively evaluate the ability of the subreddit vectors to encode semantic relations, we created a list of subreddit combinations where we have a strong expectation for the outcome subreddit. Conveniently, sport, location, and team subreddits have a natural analogy structure. Specifically, for the NBA, NFL, and NHL sports leagues we created a list of geographic location subreddits (e.g. `/r/sanfrancisco`) that when combined with a league subreddit (e.g. `/r/nba`) should result in that location's local league affiliate (e.g. `/r/warriors`).[4] Performance on this task for an individual league-location pair is assessed by calculating:

$$\mathrm{median}(SR(\vec{S}, \vec{T}), SR(\vec{L}, \vec{T})) - SR(\vec{S} + \vec{L}, \vec{T})$$

Where $\vec{S}$ is the league subreddit, $\vec{L}$ is the location subreddit, and $\vec{T}$ is the target subreddit. $SR(\vec{A}, \vec{B})$ is the rank of the subreddit B when all subreddits are ordered by decreasing cosine similarity to subreddit A.

The decrease in similarity ranking for each sports league across each of the three vector representations was then evaluated for significance by

---

[3]To aid in visualization, we only project the top 5,000 and 2,500 subreddits by unique author count for the medical and music GloVe based clusters respectively.

[4]In total we use 92 league-location combinations.

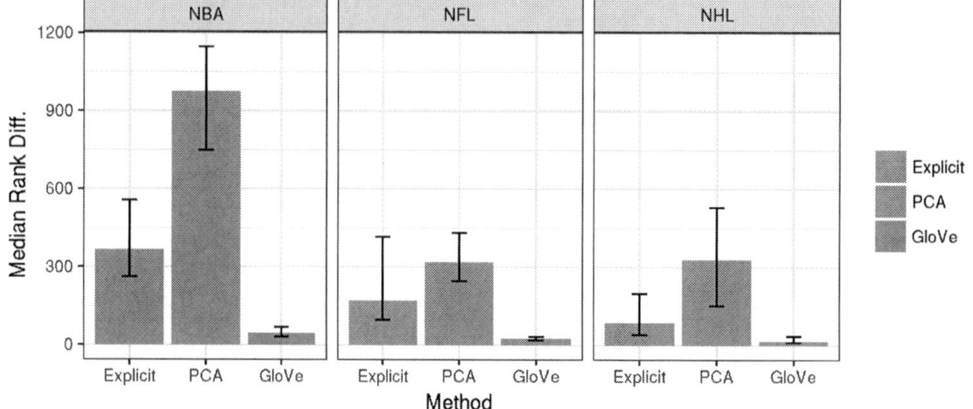

Figure 2: Comparison of different vector representation's performance for identifying local sports teams in each league.

Method	League	$\vec{S} + \vec{L}$: $\vec{T}$ Median Rank	Median Rank Diff.	p-value
Explicit	NBA	7	365.5	1.9e-9
	NFL	5	170.8	8.3e-7
	NHL	4	87.5	1.9e-9
PCA	NBA	212	976.3	4.7e-8
	NFL	13	320.1	9.3e-10
	NHL	41.5	330	3.4e-4
GloVe	NBA	7	46.5	1.8e-6
	NFL	2	25	1.5e-5
	NHL	1	16.5	1.8e-6

Table 1: Results of automated testing of subreddit vector representation semantic encodings.

a two-sided Wilcoxon signed-rank test for symmetry of the rank changes around 0. The median decrease in target subreddit rank between $SR(\vec{S} + \vec{L}, \vec{T})$ and median$(SR(\vec{S}, \vec{T}), SR(\vec{L}, \vec{T}))$ for each sports league-vector representation pair is shown in Figure 2.[5] Interestingly, both the explicit and PCA vector representations appear to perform best, but all three methods show significant performance on the task as indicated in Table 1.

Closer inspection of the results reveals though that while the PCA method has the largest improvement in target subreddit rank (Median Rank Diff. in Table 1), it also has the highest median subreddit ranks for the target subreddits after performing subreddit algebra of the three methods ($\vec{S} + \vec{L}$: $\vec{T}$ Median Rank in Table 1). This observation suggests that while the PCA representations benefit the most from algebra they also have the least accuracy for identifying the target subreddit

overall.[6] In contrast, for algebra using either the explicit or GloVe vector representations, the target subreddit is often the most similar result.

4.3 Selected Semantic Examples

In addition to the automated test, we also identified several interesting analogy tasks to run using subreddit algebra.[7] Because we do not necessarily have subreddits for representing concepts such as "man" or "woman" we cannot reproduce exactly classic cases like $king - man + woman = queen$, but for the cases where we could form robust analogies the results are encouraging, as shown in Figure 3.

Of note is that we can reproduce country:capital relationships similar to those found in word embeddings using community participation across subreddits and also can reproduce analogies that

---

[5]More specifically the Hodges-Lehmann pseudomedian, with 95% CI

[6]Also, PCA based representations do not necessarily have the linear substructure seen in GloVe embeddings.

[7]We use the explicit representations here.

```
/r/berlin - /r/germany + /r/unitedkingdom = /r/london
/r/chicagobulls - /r/chicago + /r/minnesota = /r/timberwolves
/r/running + /r/weightlifting = /r/fitness
/r/personalfinance - /r/frugal = /r/wallstreetbets
/r/books + /r/fiction = /r/HFnovels
```

Figure 3: Selected semantic algebra examples.

subtract a component (Chicago) of a whole (Chicago Bulls NBA team) and add a different location (Minnesota) to get that locality's NBA team (Minnesota Timberwolves). We can also find communities specific to medium-genre combinations such as the historical fiction book community `/r/HFnovels`. Finally, we see some surprising examples, such as subtracting the community for frugality from the community for managing personal finances results in the community for taking extreme risks on the stock market, `/r/wallstreetbets`.

5 Conclusions

Our work here shows that vector representations of communities can encode meaningful analogies and semantic relationships in the same way as has been previously seen for words. Notably, the explicit vector representations perform competitively with the GloVe embeddings on the semantic task we tested, suggesting that the semantic meanings are present in the raw vectors and are simply preserved through the embedding process. Future directions we are pursuing involve supplementing the vector representations with data on comment voting scores, using posts or views in lieu of or supplementally to comments and looking at diachronic subreddit embeddings to analyze the patterns of subreddit relationships over time.

Acknowledgments

We would like to thank Will Hamilton for his valuable comments and suggestions on the manuscript.

References

Alexa. 2017. http://www.alexa.com/siteinfo/reddit.com. *Alexa Rankings* .

Ehsaneddin Asgari and Mohammad R. K. Mofrad. 2015. Continuous distributed representation of biological sequences for deep proteomics and genomics. *PLOS ONE* 10(11):1–15. https://doi.org/10.1371/journal.pone.0141287.

John A. Bullinaria and Joseph P. Levy. 2007. Extracting semantic representations from word co-occurrence statistics: A computational study. *Behavior Research Methods* 39(3):510–526. https://doi.org/10.3758/BF03193020.

Aditya Grover and Jure Leskovec. 2016. node2vec: Scalable feature learning for networks. *CoRR* abs/1607.00653. http://arxiv.org/abs/1607.00653.

William L. Hamilton, Justine Zhang, Cristian Danescu-Niculescu-Mizil, Dan Jurafsky, and Jure Leskovec. 2017. Loyalty in online communities. *CoRR* abs/1703.03386. http://arxiv.org/abs/1703.03386.

Omer Levy, Yoav Goldberg, and Ido Dagan. 2015. Improving distributional similarity with lessons learned from word embeddings. *Transactions of the Association for Computational Linguistics* 3:211–225. https://transacl.org/ojs/index.php/tacl/article/view/570.

Laurens van der Maaten and Geoffrey Hinton. 2008. Visualizing data using t-sne. *Journal of Machine Learning Research* 9(Nov):2579–2605.

Tomas Mikolov, Kai Chen, Greg Corrado, and Jeffrey Dean. 2013a. Efficient estimation of word representations in vector space. *CoRR* abs/1301.3781. http://arxiv.org/abs/1301.3781.

Tomas Mikolov, Wen-tau Yih, and Geoffrey Zweig. 2013b. Linguistic regularities in continuous space word representations. In *Hlt-naacl*. volume 13, pages 746–751.

Edward Newell, David Jurgens, Haji Saleem, Hardik Vala, Jad Sassine, Caitrin Armstrong, and Derek Ruths. 2016. User migration in online social networks: A case study on reddit during a period of community unrest.

Randal Olsen and Zachary Neal. 2015. Navigating the massive world of reddit: using backbone networks to map user interests in social media. *PeerJ Computer Science* .

Jeffrey Pennington, Richard Socher, and Christopher D. Manning. 2014. Glove: Global vectors for word representation. In *Empirical Methods in Natural Language Processing (EMNLP)*. pages 1532–1543. http://www.aclweb.org/anthology/D14-1162.

Bryan Perozzi, Rami Al-Rfou, and Steven Skiena. 2014. Deepwalk: Online learning of social representations. *CoRR* abs/1403.6652. http://arxiv.org/abs/1403.6652.

Andrew Perrin. 2015. Social media usage: 2005-2015. *PewResearchCenter* .

A Supplemental Material

All code and league-location-team combinations are available at `https://github.com/trevormartin/papers`.

Telling Apart Tweets Associated with Controversial versus Non-Controversial Topics

Aseel Addawood
Illinois Informatics Institute
University of Illinois at Urbana-Champaign
aaddaw2@illinois.edu

Rezvaneh Rezapour
School of Information Sciences
University of Illinois at Urbana-Champaign
rezapou2@illinois.edu

Omid Abdar
Department of Linguistics
University of Illinois at Urbana-Champaign
abdar2@illinois.edu

Jana Diesner
School of Information Sciences
University of Illinois at Urbana-Champaign
jdiesner@illinois.edu

Abstract

In this paper, we evaluate the predictability of tweets associated with controversial versus non-controversial topics. As a first step, we crowd-sourced the scoring of a predefined set of topics on a Likert scale from non-controversial to controversial. Our feature set entails and goes beyond sentiment features, e.g., by leveraging empathic language and other features that have been previously used, but are new for this particular study. We find focusing on the structural characteristics of tweets to be beneficial for this task. Using a combination of emphatic, language-specific, and Twitter-specific features for supervised learning resulted in 87% accuracy (F1) for cross-validation of the training set and 63.4% accuracy when using the test set. Our analysis shows that features specific to Twitter or social media in general are more prevalent in tweets on controversial topics than in non-controversial ones. To test the premise of the paper, we conducted two additional sets of experiments, which led to mixed results. This finding will inform our future investigations into the relationship between language use on social media and the perceived controversiality of topics.

1 Introduction

The micro-blogging platform Twitter is a central venue for online discussions and argumentation. This service has also been widely used to disseminate information during emergencies and natural disasters, and to mobilize support for social and political movements (Lotan, Graeff, Ananny, Gaffney, & Pearce, 2011). As with many other outlets of public opinion, Twitter features the emergence of polarization around controversial issues (Addawood & Bashir, 2016; Garimella, De Francisci Morales, Gionis, & Mathioudakis, 2016), and provides a forum where people can express their opinions, which may be conflicting (Pennacchiotti & Popescu, 2010).

This paper focuses on the classification of tweets on topics that are perceived as controversial versus non-controversial. A distinction needs to be made between controversiality and controversy. "Controversy" can be understood as the dyadic or social act of discussing or arguing about an issue (Chen & Berger, 2013). This concept is not addressed in this paper. "Controversiality" means that multiple, potentially conflicting or opposing, viewpoints or opinions have been expressed on a given topic, and people may argue about them or not (Dori-Hacohen, Yom-Tov, & Allan, 2015). In this article, we focus on detecting tweets associated with controversial versus non-controversial topics. Our goal is to gain a better understanding of language-related and tweet-related features that people use in tweets on controversially versus non-controversially perceived topics.

The identification and characterization of controversial topics is difficult for several reasons. First, what is regarded as controversial depends on the senders and receivers of information as well as on the context of a topic in terms of space and time. Second, understanding or even resolving controversies on the individual level may require expertise that may not be part of everybody's general knowledge; making the construction of con-

Proceedings of the Second Workshop on Natural Language Processing and Computational Social Science, pages 32–41,
Vancouver, Canada, August 3, 2017. ©2017 Association for Computational Linguistics

sensus challenging in terms of creating a comprehensive and shared knowledge base in the first place. Third, the potentially continuously evolving nature of information and knowledge further adds to this challenge.

Previous research used Twitter for detecting both controversy and controversiality (Conover et al., 2011; Garimella et al., 2016; Pennacchiotti & Popescu, 2010). To date, much of the previous research on controversiality has used data from political debates (Adamic & Glance, 2005; Conover et al., 2011; Mejova, Zhang, Diakopoulos, & Castillo, 2014; Morales, Borondo, Losada, & Benito, 2015), news (Awadallah, Ramanath, & Weikum, 2012; Choi, Jung, & Myaeng, 2010; Mejova et al., 2014), and social media, such as blogs (Adamic & Glance, 2005), and Wikipedia (Dori-Hacohen & Allan, 2013; Kittur, Suh, Pendleton, & Chi, 2007; Rad & Barbosa, 2012).

To detect tweets about controversial versus non-controversial topics, we first built a questionnaire to identify such topics that are discussed in the U.S. by using social media and crowdsourcing. We then collected a total of 247,340 tweets from between January 1 to November 28 of 2016. Our research focuses on the underlying characteristics of tweets and demonstrates that the considered features are useful for distinguishing tweets on controversial versus non-controversial topics.

The rest of the paper is organized as follows: The literature review discusses how this work fills a gap in prior work. The data section describes the topic and corpus selection. In the method section, we explain the feature selection and classification. We then report the results of our empirical evaluation of the classifier. We conclude with a discussion of possible improvements and directions for future work.

2   Literature Review

2.1   Controversiality Detection in Online News

To quantify controversiality in online news, Choi, Jung, and Myaeng (2010) leveraged positive and/or negative sentiment words to compute the degree of controversiality. Mejova and colleagues (2014) report a high correlation between a) controversial issues and b) the use of negative affect and biased language. Awadallah and colleagues (2012) describe a method where opinion holders and their opinions as extracted facets from Web result snippets were identified through an iterative process based on a seed set of patterns that describe expressions in either support or opposition to an idea.

2.2   Controversiality Detection Using Other Sources

Some prior work on detecting controversiality leveraged Wikipedia, where structured data and revision histories provide relevant data related to conflicting opinions (Kittur et al., 2007). Using Wikipedia data, Rad and Barbosa (2012) compared five methods for identifying and modeling controversy and controversiality. Das and colleagues (2013) used controversy detection as one step in studying content manipulation by Wikipedia administrators. Knowledge about controversial articles on Wikipedia has been utilized to evaluate the level of controversy of other documents (e.g., web pages) (Dori-Hacohen & Allan, 2013). Finally, Wikipedia has been leveraged for developing a lexicon or hierarchy for controversial words and topics (Awadallah et al., 2012; Pennacchiotti & Popescu, 2010).

Another line of work has focused on controversy detection in blogs. Mishne and Glance (2006) present a large-scale study of blog comments and their relation to corresponding articles. They addressed the task of finding comment threads indicating a controversy as a text classification problem.

Finally, Tsytsarau, Palpanas, and Denecke (2011) focused on finding sentiment-based contradictions at scale by using data sets as disparate as drug reviews, comments to YouTube videos, and comments on Slashdot posts. Even though sentiment analysis seems an intuitive component for detecting multiple viewpoints (Choi et al., 2010; Pennacchiotti & Popescu, 2010), some researchers have argued that this technique is not sufficient and may not be the right metric with which to measure controversiality (Awadallah et al., 2012; Dori-Hacohen & Allan, 2013; Mejova et al., 2014).

2.3   Controversiality Detection in Twitter

The work closest to ours is that by Pennacchiotti and Popescu (2010), where they sought to detect controversiality about selected celebrities and events associated with them based on Twitter data. Their study measures the presence of terms explicitly associated with controversiality in celebrity-related tweets, resulting in an average precision of up to 66% in predicting controversiality. The authors operationalized this task as a regression problem to predict a controversiality score of each tweet that mentions a specific celebrity and terms based on a list of controversial topics from Wikipedia. By contrast, we conceptualize this task as a classification problem where we predict if a tweet is about a controversial or a non-controversial topic. We do not address or measure if a tweet or sequence of tweets is controversial, in fact, we do not assume a relationship between the controversiality of tweets and of topics, and vice versa. While the work by Pennacchiotti and Popescu focused on celebrities, we address a broader range of topics.

Our work also relates to that of Conover et al. (2011), who studied controversy in political communication about congressional midterm elections using Twitter data. They found a highly segregated partisan structure (present in the retweet graph, but not in the mention graph), and limited connectivity between left- and right-leaning users.

Overall, we build upon previous work by adding additional features for the given task. We do not solely rely on sentiment analysis, but also extract other features. We also develop a lexicon to identify emphatic language used in tweets on the considered topics based on prior literature, and supplemented that with an existing lexical resource for profanity.

3 Data

3.1 Topic Selection

To identify a set of controversial and non-controversial topics, we first searched controversy-related web sources (i.e. Procon.org), Wikipedia controversiality lists, news media websites, and blogs. The results of this initial search helped us to develop eight claim statements (one statement per topic) on topics (see Table 1).

After formulating these statements, two online surveys were conducted in which the participants rated the statements pertaining to different topics on a 5-point scale ranging from controversial to non-controversial. Participants were randomly assigned to evaluate four out of the eight statements. Table 1 shows the selected topics and associated statements used in the survey.

The first questionnaire was run on Amazon's Mechanical Turk service (MTurk), an online crowdsourcing system. MTurk participants were compensated with $0.10 USD per survey. The survey was available only to U.S. residents with at least 95% approval rating (a screening option that is provided by MTurk). A total of 197 surveys was received from MTurkers, and 172 of them were valid. A response is considered invalid if it did not contain complete answers or was not validated through a validation question.

The second questionnaire was distributed on social media, specifically on Facebook and Reddit. Participants were not compensated for their contribution due to the need of preserving their anonymity. Empty responses and responses that did not contain complete answers were eliminated. A total of 120 responses was received and out of those, 71 were completed. In total (considering both surveys), a total of 243 valid responses was collected. The surveys were conducted over a period of three weeks in October 2016.

To measure the controversiality of a statement, participants were asked to rate how controversial they believed a statement was on a 5-point Likert scale (5 = "very controversial", 1= "not controversial at all"). Based on the participants' average rating of the presented topics (see Table 1), the three-top controversial and non-controversial topics were selected for further analysis: The controversial topics were (a) individual privacy versus national security, (b) the link between vaccination and autism, and (c) gun control. The non-controversial topics were (a) usage of seatbelts,

Categorization	Exemplary Topic	Statement	AVG
Controversial	Privacy	*"Citizen privacy takes precedence over national security"*	3.73
	Vaccine	*"MMR vaccine causes autism"*	3.63
	Gun control	*"Access to guns should be more restricted"*	4.10
Non-controversial	Seatbelts	*"Seat belt use can save lives in car accidents"*	1.30
	Child education	*"Every child should have access to education"*	1.49
	Sun exposure	*"Skin damage from excessive sun exposure"*	1.43

Table 1: Controversial and non-controversial topics considered in this study.

(b) access to education for children, and (c) detrimental effects of sun exposure.

3.2 Corpus Selection

We used Crimson Hexagon (Etlinger & Amand, 2012), a social media analytics tool, to collect public tweets posted in the time window from January 1, 2016 through November 28, 2016 on the given topics, based on queries we formulated. The sample only included tweets from accounts that set English as their language and that were geo-located in the U.S. The total number of collected and downloaded tweets is shown in Table 2. Out of the total 246,869 unique tweets that were collected, 148,677 were on controversial topics, and 98,208 were on non-controversial topics.

4 Method

4.1 Feature Selection

User-generated text can express various different thoughts in controversial and non-controversial tweets (Davidov, Tsur, & Rappoport, 2010). Our feature selection was motivated by the assumption that features that capture these thoughts would be effective for our classification task. Some of our features, e.g. sentiment (Pennacchiotti & Popescu, 2010), have been previously used for analyzing Twitter data, while others are novel for this task, and are motivated by pragmatic research into linguistic mechanisms related to engagement in controversial talk.

Emphatic Features

Lexical Emphasis: In the pragmatics literature, it is believed that throughout conversation, speakers have a desire for their thoughts and beliefs to be accepted by their audience (Roberts, 1992). Since controversial topics can be expected to result in disagreement or dissent, we expect tweets on these topics to have a heavier reliance on emphatic language. Based on this intuition, we developed a lexicon to help detecting instances of lexical emphasis. We used a taxonomic grammar of English (Celce-Murcia, Larsen-Freeman, & Williams, 1999) to source a list of emphatic words, including emphatic adjectives (e.g., "awful," "horrible," "great," "fantastic," "superb," etc.) and intensifying adverbs (e.g., "perfectly," "extremely," "insanely," "ridiculously," etc.). We added these words to a lexicon of profanity in English (Ahn., n.d.), which was used since the use of swear words has shown to reflect the emotional state of the speaker (Jay & Janschewitz, 2008).

Orthographic-Based Emphasis: Emphasis can also be achieved via orthographic stylistic expressions, including punctuation and upper casing (Davidov et al., 2010). We recorded instances of uppercase words. Social media users also occasionally use repeated exclamation marks to show sarcasm or emphasis. We recorded all instances of the use of one or more exclamation marks in tweets.

Language-Specific Features

Since a previous study showed that using lexical and syntactic features improve the accuracy of detecting controversy (Allen, Carenini, & Ng, 2014), we built upon this finding, but relied on a wider range of language specific features, namely grammatical and psychological features. We used the Python NLTK library (Bird, Klein, & Loper, 2009) and custom python scripts for grammatical features, and LIWC (Linguistic Inquiry and Word Count) (Pennebaker, Booth, & Francis, 2007) for psychological features.

Psychological Features: Controversial topics lead to disagreements in the audience (Dori-Hacohen et al., 2015), and controversial conversations can create misalignment effects that speakers might mitigate (Roberts, 1992). While the exact nature of how these effects occur in conversation can be hard to pinpoint, we included a set of psychological features as defined and provided by LIWC to help in capturing some of these effects from tweets. We extracted instances of the following selected categories available in LIWC (Pennebaker et al., 2007): (a) "Cognition Processes" such as words related to insight, cause, discrepancies, degree of certitude, and difference, (b) "Informal Language Markers" such as assents, fillers, and swear words, (c) "Personal Concerns" such as words related to work, leisure, home, money,

Topic	Number of Download	# After Removing duplicates
Privacy	99,549	73,593
Vaccine	63,137	41,005
Gun control	50,000	34,490
Seatbelts	89,912	73,271
Child education	46,931	10,808
Sun exposure	20,528	14,173

Table 2: Total number of tweets after removing duplicates.

Features	NB			DT			SVM		
	P	**R**	**F1**	**P**	**R**	**F1**	**P**	**R**	**F1**
Baseline (Twitter)	62.7	49.0	41.7	69.1	69.4	68.9	65.8	66.0	64.3
Twitter + Emphatic	63.2	50.3	44.2	69.8	70.1	69.7	65.8	66.0	64.3
Twitter + Language-Specific	77.6	77.7	77.4	87.6	87.6	87.6	86.3	86.4	86.3
Twitter + Emphatic+ Language-Specific	77.6	77.7	77.4	87.7	87.7	87.7	86.4	86.4	86.4

Table 3: Results of NB, DT, and SVM using 10-fold cross validation (values are %).

religion, and death, (d) "Social Words," such as words related to family and friends, (e) "Drives," which are words related to affiliation, achievement, power, risk and reward, (f) "Clout", (g) "Tone", (h) "Authenticity", and (i) "Analytical Thinking". LIWC is a dictionary-based tool which associates words with categories. As in the previous step, the presence of various words (in the respective category) is calculated per tweet and then normalized by tweet length.

Grammatical Features: We extracted or calculated the (a) presence of different parts of speech, (b) tweet length, (c) ratio of various pronouns, (d) time orientation of tweets as past, present, or future, calculated using different verb tenses and related adverbs, (e) ratio of comparisons, interrogatives, numbers and quantifiers, (f) sentiment of the tweets from Crimson Hexagon, and (g) the subjectivity or objectivity of tweets, using the MPQA subjectivity lexicon (Wilson, Wiebe, & Hoffmann, 2005). To capture the above-mentioned categories (c, d, e), we counted the number of related words in each tweet and normalized the counts by tweet length.

Twitter-Specific Features

Some text level attributes are specific to Twitter, such as mentions, URLs, and hashtags. Before preprocessing the data, we calculated the number of occurrences of each of these features in a tweet and added them to the set of attributes. We also incorporated the number of repetitions of each tweet in our data as a feature before removing the repeated tweets. In addition, we considered the gender, number of tweets, number of followers, and followings of accounts where available through Crimson Hexagon as Twitter-specific features. The gender of the authors was retrieved from Crimson Hexagon, where gender is calculated using "the distribution of the author names in census data and other public records" (Etlinger & Amand, 2012).

Overall, we considered a total of 90 features. We chose not to use some common features such as bag of word and top TF-IDF words to avoid overly strong domain dependence and topic specificity of the classifier.

4.2 Classification

After preprocessing and before building the classification models, we divided the data into training and testing data. Both sets included controversial and non-controversial topics. After dividing the data, the training set included the tweets from two controversial and two non-controversial topics: Privacy and Vaccines (controversial), and Seatbelts and Child education (non-controversial). The tweets from the other two topics, Gun control (controversial) and Sun exposure (non-controversial), were included in the test set.

As a first step, we compared classifiers that have frequently been used in related work: Naïve Bayes (NB) as used in Teufel and Moens (2002), Support Vector Machines (SVM) as used in Liakata and colleges (2012), and Decision Trees (DT, J48) as used in Castillo, Mendoza and Poblete (2011). We used Weka (Hall et al., 2009) and an R machine learning package (e1071) (Dimitriadou, Hornik, Leisch, Meyer, & Weingessel, 2011) as implementations of these classifiers.

To find the best features, we first built a baseline model using Twitter-specific features only. We then added the other two features to the baseline to find the impact of each set. Next, we conducted 10-fold cross-validation to find the best combination of features to train the model, and then used the best trained model on the test set to evaluate the predictability of tweets on controversial vs. non-controversial topics. In addition, before classifying the tweets, we chose the most efficient features using Information Gain (Eq.1).

Classification Sets	Topics	NB			DT			SVM		
		P	R	F1	P	R	F1	P	R	F1
Train set (10-fold)	Privacy, Child Education, Seatbelts, and Vaccine	77.6	77.7	77.4	87.7	87.7	**87.7**	86.4	86.4	86.4
Test set	Gun Control and Sun exposure	60	61.3	60.5	66.5	60	61.7	66.5	62	**63.4**

Table 4: Results of the best NB, DT, and SVM models on the test set.

$$InfoGain\,(Class, Attibute) = H(Class) -$$
$$H(Class|Attribute) \qquad\qquad (1)$$

To assess the accuracy of the predictions, we used the standard metrics of precision (P), recall (R), and F-score (with $\beta = 1$) (F1). Table 3 lists the results of all features and classification algorithms.

5 Results

5.1 Classification

As shown in Table 3, the best performance of the baseline model (Twitter-specific features only) was achieved by the DT classification algorithm (69.9% F1-score). Adding the emphatic feature to the baseline increased the performance of DT and NB by around 1-2%, but did not change the result of the SVM classification. Adding language-specific features to the baseline only resulted in a jump in the performance of all three classifiers: The Precision, Recall, and F1-scores of all classifiers increased by 14-33%, which shows the effectiveness of this set of features (Table 3). Finally, combining all three features slightly increased the performance of DT and SVM by around 0.01%, but the performance of NB did not change. Overall, as the last row of Table 3 shows, we found the combination of all three features to provide the best performance.

After training, we tested the classifiers on the remaining two held out topics (test set) as a means of evaluating the best model (the combination of all three classes of features) in new controversial vs. non-controversial topics. As shown in Table 4, SVM outperformed the other models, and achieves a final average F1-score of 63.4%.

5.2 Feature Analysis

The Twitter-specific, emphatic, and language-specific features are the most helpful ones for the classification given task. To find the most effective attributes of each feature set, we ranked the attributes by their information gain score (Eq. 1). The attributes with the highest scores are listed in Table 5. The baseline model consists of nine attributes. From those, "Following" and "URL" are the highest ranked attributes. After combining Twitter-specific with emphatic features, "Following" and "URL" from the baseline model remained the top-ranked attributes, and "Uppercase words" benefitted the model more than other emphatic attributes. "Lexical emphasis" also ranked among the top ten attributes of this feature set. Also, we find that Twitter-specific features are more helpful for the detection tweets on controversial than non-controversial topics (Table 6).

The top ten attributes of the Twitter + Language-specific and the Twitter + Emphatic + Language-specific model were dominated by the language-specific features, both their grammatical and psychological attributes.

Regarding the emphatic features, the results show that the ratio of "Uppercase letters" is higher in tweets on controversial topics, while tweets on non-controversial topics have slightly more "Lex-

Feature Sets	Top-Ranked Attributes *(in order of internal ranking from left to right)*
Baseline (Twitter)	Following, URL, Followers, Hashtag, Mention, Gender, Posts, tweet count, Re-tweet
Twitter + Emphatic	Following, URL, Uppercase, Followers, Hashtag, Mention, Lexical emphasis, Gender, Posts, tweet count
Twitter + Language-Specific	Risk, Six letter, Personal pronoun, Adjective, Sentiment, I, Clout, Punctuation, Dictionary words, Authenticity
Twitter + Emphatic + Language-Specific	Risk, Six letter, Personal pronoun, Adjective, Sentiment, I, Clout, Punctuation, Dictionary words, Authenticity

Table 5: Top-ranked attributes of each feature set based on information gain score.

Feature	Contro. AVG±STD	Non-Contro. AVG±STD
Emphatic Features		
Lexical emphasis	0.66±0.88	**0.82±0.97**
Uppercase	**0.75±2.023**	0.48±1.83
# Exclamation	0.12±0.425	**0.17±0.47**
Language-Specific Features		
Personal pronoun	3.81±5.07	**9.50±8.28**
Preposition	8.69±5.84	**9.80±6.92**
Auxiliary verb	5.26±5.49	**5.97±6.05**
Adverb	2.78±4.19	**3.69±5.007**
Conjunction	2.85±3.94	**3.79±4.65**
Analytic	**74.65±28.33**	63.45±33.43
Authentic	21.59±28.65	**39.81±38.97**
Sentiment	**-0.23±0.61**	-0.08±0.69
Power	**4.55±5.14**	3.02±5.31
Risk	**3.92±4.40**	0.86±2.37
Focus past	1.58±3.20	**2.19+4.24**
Focus present	7.08±6.43	**9.07±7.77**
Focus future	0.67±1.96	**0.94±2.51**
Money	**0.60±1.94**	0.48±2.06
Religion	**0.19±1.11**	0.18±1.26
Death	**0.29±1.30**	0.23±1.26
Twitter-Specific Features		
Retweet	**0.0004±0.02**	0.00015±0.012
Mention	**0.42±0.49**	0.29±0.455
Hashtag	**0.315±0.46**	0.21±0.41
URL	**0.54±0.497**	0.37±0.48

Table 6: Data-driven feature analysis.

		CT 1-vs-all	NCT 1-vs-all
CT	Privacy	86.5	80.6
	Vaccine	78.0	74.4
	Gun control	83.4	77.2
NCT	Education	84.2	86.1
	Sun exposure	77.4	80.2
	Seatbelts	72.7	76.3

Table 7: Classification results 1-vs-all

(F1-measure values are %).

ical emphasis" and "Exclamation marks" (Table 6). This result might seem counterintuitive since we expected this set of features to be more significant for controversial topics. Furthermore, the results show that controversial topics have a higher ratio of negative sentiment (Table 6). Our findings support the insight from prior work that sentiment is a helpful feature for controversiality detection, but needs to be supplemented with other features (Awadallah et al., 2012; Dori-Hacohen & Allan, 2013; Mejova et al., 2014). Looking into some of the tweets on one of the non-controversial topic, i.e., "Seatbelts", we saw that these statements reflected an awareness of the dangers, risks, and negative outcomes that could result from ignoring seatbelts. In other words, deviations from socially agreed upon consensus or norms might spur atten-tion and dissent. Alternatively, when tweeting about non-controversial issues, people might focus on controversial sub-aspects, for example, because they are lingering or emerging. Further research is needed to explain our observations and the engagement with non-controversial themes on social media.

5.3 Testing the Premise of the Project

One potential critique of our study could be that we predict sets of topics rather than overarching, unifying characteristics (controversiality versus non-controversiality) of these set of topics. If that was true, then predicting tweets on controversial topics *CT* based on tweets from other controversial topics *OCTs* should result in higher accuracy than predicting tweets on *CT* based on tweets from non-controversial topics *NCT*. Analogously, predicting tweets on *NCT* based on tweets on other non-controversial topics *ONCTs* should result in higher accuracy than predicting tweets on *NCT* based on tweets on *CT*. We tested the premise of this paper by applying this logic in two ways.

First, we used a "one-versus-all" approach. Using all features, we built binary classifiers (using Naïve Bayes) for each type (CT, NCT) using the tweets on the other CTs or NCTs (the two remaining other topics from the same type, and three from the opposing type), and conducted 10-fold cross validation. Table 7 shows the resulting F-measure values. Using this test, we find that indeed, NCTs are predicted with higher accuracy when learning from tweets from other NCTs than CTs and vice versa in all tested cases, which support the general premise of this paper. This methodology is aligned with the learning methodology used in this paper (Table 3 and 4) where we perform binary classification to predict CT vs. NCT, the difference is that in this additional test, we predict only CT or only NCT.

Topic (CT)	Controversial topics	Non-Controversial topics (NCT)		
		(education, sun)	*(education, seatbelt)*	*(seatbelt, sun)*
Privacy	79.8	77.6	81.2	76.3
Vaccine	69.6	69.5	71.5	65. 2
Gun Control	70.9	69.7	72.0	74.7

Table 8: Prediction results for each CT from the other two CT as well as from all NCT (F1-measure values are %).

Topic (NCT)	Non-Controversial topics	Controversial topics (CT)		
		(privacy, vaccine)	*(privacy, gun)*	*(vaccine, gun)*
Education	88	83.8	81.1	80.1
Sun exposure	75.4	73.4	76.3	74.2
Seatbelt	64.9	68.7	77.3	69

Table 9: Prediction results for each NCT from the other two NCT as well as from all CT (F1-measure values are %).

Second, we predicted each CT from the other two CTs as well as from all NCTs (Table 8). Analogously, we predicted each NCT from the other two NCTs as well as from all CTs (Table 9). This methodology deviates from the learning methodology used in this paper (Table 3 and 4) in that it uses a more detailed approach to predict a single class. Therefore, this test challenges the premise of the paper more strongly or from a different methodological viewpoint than the main method, while the first premise validates our test. The results (Tables 8, 9) show that for each set of experiments, 5 of 9 test cases support the premise of this paper, and 4 out of 9 do not. Table 9 further shows that there might be topic related effects: Seatbelt, a NCT, is easier to be predicted from tweets associated with CT than tweets from NCT. These outcomes call for further research, including pragmatic analysis, into tweet characteristics that indicate tweet association with the controversiality of topics.

6 Discussion

Since noticing controversiality can be a hard task for individuals, we developed a supervised model that detects tweets associated with controversial versus non-controversial topics on Twitter. As a prerequisite for this study, we conducted an online survey where participants rated the controversiality level of sentences related to a selected set of topics. We then selected the topics that the crowd considered as most and least controversial. We trained and evaluated a classifier using three feature sets (Twitter-specific, emphatic, and language-specific features). We considered features new for this particular task, and the linguistic robustness of these features is backed by pragmatic research into the nature of disagreement between speakers during controversial talk (Roberts, 1992).

The considered features proved to be informative for the classification task, albeit with varying degrees of contribution: Twitter-specific attributes such as mentions, URLs, and hashtags helped to build a baseline that performed at 69.9% (F1 score) using the DT algorithm. This finding might be accounted for by the sociolinguistic insight that linguistic communication is socially distributed (Cox, 2005). In other words, Twitter users conform to social stylistic norms of using social media (enabled) features. Moreover, these features were more indicative of controversial than non-controversial topics, which may indicate that social media provides features that people use when making statements related to controversial themes (Table 6).

Emphatic features provide a small contribution to this task (about 1-2% increase in F1 when using DT and NB models). Such features have been previously used for the detection of sarcasm from social media text data (Davidov et al., 2010). Our results suggest that this feature can also improve the detection of controversiality (Table 6), which may be due to social stylistics or an element of sarcasm in the tweets, among other possible reasons. Finally, incorporating grammatical and psychological language-specific attributes resulted in a sizeable increase in the performance of all classifier models. These attributes are not equally distributed across the two types of labels.

7 Conclusion and Future Work

Our results show that focusing on the structural characteristics of tweets offers a means of detecting tweets associated with controversial versus non-controversial topics. This work is limited in several ways. Linguistic and stylistic attributes of language use are subject to temporal and regional variations. Also, some of the features that we considered are not only affected by whether a tweet is related to a controversial topic or not, but also by the context and subject of the tweet. Even given these limitations, we believe this study expands prior work by a) distinguishing between controversy (a communication act or a social interaction, not addresses herein) and controversiality (an aggregate effect of potentially unrelated personal utterances, the object of study in this paper), and b) analyzing the contribution of features that can be assumed—based on prior work and theory—to help distinguish tweets on controversial versus non-controversial topics.

This work raises questions to be addressed in future research. First, we plan to test this approach on other social media platforms in order to study the utility and validity of these features across various outlets. Second, we intend to combine our data mining approach with close reading and qualitative text analysis techniques to explain the counterintuitive effects we have been observing, and to identify the relationship between a) expressions of consensus and dissent on the tweet level, and b) controversiality versus non-controversiality of topics.

Finally, yet importantly, the tests for validating the premise of the paper have provided mixed results: One strategy (one versus all) confirmed our basic idea and goal for all tested cases. This congruence might be due to the fact that the underlying strategy for partitioning the data and predicting classes was similar to the learning methodology. The second strategy (predicting NCT based on other NCTs versus all CTs, and vice versa) partially challenged our premise (confirmed it for 56% of the test cases, rejected for the other 44%). This test used a different logic than the learning experiments. We plan to further investigate the reasons for these discrepancies to inform our future work on identifying controversiality on social media.

Acknowledgment

We thank Professor Corina Roxana Girju from the Linguistics department at UIUC for her helpful insight and direction.

References

Adamic, L. A., & Glance, N. (2005). *The political blogosphere and the 2004 US election: Divided they blog*. In Proceedings of the 3rd International Workshop on Link Discovery, ACM.

Addawood, A. A., & Bashir, M. N. (2016). *"What is your evidence?" A study of controversial topics on social media*. In Proceedings of the 3rd Workshop on Argument Mining, ACL.

Ahn., L. v. (n.d.). Offensive/Profane Word List [Lexicon]. Retrieved from https://www.cs.cmu.edu/~biglou/resources/bad-words.txt

Allen, K., Carenini, G., & Ng, R. T. (2014). *Detecting Disagreement in Conversations using Pseudo-Monologic Rhetorical Structure*. In Proceedings of the 2014 Conference on Empirical Methods in Natural Language Processing (EMNLP), ACL.

Awadallah, R., Ramanath, M., & Weikum, G. (2012). *Harmony and dissonance: Organizing the people's voices on political controversies*. In Proceedings of the 5th ACM International Conference on Web Search and Data Mining (WSDM), ACM.

Bird, S., Klein, E., & Loper, E. (2009). *Natural language processing with Python: Analyzing text with the natural language toolkit*: O'Reilly Media, Inc.

Castillo, C., Mendoza, M., & Poblete, B. (2011). *Information credibility on Twitter*. In Proceedings of the 20th International Conference on World Wide Web (WWW), ACM.

Celce-Murcia, M., Larsen-Freeman, D., & Williams, H. A. (1999). *The Grammar Book: An ESL/EFL Teacher's Course*. Boston, MA: Heinle & Heinle.

Chen, Z., & Berger, J. (2013). When, why, and how controversy causes conversation. *Journal of Consumer Research, 40*(3), 580-593.

Choi, Y., Jung, Y., & Myaeng, S.-H. (2010). *Identifying controversial issues and their subtopics in news articles*. In Proceedings of the Pacific-Asia Workshop on Intelligence and Security Informatics, Springer.

Conover, M., Ratkiewicz, J., Francisco, M. R., Gonçalves, B., Menczer, F., & Flammini, A. (2011). *Political Polarization on Twitter*. In Proceedings of the AAAI Conference on Weblogs and Social Media (ICWSM), AAAI.

Cox, A. (2005). What are communities of practice? A comparative review of four seminal works. *Journal of Information Science, 31*(6), 527-540.

Das, S., Lavoie, A., & Magdon-Ismail, M. (2013). *Manipulation among the arbiters of collective intelligence: How Wikipedia administrators mold public opinion*. In Proceedings of the 22nd ACM International Conference on Information & Knowledge Management (CIKM), ACM.

Davidov, D., Tsur, O., & Rappoport, A. (2010). *Semi-supervised recognition of sarcastic sentences in Twitter and amazon*. In Proceedings of the 14th Conference on Computational Natural Language Learning, ACL.

Dimitriadou, E., Hornik, K., Leisch, F., Meyer, D., & Weingessel, A. (2011). Misc Functions of the Department of Statistics (e1071), TU Wien. *R package version*, 1-6.

Dori-Hacohen, S., & Allan, J. (2013). *Detecting controversy on the web*. In Proceedings of the 22nd ACM International Conference on Information & Knowledge Management (CIKM), ACM.

Dori-Hacohen, S., Yom-Tov, E., & Allan, J. (2015). *Navigating controversy as a complex search task*. In Proceedings of the ECIR Supporting Complex Search Task Workshop, Elsevier.

Etlinger, S., & Amand, W. (2012). Crimson Hexagon [Program documentation]. Retrieved from http://www.crimsonhexagon.com/wp-cotent/uploads/2012/02/CrimsonHexagon_Altimeter_Webinar_111611.pdf

Garimella, K., De Francisci Morales, G., Gionis, A., & Mathioudakis, M. (2016). *Quantifying controversy in social media*. In Proceedings of the 9th ACM International Conference on Web Search and Data Mining (WSDM), ACM.

Hall, M., Frank, E., Holmes, G., Pfahringer, B., Reutemann, P., & Witten, I. H. (2009). The WEKA data mining software: An update. *ACM SIGKDD Explorations Newsletter, 11*(1), 10-18.

Jay, T., & Janschewitz, K. (2008). The pragmatics of swearing. *Journal of Politeness Research. Language, Behaviour, Culture, 4*(2), 267-288.

Kittur, A., Suh, B., Pendleton, B. A., & Chi, E. H. (2007). *He says, she says: Conflict and coordination in Wikipedia*. In Proceedings of the SIGCHI Conference on Human Factors in Computing Systems, ACM.

Liakata, M., Saha, S., Dobnik, S., Batchelor, C., & Rebholz-Schuhmann, D. (2012). Automatic recognition of conceptualization zones in scientific articles and two life science applications. *Bioinformatics, 28*(7), 991-1000.

Lotan, G., Graeff, E., Ananny, M., Gaffney, D., & Pearce, I. (2011). The Arab Spring the revolutions were tweeted: Information flows during the 2011 Tunisian and Egyptian revolutions. *International Journal of Communication, 5*, 31.

Mejova, Y., Zhang, A. X., Diakopoulos, N., & Castillo, C. (2014). Controversy and sentiment in online news. *Computation+Journalism Symposium*.

Mishne, G., & Glance, N. (2006). *Leave a reply: An analysis of weblog comments*. In Proceedings of the 3rd Annual Workshop on The Weblogging Ecosystem, (WWW), ACM.

Morales, A., Borondo, J., Losada, J. C., & Benito, R. M. (2015). Measuring political polarization: Twitter shows the two sides of Venezuela. *Chaos: An Interdisciplinary Journal of Nonlinear Science, 25*(3), 033114.

Pennacchiotti, M., & Popescu, A.-M. (2010). *Detecting controversies in Twitter: A first study*. In Proceedings of the NAACL HLT 2010 Workshop on Computational Linguistics in a World of Social Media, ACL.

Pennebaker, J. W., Booth, R. J., & Francis, M. E. (2007). Linguistic inquiry and word count: LIWC [Computer software]. *Austin, TX: liwc. net.*

Rad, H. S., & Barbosa, D. (2012). *Identifying controversial articles in Wikipedia: A comparative study*. In Proceedings of the 8th Annual International Symposium on Wikis and Open Collaboration, ACM.

Roberts, J. (1992). Face-threatening acts and politeness theory: Contrasting speeches from supervisory conferences. *Journal of Curriculum and Supervison, 7*(No 3), 287-301.

Teufel, S., & Moens, M. (2002). Summarizing scientific articles: Experiments with relevance and rhetorical status. *Computational Linguistics, 28*(4), 409-445.

Tsytsarau, M., Palpanas, T., & Denecke, K. (2011). *Scalable detection of sentiment-based contradictions*. In Proceedings of the DiversiWeb 2011: 1st International Workshop on Knowledge Diversity on the Web, in conjunction with WWW, ACM.

Wilson, T., Wiebe, J., & Hoffmann, P. (2005). *Recognizing contextual polarity in phrase-level sentiment analysis*. In Proceedings of the Conference on Human Language Technology and Empirical Methods in Natural Language Processing, ACL.

Cross-Lingual Classification of Topics in Political Texts

Goran Glavaš, Federico Nanni, and Simone Paolo Ponzetto
Data and Web Science Group
Faculty of Business Informatics and Mathematics
University of Mannheim
B6, 26, DE-68159, Mannheim, Germany
{goran, federico, simone}@informatik.uni-mannheim.de

Abstract

In this paper, we propose an approach for cross-lingual topical coding of sentences from electoral manifestos of political parties in different languages. To this end, we exploit continuous semantic text representations and induce a joint multilingual semantic vector spaces to enable supervised learning using manually-coded sentences across different languages. Our experimental results show that classifiers trained on multilingual data yield performance boosts over monolingual topic classification.

1 Introduction

Political parties are at the core of contemporary democratic systems. Election programs (the so-called *manifestos*), in which parties declare their positions over a range of topics (e.g., foreign policies, welfare, economy), are a widely used information source in political science. Within the Comparative Manifesto Project (CMP) (Volkens et al., 2011), political scientists have been collecting and topically coding manifestos from countries around the world for almost two decades now.

Manual topic coding of manifesto sentences, following the Manifesto Coding scheme with more than fifty fine-grained topics, grouped in seven coarse-grained topics (e.g, External Relations, Economy),[1] is time consuming and requires expert knowledge (King et al., 2017). Moreover, it is difficult to ensure annotation consistency, especially across different countries and languages (Mikhaylov et al., 2012). Nonetheless, manually coded manifestos remain the crucial data source for studies in computational political science (Lowe et al., 2011; Nanni et al., 2016).

---

[1] https://manifestoproject.wzb.eu/coding_schemes/mp_v5

In order support manual coders and mitigate the issues pertaining to manual coding, researchers have employed automatic text classification to topically label political texts (Karan et al., 2016; Zirn et al., 2016). Existing classification models utilize discrete representation of text (i.e., bag of words) and can thus exploit only monolingual data (i.e., train and predict same language instances).

In contrast, in this work, we aim to exploit multilingual data – topically-coded CMP manifestos in different languages. We propose a classification model that can be trained on multilingual corpus of political texts.To this effect, we induce semantic representations of texts from ubiquitous word embeddings (Mikolov et al., 2013b; Pennington et al., 2014) and induce a joint multilingual embedding space via the linear translation matrices (Mikolov et al., 2013a). We then experiment with two classification models, support vector machines (SVM) and convolutional neural network (CNN) that use embeddings from the joint multilingual space as input. Experimental results offer evidence that topic classifiers leveraging multilingual training sets outperform monolingual classifiers.

2 Related Work

The recent adoption of NLP methods had led to significant advances in the field of Computational Social Science (CSS) (Lazer et al., 2009) and political science in particular (Grimmer and Stewart, 2013). Among other tasks, researchers have addressed the identification of political differences from text (Sim et al., 2013; Menini and Tonelli, 2016), positioning of political entities on a left-right spectrum (Slapin and Proksch, 2008; Glavaš et al., 2017), as well as the detection of political events (Nanni et al., 2017) and prominent topics (Lauscher et al., 2016) in political texts.

For what concerns the analysis of manifestos,

Proceedings of the Second Workshop on Natural Language Processing and Computational Social Science, pages 42–46,
Vancouver, Canada, August 3, 2017. ©2017 Association for Computational Linguistics

previous studies have focused on topical segmentation (Glavaš et al., 2016) and monolingual (English) classification of sentences into coarse-grained topics (Zirn et al., 2016). Because manifesto sentences are short and short text classification is inherently challenging due to limited context, Zirn et al. (2016) proposed to apply a global optimization step (performed via Markov Logic network) on top of independent topic decisions for sentences. Numerous supervised models have also been proposed for classification of other types of political text (Purpura and Hillard, 2006; Stewart and Zhukov, 2009; Verberne et al., 2014; Karan et al., 2016, *inter alia*). However, these models also represent texts as sets of discrete words which directly limits their applicability to monolingual classification settings only.

3 Cross-lingual Classification

We first explain how we induce the joint multilingual embedding space and then describe the two classification models we experimentally evaluated.

3.1 Multilingual Embedding Space

Words from different languages can be semantically compared only if their embeddings come from the same multidimensional semantic space. However, independent training of monolingual word embeddings, as obtained by running embedding models (Mikolov et al., 2013b; Pennington et al., 2014) on large monolingual corpora, will result in completely unassociated spaces between the languages (e.g., the English embedding of *"bad"* will not be similar to the German embedding of *"schlecht"*).

Consequently, to enable a unified representation of texts in different languages, we must first map different monolingual embedding spaces to a joint multilingual space in which words from different languages will become semantically comparable. To this end, we set the semantic space of one language as the *target embedding space*) and translate vectors of all words from all other languages to the target space. The translation is performed using the linear translation model proposed by Mikolov et al. (2013a), who observed that there exists a linear translation between embedding spaces independently trained on different corpora.

Given a set of N word translations pairs $\{w_{s_i}, w_{t_i}\}_{i=1}^{N}$, we learn a translation matrix $\mathbf{M}$ that projects the embedding vectors from the *source space* to the *target space*. Let $\mathbf{S}$ be the matrix composed of embeddings of all source words w_{s_i}

from translation pairs and $\mathbf{T}$ be the matrix made of embeddings of corresponding target words w_{t_i}. Unlike the original work (Mikolov et al., 2013a), and following the observations from Glavaš et al. (2017), we do not learn the translation matrix $\mathbf{M}$ via iterative numeric optimization, but analytically by multiplying the Moore-Penrose pseudoinverse of the source matrix $\mathbf{S}$ ($\mathbf{S}^{+}$) with the target matrix $\mathbf{T}$, i.e., $\mathbf{M} = \mathbf{S}^{+} \cdot \mathbf{T}$. The translation matrices obtained via the pseudoinverse seem to be of same quality as those obtained through numeric optimization (Glavaš et al., 2017).

3.2 Classification Models

We experiment with two classification models that are able to take text embeddings as input for classification – SVM and CNN. Taking embeddings as input, models are fully agnostic of the language of text instances. Therefore, we must ensure that representations of all instances are translated to the joint multilingual embedding space before we feed them to the classifiers.

3.2.1 Convolutional Neural Network

Recently, convolutional neural networks (LeCun and Bengio, 1998, CNN) have yielded best performance on many text classification tasks (Kim, 2014; Severyn and Moschitti, 2015). CNN is a feed-forward neural network consisting of one or more convolution layers. Each convolution layer consists of a set of filters matrices (parameters of the model optimized during training). In text classification, the convolution operation is computed sequentially between each filter matrix and each slice (of the same size as filter) of the embedding matrix representing the input text. Each convolution layer is coupled with a pooling layer, in which only the subset of largest convolution scores produced by each filter is retained and used as input either for the next convolution layer or the final fully-connected prediction layer. With such architecture, CNN captures local aspects of texts, i.e., the most informative k-grams (where k is the filter size) in the input text with respect to the classification task. Following previous work (Kim, 2014; Severyn and Moschitti, 2015), we train CNNs with a single convolution and single pooling layer.

The input representation of each text instance for the CNN is a sequence of word embeddings – i.e., each text instance is represented with a $N \times K$ matrix, with N being the length of the text and K the length of word embeddings. CNN requires the input matrices to have the same size for all training instances. Thus, all text instances must be adjusted so that they are of the same length. In all our experiments, we set N to the number of tokens of the longest text in the dataset. We then pad all other sentences with a special padding token (which is assigned a random embedding vector), in order to make them N tokens long as well.

3.2.2 SVM with Sentence Embeddings

The second model we employ is SVM classifier. Since (1) SVMs, unlike CNN, cannot take a matrix as input and (2) concatenating embedding vectors of sentence words into one large embedding vector would result in a too large feature space, we first compute the aggregated embedding vector of the sentence from the embeddings of its constituent words and then feed this aggregate sentence embedding to the SVM classifier. The sentence embedding is a weighted continuous bag of words (WCBOW) aggregation of word embeddings:

$$WCBOW(t_1, \ldots, t_k) = \frac{1}{\sum_{i=1}^{k} w_i} \sum_{i=1}^{k} w_i e(t_i)$$

where t_i is the i-th token of the input text, $e(t_i)$ is the word embedding of the token t_i, and weight w_i is the TF-IDF score of the token-sentence pair, used to assign more importance to more informative words. Considering that the resulting sentence embedding is a low-dimensional (e.g., 100 dimensions) dense numeric vector, we opted for the SVM classifier with non-linear RBF kernel.

4 Evaluation

We first describe the multilingual dataset of manually topically-coded manifestos. We then describe the experimental setting and finally present and discuss the results.

4.1 Dataset

We collected all available manually topically-coded manifestos in four different languages: English (20196 annotated sentences), French (4808), German (48117), and Italian (4370). In order to compare the results across languages more clearly, we opted for a language-balanced dataset, containing the same number of instances in all four languages. Thus, we randomly sampled 4370 (number of annotated sentences in Italian, the lowest number across the four languages) sentences from English, French,

Topic	% of Sentences
External Relations	10%
Freedom & Democracy.	8%
Political System	10%
Economy	24%
Welfare & Quality of Life	28%
Fabric of Society	11%
Social Groups	9%

Table 1: Topic distribution in the dataset.

Translation	P@1 (%)	P@5 (%)
DE → EN	31.6	52.6
FR → EN	38.3	55.6
IT → EN	34.4	50.8

Table 2: Quality of translation matrices.

and German manifestos. The distribution of sentences over the seven coarse-grained manifesto topics in the obtained dataset is shown in Table 1. We next split the dataset into the train, development, and test portion (70%-15%-15% ratio).[2]

4.2 Experimental Setting

Embeddings and translation matrices. We obtained the pre-trained monolingual word embeddings for all four languages: CBOW embeddings (Mikolov et al., 2013b) for German (100 dim.), Italian (300 dim.), and French (300 dim.) and GloVe embeddings (Pennington et al., 2014) for English (100 dim.). We created the multilingual embedding space by mapping embeddings of other three languages to the English embedding space.[3]

We obtained the word translation pairs, required to learn the translation matrices by translating 4200 most frequent English words to the other three languages using Google Translate. We then used 4000 pairs to train each of the translation matrices (DE → EN, FR → EN, and IT → EN) and remaining 200 pairs for evaluation of translation quality. The quality of obtained translation matrices is shown in Table 2 in terms of P@1 and P@5.

Evaluation settings. Our primary goal is to evaluate whether the cross-lingual models, which are able to use instances in different languages for training perform better than models using only instances

---

[2]We make the dataset freely available at `https://tinyurl.com/ml835s8`

[3]Glavaš et al. (2017) showed that using monolingual embeddings of different sizes trained with different algorithms has no negative effect on learned translation matrices.

Setting	Model	EN	DE	FR	IT
Mono-L	Linear SVM (BoW)	.54	**.44**	.63	.53
	SVM RBF (emb)	.43	.31	.42	.37
	CNN	.57	.41	.59	.33
Cross-L	SVM RBF (emb)	.30	.30	.49	.40
	CNN	**.59**	.40	**.86**	**.84**

Table 3: Topic classification results.

from one language (i.e., train and test sentences of same language). To this end, we evaluate both models, SVM and CNN, in both the *monolingual* and *cross-lingual* setting. In the monolingual setting (Mono-L), the models are respectively trained, optimized, and evaluated on train, validation, and test instances of the same language. In the cross-lingual setting (Cross-L), we train the models on the union of training instances of all four languages. On one hand, the Cross-L training set is four times larger than each individual Mono-L training set. On the other hand, instances of the same topic should be more heterogeneous as they (1) originate from different languages and (2) were obtained via imperfect embedding translation (except for English). In addition to the models from Section 3.2, in the Mono-L setting, as a baseline, we evaluate a simple linear SVM with bag-of-words features.

Model optimization. We learn the CNN parameters using the RMSProp algorithm (Tieleman and Hinton, 2012). In all experiments, we optimize the models' hyperparameters (C and γ for RBF kernel SVM, filter sizes, number of filters, and dropout rate for CNN) on the corresponding (monolingual) validation portion of the dataset. We then report the performance of the model with optimal hyperparameter values on the corresponding (monolingual) test set.

4.3 Results and Discussion

In Table 3 we show the topic classification performance of the models, in terms of F_1 score (micro-averaged over all seven topic classes). Considering the predictions for individual topics, all models, unsurprisingly, yielded best performance for the two classes with largest number of instances in training sets: *Economy* and *Welfare & Quality of Life*.

In the monolingual setting (Mono-L), surprisingly, the baseline SVM using lexical features seems to perform better than both embedding-based RBF-kernel SVM and CNN. Since the RBF-kernel SVM with aggregate embedding features displays poor performance in the cross-lingual setting as well, we speculate that the aggregate sentence embeddings are semantically too fuzzy (especially for long sentences) and consequently less informative for discriminating the political topics. On the other hand, CNN shows improvements in performance when trained using the multilingual training set (for all languages except German). We believe that the monolingual training sets are simply too small to successfully learn the good values for CNN parameters. Cross-L performance of CNN models shows the benefits of using multilingual training data for topic classification, enabled through the induction of the joint multilingual embedding space.

We observe that the Cross-L prediction performance across languages varies dramatically. When trained on Cross-L training set, CNN shows small prediction improvement for English, no improvement for German, and drastic improvements for French and Italian. We believe that this large variance across languages can be credited to different levels of (in)consistency in manual topic annotations. Political scientists working with CMP data have already observed substantial inconsistencies in manual topic coding of manifestos (Mikhaylov et al., 2012; Gemenis, 2013). Our results suggest that German and English annotations are significantly less consistent than French and Italian. CMP started coding French and Italian manifestos only recently (in 2012 and 2013, respectively), whereas the German and English manifestos have been coded for almost two decades. Being coded over a much longer period of time, German and English manifestos (1) cover a wider span of political issues (with more language variation) and (2) have been coded by a larger number of coders over the years. Both these factors inevitably lead to less consistent topic annotations. Additional inconsistency for English manifestos possibly stems from different countries of their origin (USA, UK).

5 Conclusion

In this paper we proposed an approach for automated cross-lingual topical coding of political manifestos. We exploit continuous semantic text representations (i.e., embeddings) and induce a joint multilingual spaces, allowing us to train topic classifiers on manually coded data from different languages. Obtained experimental results show that the classifiers trained on a multilingual data outperform monolingual topic classifiers.

References

Kostas Gemenis. 2013. What to do (and not to do) with the comparative manifestos project data. *Political Studies* 61(1 suppl):3–23.

Goran Glavaš, Federico Nanni, and Simone Paolo Ponzetto. 2016. Unsupervised text segmentation using semantic relatedness graphs. In **SEM*. pages 125–130.

Goran Glavaš, Federico Nanni, and Simone Paolo Ponzetto. 2017. Unsupervised cross-lingual scaling of political texts. In *EACL*.

Justin Grimmer and Brandon M Stewart. 2013. Text as data: The promise and pitfalls of automatic content analysis methods for political texts. *Political Analysis* 21(3):267–297.

Mladen Karan, Daniela Širinić, Jan Šnajder, and Goran Glavaš. 2016. Analysis of policy agendas: Lessons learned from automatic topic classification of croatian political texts. In *LaTeCh*.

Yoon Kim. 2014. Convolutional neural networks for sentence classification. In *EMNLP*. Doha, Qatar.

Gary King, Patrick Lam, and Margaret Roberts. 2017. Computer assisted keyword and document set discovery from unstructured text. *American Journal of Political Science* .

Anne Lauscher, Federico Nanni, Pablo Ruiz Fabo, and Simone Paolo Ponzetto. 2016. Entities as topic labels: combining entity linking and labeled lda to improve topic interpretability and evaluability. *Italian Journal of Computational Linguistics* 2(2):67–88.

David Lazer, Alex Sandy Pentland, Lada Adamic, Sinan Aral, Albert Laszlo Barabasi, Devon Brewer, Nicholas Christakis, Noshir Contractor, James Fowler, Myron Gutmann, et al. 2009. Life in the network: the coming age of computational social science. *Science (New York, NY)* 323(5915):721.

Yann LeCun and Yoshua Bengio. 1998. The handbook of brain theory and neural networks. MIT Press, Cambridge, MA, USA, chapter Convolutional Networks for Images, Speech, and Time Series.

Will Lowe, Kenneth Benoit, Slava Mikhaylov, and Michael Laver. 2011. Scaling policy preferences from coded political texts. *Legislative studies quarterly* 36(1):123–155.

Stefano Menini and Sara Tonelli. 2016. Agreement and disagreement: Comparison of points of view in the political domain. In *Coling*. pages 2461–2470.

Slava Mikhaylov, Michael Laver, and Kenneth R Benoit. 2012. Coder reliability and misclassification in the human coding of party manifestos. *Political Analysis* .

Tomas Mikolov, Quoc V. Le, and Ilya Sutskever. 2013a. Exploiting similarities among languages for machine translation. *CoRR* .

Tomas Mikolov, Ilya Sutskever, Kai Chen, Greg S Corrado, and Jeff Dean. 2013b. Distributed representations of words and phrases and their compositionality. In *NIPS*. pages 3111–3119.

Federico Nanni, Simone Paolo Ponzetto, and Laura Dietz. 2017. Building entity-centric event collections. JCDL.

Federico Nanni, Cäcilia Zirn, Goran Glavaš, Jason Eichorst, and Simone Paolo Ponzetto. 2016. Topfish: topic-based analysis of political position in us electoral campaigns. In *PolText*.

Jeffrey Pennington, Richard Socher, and Christopher D Manning. 2014. Glove: Global vectors for word representation. In *EMNLP*. pages 1532–1543.

Stephen Purpura and Dustin Hillard. 2006. Automated classification of congressional legislation. In *Proceedings of the 2006 international conference on Digital government research*. Digital Government Society of North America, pages 219–225.

Aliaksei Severyn and Alessandro Moschitti. 2015. Twitter sentiment analysis with deep convolutional neural networks. In *SIGIR*.

Yanchuan Sim, Brice Acree, Justin H Gross, and Noah A. Smith. 2013. Measuring ideological proportions in political speeches. In *EMNLP*.

Jonathan B Slapin and Sven-Oliver Proksch. 2008. A scaling model for estimating time-series party positions from texts. *American Journal of Political Science* 52(3):705–722.

Brandon M Stewart and Yuri M Zhukov. 2009. Use of force and civil–military relations in russia: an automated content analysis. *Small Wars & Insurgencies* 20(2):319–343.

Tijmen Tieleman and Geoffrey Hinton. 2012. Lecture 6.5-rmsprop: Divide the gradient by a running average of its recent magnitude. Technical Report 2.

Suzan Verberne, Eva Dhondt, Antal van den Bosch, and Maarten Marx. 2014. Automatic thematic classification of election manifestos. *Information Processing & Management* 50(4):554–567.

Andrea Volkens, Onawa Lacewell, Pola Lehmann, Sven Regel, Henrike Schultze, and Annika Werner. 2011. The manifesto data collection. *Manifesto Project (MRG/CMP/MARPOR), Berlin: Wissenschaftszentrum Berlin für Sozialforschung (WZB)* .

Cäcilia Zirn, Goran Glavaš, Federico Nanni, Jason Eichorts, and Heiner Stuckenschmidt. 2016. Classifying topics and detecting topic shifts in political manifestos. In *PolText*.

Mining Social Science Publications for Survey Variables

Andrea Zielinski and **Peter Mutschke**
GESIS - Leibniz Institute for the Social Sciences
Unter Sachsenhausen 6-8
50667 Cologne, Germany
`[andrea.zielinski,peter.mutschke]@gesis.org`

Abstract

Research in Social Science is usually based on survey data where individual research questions relate to observable concepts (variables). However, due to a lack of standards for data citations a reliable identification of the variables used is often difficult. In this paper, we present a work-in-progress study that seeks to provide a solution to the variable detection task based on supervised machine learning algorithms, using a linguistic analysis pipeline to extract a rich feature set, including terminological concepts and similarity metric scores. Further, we present preliminary results on a small dataset that has been specifically designed for this task, yielding a significant increase in performance over the random baseline.

1 Introduction

In face of the growing number of scientific publications, Text Mining (TM) becomes increasingly important to make hidden knowledge explicit. A particular challenge in this regard is to identify research data citations in scholarly publications, due to their wide variety, ranging from quotations to free paraphrases. The problem of detecting dataset references in Social Science publications has been addressed so far by Boland et al. (2012) who mine patterns for discovering dataset citations in full texts to link them to the corresponding entries in a Social Science dataset repository. The recognition, however, has been done just on study name level, in the Social Sciences typically a survey study, e.g. the International Social Survey Programme ISSP. Survey studies, however, usually consist of several hundreds of concepts, so-called variables, each of them representing a single survey question (e.g. *Do you believe in Heaven?*). Therefore, from the perspective of the Social Sciences, having a linkage just to the entire study would not be sufficient to clearly identify the data actually used. For this, identifying the precise variable, the precise subset of variables respectively that was referenced, is strongly needed.

A fine-grained linking between publications and data on the level of variables would have a number of benefits to researchers: It would enable indexing publications by survey variables and discovering publications that discuss the concept of interest (a particular variable). Moreover, it would facilitate a monitoring of the relevance of topical issues (by tracking the use of variables for research) as well as detecting research gaps (by tracking the variables not being addressed by researchers).

The problem, however, is that even though variables are usually assigned a code and a label (e.g. *V39: Belief in life after death* or *V40: Believe in Heaven* from the ISSP 1998 study) as well as the question text from the questionnaire, in practice, authors often do not adhere to citation standards, neither for study names nor for variables. Instead, authors tend to use variations of label and/or question text or combine several variables in one phrase (such as *"...belief in afterlife and Heaven..."* (Neporov and Nepor, 2009)).

In this paper, we introduce the novel task of identifying variables which we define as a multi-label classification task, drawing on ideas from Paraphrase Identification, Citation Matching, and Answer Retrieval in a Question Answering (QA) scenario. Given a set of survey variables, the system needs to examine if one or more of them are mentioned in a text. The task is particularly challenging for the following reasons: The scholarly publications are heterogeneous, covering various styles and topics, and noisy due to pdf-to-text conversion. Moreover, training data is sparse. There-

47

Proceedings of the Second Workshop on Natural Language Processing and Computational Social Science, pages 47–52,
Vancouver, Canada, August 3, 2017. ©2017 Association for Computational Linguistics

fore, it is crucial to investigate how existing methods in the field of NLP can be applied to our use case. We present a work-in-progress study that seeks to provide a solution to the variable detection task based on supervised ML, using a linguistic analysis pipeline to extract indicative features, ranging from surface-oriented to lexical semantic features.

The overall task can be interpreted either as an information retrieval task, trying to return the most relevant spans of text, as exemplified in TREC QA track (Voorhees, 1999), or as the task to assess the semantic similarity between two (generally very short) text pairs (Agirre et al., 2013). Both approaches can also be combined, i.e. by filtering out good candidates from (possibly huge) document collections in the first stage, and using higher-level semantic processing tools in the second step in order to increase precision.

The paper is organized as follows: Section 2 presents related work, Section 3 describes the Social Science use case, Section 4 reports on two basic approaches to the task, summarizing their underlying resources and tools, Section 5 shows the experiments and discusses the results. Finally, Section 6 draws the conclusions and shows future directions.

2   Related Work

Variable Detection is a new task, yet closely related to several existing lines of work in the field of NLP. At its core it is detecting the similarity between sentences, involving the complex task of textual entailment recognition and paraphrase detection at the upper end of the spectrum and string matching, prominent for, *e.g.*, detecting plagiarism, at the lower end of it.

In the Pascal Challenge *Recognizing Textual Entailment (RTE)* (Dagan et al., 2006), QA systems have been designed to identify texts that entail a hypothesized answer (T) to a given question (H). The best results were obtained by lexically-based systems without deeper semantic reasoning, relying on ML techniques, similarity measures (string, lexical and syntactic-based), knowledge resources (e.g., WordNet, paraphrase corpora) and linguistic analysis (*e.g.* Punyakanok et al. (2004) compute the tree edit distance between the dependency trees of the question and answer, and Bouma et al. (2005) use deep syntactic parsing and distributional similarities from external cor-

pora). Even though results to the RTE task in general were modest with accuracy scores between 50-60%, for specific task settings, they could bring accuracy gains: Harabagiu (2006) report an increase in performance from 30.6% to 42.7% on an open-domain QA task.

An important component for any QA system is sentence retrieval, since answers occur locally in a text. The systems' performance is generally evaluated by means of the mean reciprocal rank (MRR) of top k sentences retrieved as answers to a question. The problem of re-ranking pairs of short texts has been addressed by Severyn et al. (2015) who build a convolutional neural network architecture. When augmenting the deep learning model with word overlap features the model achieves an improvement of 3% in MAP and MRR on the TREC QA task. For the same task, an increase in performance could also be observed by Bordes et al. (2014) by adopting deep learning techniques. The authors set up a compositional embedding model, projecting question and answer pairs into a joint space. Kusner et al. (2015) define a distance metric between text documents, *i.e.* the Word Mover's Distance. The metric utilizes *word2vec* word embeddings pre-trained on the Google News Corpus to address the vocabulary mismatch problem. The authors report that WMD achieves an error reduction of up to 10% for the k-nearest neighbor document classification task as compared to traditional approaches, outperforming LDA.

An overview of the plagiarism detection competition in PAN-PC11 is given in Potthast (2011). Best results on extrinsic plagiarism, with a focus on cases made up of < 50 words, achieve 14% recall and 70% precision (evaluated on a character basis). A more fine grained typology of plagiarism is given in (cf. Baron (2013)) who reports that while *copy&paste* plagiarism can be detected reliably using VSMs, fingerprinting or substring matching methods, cases involving the recognition of text segments that are paraphrases, are extremely hard to detect. On the P4P corpus - a subset of the PAN-PC-10 Corpus - a modest recall of 12% could be achieved by Costa-Jussà (2010) for the best performing system.

3   Task Description

Identifying mentions of survey variables in texts can be defined as a multi-label classification problem: given a set of sentences $S \subseteq \{s_1, .., s_i\}$ and variables $V \subseteq \{v_1, .., v_j\}$, we need to build a classifier function $h : S \rightarrow V$. Each variable v has a unique label (*i.e.* a class) characterizing its semantics. Each sentence s is represented by a single instance which can be associated with one (or more) class label(s), including *non-related* as a label. Usually, the number of labels assigned to s is relatively small. Since the link between a publication and a study has been established beforehand, the set of labels can be reduced to those that occur in the respective study.

A gold standard corpus entitled *ALLBUS-English* and *ALLBUS-German* has been compiled and annotated by two Social Sciences students. In doing so, they have taken the specific document context as well as dependencies among variables belonging to the same study into account. Identical survey variables (ca. 8%) have been clustered beforehand. The corpus is composed of sentences labeled with any of the 62 (88) variables from the underlying survey studies, yielding 66 (98) sentences classified as relevant, while the vast majority of sentences is unrelated, i.e. 4.585 (8.351) sentences for English and German respectively. Average density of labels is 1.02 and average length of a variable text is about 14.3 tokens per sentence. A typical example showing how variable references can differ from their data catalog entry is provided below:

Reference: *"Foreigners should not be allowed to engage in political activities."*
Survey_Variable_v45-ALLBUS-ZA4500:
"Please tell me for each statement to what extent you agree with it. [..]. *Foreigners living in Germany should be prohibited from taking part in any kind of political activity* in Germany."

A first empirical investigation revealed different types of variable references, most prominently:

- Citations, reported speech, *i.e.*, either exact copies of a text fragment or marked by quotation marks (such as "Foreigners" from the above example)

- Lexical modifications, due to synonym substitution or compounding, along with negation: "should be prohibited" (Survey) vs. "should not be allowed" (Reference), "taking part in" (Survey) vs. "to engage in" (Reference)

- Morphological variations: "political activity" (Survey) vs. "political activities" (Reference)

- Trend to shorten and summarize the variable: "belief in life after death" (Survey) vs. "belief in afterlife" (Reference)

- Word order modifications along with verb/noun conversions and omissions: "life after" (Survey) vs. "afterlife" (Reference), omission of "in Germany" in the above example.

4 Approaches for Variable Detection

In our experiments, we tested (**A**) a supervised ML model based on a Bag of Words (BoW) representation, using linguistic and conceptual features, and integrating external knowledge resources, and (**B**) a supervised ML model using real-valued feature vectors derived from computing semantic similarity metrics for pairs of variables and sentences. In both approaches, **A** and **B**, documents are first preprocessed and the variable lists are retrieved from the data catalog. Then, a rich set of features is computed from sentences and variables.

4.1 Feature Extraction

For pre-processing, we use a pipeline of tools from DKPro (de Castilho and Gurevych, 2014) that supports tokenization, lemmatization, part-of-speech tagging and Named Entity Recognition. For text segmentation, *i.e.* extracting sentences from sections and paragraphs, we use a pdf-to-text converter. Titles as well as tables are largely ignored.

For approach **A** we integrate general lexical resources as well as the thesaurus for the Social Sciences *TheSoz* (Zapilko et al., 2013), extracting the following features from sentences and variables:

- Tokens, lemmas, PoS using Schmid (1995)

- Named Entities using *Stanford NER* (Finkel et al., 2005; Faruqui and Padó, 2010)

- Term filter, selecting lemmas with PoS=Noun, Verb, Adjective (idf-weighted)

- Keyword terms, synonyms and hypernyms from *TheSoz*

- Synonyms, hypernyms as well as derivational variants from *WordNet* (Fellbaum, 1998; Hamp and Feldweg, 1997)

For **B** we rely on a set of similarity distance metrics provided by DKPro Similarity (Bär et al., 2013) and by the Evaluation Framework for Statistical Machine Translation. In particular, the *METEOR* metric has proven to yield competitive results in the paraphrase detection task (Pado et al., 2014). Extracted features from all the S-V-pairs are:

- *DKPro Similarity* metrics such as character and word n-grams (1,2,3,4), greedy string tiling, longest common subsequence (Bär et al., 2013).

- *BLEU*: maximum n-gram order of 4 (Papineni et al., 2002).

- *METEOR*, using the standard setting with normalization and all variants *exact, stem, synonym and paraphrase* (Banerjee and Lavie, 2005) with extended *DBnary* for German (Elloumi et al., 2015).

4.2 Classification Algorithms

For approach **A**, we use a BoW representation of features from 4.1 and experiment with 3 learning algorithms from the ML framework WEKA (Witten et al., 1999), Naive Bayes, KNN and SVM linear. In order to rank candidate sentences, *i.e.* all sentences not classified as *non-related*, we use the Nearest Neighbor algorithm which returns the closest instances for V based on majority voting. KNN already provides a simple, yet effective solution to the multi-label problem.

In **B**, similarity is encoded in the similarity scores (cf. 4.2). Generally, for a new task, finding the best measures and thresholds is difficult, since no prior heuristics exist. In order to find out which scores correlate most with human judgments, we computed the Pearson correlation coefficient $r_{S,V}$.

5 Experiments and Results

5.1 Supervised ML model based on BoW (A)

The variables' texts were used to train a set of classifiers, resulting in one classifier per variable. For our experiments, we first tested one single feature set at a time, in order to determine which feature sets are most effective for the task. Then, we also combined all features to find out if this increases classifier performance, iterating over the set of ML algorithms. In order to be able to detect irrelevant

sentences, we introduced some noise (1% *non-related*) from withheld sentences. Testing was carried out on the entire German and English ALLBUS corpus (disjoint from the training set).

Results are given in Table 1, showing a significant increase in recall (by a factor of 14) and precision (by a factor of 6) for English. Likewise for German, recall could be enhanced (by a factor of 9) and precision (by a factor of 5) over the random baseline. Results obtained for English are consistently above the keyword match baseline (cf. (Light et al., 2001)).

An interesting finding is that domain-specific *TheSoz* terms achieve a relatively high performance, in particular for German. In combination with *WordNet* terms, synonyms bring most gain, followed by hypernyms and derivations. Also, the performance of classifiers varies considerably. We observed that when running multiple classifiers in an ensemble, different result sets could be retrieved, increasing recall. Adding features derived from the answers of the variables improved recall slightly. Overall, the percentage of missed items is relatively high, because key correspondences were not always detected. For instance, the system failed to bridge from *people from EU countries coming to work here* to *EU workers* in the example below.

> **Reference**: "To measure anti-immigrant sentiments, [..] regarding citizens' beliefs about immigration for four groups: asylm seekers, *EU workers*, non-EU workers and ethnic Germans. []"
> **Survey_Variable_v121-ALLBUS-ZA3450**: "[]. What is your opinion about this for *people from EU countries* coming *to work* here?"

Furthermore, we applied NN search and ranking algorithm on the combined feature set up to rank 100. Results reveal that most mentions of variables are among the top 10. Overall, MAP is higher for English than for German due to the higher coverage of lexico-semantic resources. Note that the class distributions also vary.

5.2 Supervised ML model on similarity metrics (B)

For this experiment, we aimed for a balanced dataset consisting of all positive pairings (from our gold standard) and adding randomly generated combinations of S-V pairings to constitute the *non-related* class (with 10-fold cross-validation).

Corpus	ALLBUS English						ALLBUS German					
Classifier	KNN		Naive Bayes		Linear SVM		KNN		Naive Bayes		Linear SVM	
Performance	MAP	MAR	MAP	MAR	MAP	MAR	MAP	MAR	MAP	MAR	MAP	MAR
Token	0.03	0.08	0.03	0.03	0.04	0.05	0.03	0.06	0.01	0.01	0.02	0.04
Lemma	0.06	0.06	0.03	0.03	0.06	0.06	0.02	0.06	0.03	0.03	0.02	0.03
Terms	0.06	0.09	0.02	0.03	0.05	0.06	0.03	0.08	0.01	0.01	0.03	0.09
NER	0.02	0.02	0.02	0.02	0.02	0.02	0.02	0.03	0.01	0.01	0.02	0.03
TS-S	0.04	0.08	0.02	0.02	0.04	0.08	**0.05**	**0.10**	0.01	0.01	**0.05**	**0.10**
WN-S	0.08	0.11	0.03	0.10	0.07	0.12	0.04	0.07	0.02	0.06	0.04	0.07
WN-H	0.06	0.13	0.02	0.05	0.06	0.13	0.03	0.07	0.02	0.03	0.02	0.08
WN-D	0.06	0.14	0.02	0.05	0.07	0.13	0.03	0.04	0.01	0.01	0.03	0.08
ALL	0.07	0.14	**0.09**	**0.22**	**0.09**	0.15	**0.05**	0.07	0.01	0.04	0.04	0.07

Table 1: Performance on ALLBUS for different Feature Sets (Terms; NER: *Stanford NER*; TS-S: *TheSoz*; WN-S: *WordNet Synonyms*; WN-H: *WordNet Hypernyms*; WN-D: *WordNet Derivations*; *All Features combined*; measures are: *Macro Average Precision (MAP); Macro Average Recall (MAR); Random Baseline English 0.016; Random Baseline German 0.011*)

Then, for all German and English pairs, the individual similarity scores for different standard metrics were computed and fed into a linear regression classifier.

Results are listed in Table 2 and indicate that overall Pearson correlation scores are relatively low - in particular for German (betw. 0.06 and 0.62). Surprisingly, robust metrics like Levenshtein yield a relatively high correlation score, outranking *METEOR*. Due to its ability to detect citations and deal with noisy input, results are overall better, while term expansion/weighting and unigram alignment cannot compensate for this.

Metrics	$\mathbf{E}\, r_{S,V}$	$\mathbf{G}\, r_{S,V}$
$LSSC$	0.92678	0.6216
LC	0.78116	0.5986
$JWSSC$	0.7332	0.5421
GTS_3	0.42132	0.4039
$JSSC$	0.22879	0.3586
GTS_2	0.28602	0.3379
$LCSC$	0.52536	0.3361
$BLEU$	0.20972	0.2648
MET_{ssp}	0.75103	0.2413
$ngram_2$	0.03662	0.2315
$ngram_3$	0.74195	0.1862
M_{ess}	0.40991	0.1666
$ngram_4$	0.09381	0.1478
GTS_4	0.75164	0.0662

Table 2: Pearson Correlation Scores (G: German; E: English; $LSSC$: Levenshtein Second String Comparator; LC: Levenshtein Comparator; $JWSSC$: JaroWinkler SecondString Comparator; GTS_*: Greedy String Tiling; $JSSC$: Jaro Second String Comparator; $BLEU$; MET_{ssp}: Meteor stem-synonym-paraphrase; $LCSC$: Longest Common Subsequence Comparator; $n-gram*$; MET_{ess}: Meteor exact-stem-synonym).

6   Conclusion and Future Work

On the variable detection task, our first experiments give insights into the performance for vari-ous NLP methods. The choice of features was motivated by empirical corpus investigations. While the dataset is relevant for the task, it is still too small to train and develop robust ML classifiers. Yet, evaluating the two approaches with different parameter settings and testing them individually provides interesting results on their own which we will use for future work. First, we will elaborate on the BoW approach, by a) integrating novel language modeling techniques (such as word embedding) to increase recall and b) enhancing term weights from external resources, since terminology proved to be important for retrieving variables. Second, we will devise specialized classifiers for the recognition of citations and reported speech for which string similarity based classifiers are well suited. Last but not least, we will adapt *METEOR* to better fit the task, e.g. optimizing the penalty score and matching, because it has a high potential for disambiguating related variables.

Acknowledgments

This work was supported by the European Union's Horizon 2020 research and innovation programme (H2020- EINFRA-2014-2) under grant agreement No. 654021 (OpenMinTeD[1]).

References

E. Agirre, D. Cer, M. Diab, A. Gonzalez-Agirre, and W. Guo. 2013. Sem 2013 shared task: Semantic textual similarity, including a pilot on typed-similarity. In **SEM 2013: The Second Joint Conference on Lexical and Computational Semantics*.

S. Banerjee and A. Lavie. 2005. Meteor: An automatic metric for mt evaluation with improved correlation

---

[1]http://openminted.eu/

with human judgments. In *Proc. of the acl workshop on intrinsic and extrinsic evaluation measures for machine translation and/or summarization.* volume 29, pages 65–72.

D. Bär, T. Zesch, and I. Gurevych. 2013. Dkpro similarity: An open source framework for text similarity. In *ACL (Conference System Demonstrations).* pages 121–126.

A. Barrón-Cedeño, M. Vila, M. Martí, and P. Rosso. 2013. Plagiarism meets paraphrasing: Insights for the next generation in automatic plagiarism detection. *Computational Linguistics* 39(4):917–947.

K. Boland, D. Ritze, K. Eckert, and B. Mathiak. 2012. Identifying references to datasets in publications. In *International Conference on Theory and Practice of Digital Libraries.* Springer, pages 150–161.

A. Bordes, S. Chopra, and J. Weston. 2014. Question answering with subgraph embeddings. *ArXiv preprint arXiv:1406.3676* .

G. Bouma, J. Mur, G. Van Noord, L. Van Der Plas, and J. Tiedemann. 2005. Question answering for dutch using dependency relations. In *Workshop of the Cross-Language Evaluation Forum for European Languages.* Springer, pages 370–379.

M. Costa-Jussà, R. Banchs, J. Grivolla, and J. Codina. 2010. Plagiarism detection using information retrieval and similarity measures based on image processing techniques-lab report for pan at clef 2010. In *CLEF (Notebook Papers/LABs/Workshops).*

I. Dagan, O. Glickman, and B. Magnini. 2006. The pascal recognising textual entailment challenge. In *Machine learning challenges. evaluating predictive uncertainty, visual object classification, and recognising tectual entailment*, Springer, pages 177–190.

R. de Castilho and I. Gurevych. 2014. A broadcoverage collection of portable nlp components for building shareable analysis pipelines. In *Proc. of the Workshop on Open Infrastructures and Analysis Frameworks for HLT (OIAF4HLT) at COLING.* pages 1–11.

Z. Elloumi, H. Blanchon, G. Serasset, and L. Besacier. 2015. Meteor for multiple target languages using dbnary. In *MT Summit 2015.*

M. Faruqui and S. Padó. 2010. Training and evaluating a german named entity recognizer with semantic generalization. In *KONVENS.* pages 129–133.

Ch. Fellbaum. 1998. *WordNet.* Wiley Online Library.

J. Finkel, T. Grenager, and Ch. Manning. 2005. Incorporating non-local information into information extraction systems by gibbs sampling. In *Proc. of the 43rd annual meeting on association for computational linguistics.* pages 363–370.

B. Hamp and H. Feldweg. 1997. Germanet. a lexical-semantic net for german. In *Proc. of ACL workshop Automatic Information Extraction and Building of Lexical Semantic Resources for NLP Applications.* pages 9–15.

S. Harabagiu and A. Hickl. 2006. Methods for using textual entailment in open-domain question answering. In *Proc. of the 21st International Conference on Computational Linguistics.* pages 905–912.

Matt Kusner, Yu Sun, Nicholas Kolkin, and Kilian Weinberger. 2015. From word embeddings to document distances. In *International Conference on Machine Learning.* pages 957–966.

M. Light, G. Mann, E. Riloff, and E. Breck. 2001. Analyses for elucidating current question answering technology. *Natural Language Engineering* 7(04):325–342.

O. Neporov and Z. Nepor. 2009. Religion: An unsolved problem for the modern czech nation. *Czech Sociological Review* 45(6):1215–1237.

S. Pado, A Stern, B. Magnini, R. Zanoli, and I. Dagan. 2014. Excitement open platform: Architecture and interfaces. In *ACL (System Demonstrations).* pages 43–48.

K. Papineni, S. Roukos, T. Ward, and W. Zhu. 2002. Bleu: a method for automatic evaluation of machine translation. In *Proc. of the 40th annual meeting on association for computational linguistics.* pages 311–318.

M. Potthast, A. Eiselt, L. A. Barrón Cedeño, B. Stein, and P. Rosso. 2011. Overview of the 3rd international competition on plagiarism detection. In *CEUR Workshop Proceedings.* CEUR Workshop Proceedings, volume 1177.

V. Punyakanok, D. Roth, and W. Yih. 2004. Mapping dependencies trees: An application to question answering. In *Proceedings of AI&Math 2004.* pages 1–10.

H. Schmid. 1995. Treetagger - a language independent part-of-speech tagger. *Proc. of Int. Conference on New Methods in Language Processing* 43:28.

A. Severyn and A. Moschitti. 2015. Learning to rank short text pairs with convolutional deep neural networks. In *Proc. of the 38th International ACM SIGIR Conf. on Research and Development in Information Retrieval.* ACM, pages 373–382.

E. Voorhees. 1999. The trec-8 question answering track report. In *Trec.* volume 99, pages 77–82.

I. Witten, E. Frank, L. Trigg, A. Hall, G. Holmes, and S. Cunningham. 1999. Weka: Practical machine learning tools and techniques with java implementations. .

B. Zapilko, J. Schaible, P. Mayr, and B. Mathiak. 2013. Thesoz: A skos representation of the thesaurus for the social sciences. *Semantic Web* 4(3):257–263.

Linguistic Markers of Influence in Informal Interactions

Shrimai Prabhumoye[*1]   Samridhi Choudhary [*1]   Evangelia Spiliopoulou [1]

Christopher Bogart [2]   Carolyn Penstein Rose [1]   Alan W Black [1]

`{sprabhum,sschoudh,espiliop,cbogart,cprose,awb}@andrew.cmu.edu`

[1] Language Technologies Institute
Carnegie Mellon University
Pittsburgh, PA 15213.

[2] Institute for Software Research
Carnegie Mellon University
Pittsburgh, PA 15213.

Abstract

There has been a long standing interest in understanding 'Social Influence' both in Social Sciences and in Computational Linguistics. In this paper, we present a novel approach to study and measure interpersonal influence in daily interactions. Motivated by the basic principles of influence, we attempt to identify indicative linguistic features of the posts in an online knitting community. We present the scheme used to operationalize and label the posts with indicator features. Experiments with the identified features show an improvement in the classification accuracy of influence by 3.15%. Our results illustrate the important correlation between the characteristics of the language and its potential to influence others.

1 Introduction

Influence is a topic of great interest in the Social Sciences. Social Influence is defined as a situation where a person's thoughts, feelings or behaviors are affected by the real or imagined presence of others (Cialdini and Goldstein, 2004). In their study of social influence research, Cialdini and Goldstein (2002) identify six basic principles that govern how one person might influence another. They are: liking, reciprocation, consistency, scarcity, social validation and authority. These principles control how influence plays out in different social situations.

The above mentioned principles constitute a solid basis for most of the work in this domain. Prior computational approaches for understanding influence, have primarily focused on influence as an explicit intention of the people involved (Tan et al., 2016a; Biran et al., 2012; Sim et al., 2016).

In this paper, we study influence from a different perspective: influence in daily, interpersonal interactions. We explore different language features based on the aforementioned theoretical principles and their correlation with influence. We attempt to extend the prior computational efforts on social influence, by using insights from the Social Sciences.

Influence can be defined and operationalized in different settings. A majority of computational work on interpersonal influence focuses on the analysis of social networks that employ probabilistic methods to analyze and maximize the flow of influence in these networks. There have been recent efforts in understanding influence in social media conversations with the aim of finding influential people (Biran et al., 2012; Quercia et al., 2011; Rosenthal and McKeown, 2016). We investigate what we can learn from language about influence from informal interactions where there is no explicit motivation to influence others. We look at user interactions in a social networking website for people interested in knitting, weaving, crocheting and fiber arts called Ravelry [1], which is a large DIY online community with tens of thousands of sub-communities within it.

In the following sections we talk about prior work on social influence and the approaches taken to study it. We describe our dataset and the task setup that allows us to measure influence. We give an overview of the linguistic features we identified, inspired from theoretical insights of social influence. Finally, we present our results and conclude with discussion.

2 Related Work

There has been a substantial amount of computational work on modeling and detecting influence that can be broadly divided in two categories: '*In-*

---

* Both authors contributed equally to this work.

[1] https://www.ravelry.com/

53

fluence in Social Networks' and '*Influence in Interactions*', each of which we discuss in this section. The aforementioned six principles play a pivotal role in defining relevant tasks for modeling and detecting influence. An example research question is: 'Do people, who are connected in a social network and who like each other, display social influence ('liking principle') through their (correlated) activities in the network?' (Anagnostopoulos et al., 2008).

2.1 Influence in Social Networks

The computational models of influence in social networks primarily focus on influence quantification and influence diffusion. Goyal et al. (2010) present different probabilistic models (static, dynamic and discrete-time models) for quantifying influence between users in Flickr. They study how people are influenced by the actions of others, especially their social contacts, when performing actions (like joining a community). Their work quantifies the interplay of the principles of Social Validation and Liking and its effects on the decisions made by community members. Tang et al. (2009) use a Topical Affinity Propagation (TAP) model to quantify topic based social influence in large networks. The model is based on the the idea that the users in a social network are influenced by others for different reasons. They attempt to differentiate social influences from different angles (topics). Anagnostopoulos et al. (2008) design time shuffling experiments to verify the existence of social influence as a driving factor behind activities observed in social networks.

Twitter has been a favorite target for such network analyses too (Weng et al., 2010; Shuai et al., 2012; Bakshy et al., 2011; Cha et al., 2010). For example, Anger and Kittl (2011) measure influence on Twitter as the social network potential of users. They look for different influence indicators, like compliance, identification, internalization and neglect.

Traditional communication theory (Rogers, 2010) has stated that a small group of individuals, called 'influentials', have better skills and excel at persuading others. Therefore, targeting these influential individuals in a network can be expected to result in a widespread chain reaction of influence with small cost (Katz and Lazarsfeld, 1966). The computational efforts based on this theory attempts to find a subset of nodes in a network (aka

seed nodes) that would maximize the diffusion or the spread of influence. Chen et al. (2009) explore different algorithms and heuristics to maximize influence in a network. Goyal et al. (2011) introduce the credit distribution model, which uses a data based approach to maximize influence by looking at historical data.

These efforts to model probability and diffusion of influence primarily focus on task-level actions relevant to the social network and not on the content of interaction between the participants. The following subsection details prior work on modeling influence based on the content of conversations.

2.2 Influence in Interactions

Bales and colleagues (Bales, 1956, 1973), developed the idea that language is a form of contribution to group interaction that functions as a resource for maintaining group cohesion. In this direction, Reid and Ng (2000) study conversations in small groups in order to investigate how conversational turns can be used to exert influence. Their analysis supports the idea that perceived influence is positively correlated with speakers' number of utterances (Ng et al., 1993) and their successful interruptions (Ng et al., 1995). They modeled influential language as language that is aligned to the norms and the goals of the group; in other words was 'prototypical' to the group. Their study found that speakers who use utterances and interruptions with high content prototypicality achieve a higher influence ranking.

Other efforts use linguistic style choices and dialog patterns to detect influence in a conversation (Sim et al., 2016; Quercia et al., 2011; Nguyen et al., 2014; Rosenthal and McKeown, 2016). They study influence and influential language through dialog structure, sentiment, valence, persuasion, agreement and control of conversational topics on online corpora. For example, Biran et al. (2012) explore communication characteristics that make someone an opinion leader or influential in online conversations. They model influential language by studying the conversational behaviors. They find that specific patterns in dialog like: initiating new topics of conversation, contributing more to dialog than others and engendering longer dialog threads on the same topic, are associated with higher influence.

Language has also been explored as a resource

for other tasks. Tan et al. (2016a), for example, explore how different language factors may indicate persuasiveness in an online community (ChangeMyView) on Reddit. They study the effect of stylistic choices in the presentation of an argument that can make it more persuasive.

As mentioned earlier, the majority of these approaches view influence as an important motivation behind the conversations. Our work attempts to study interpersonal influence as it occurs naturally among peers, without an explicit motivation to influence others. We explore the effect of language on influence, based on the theoretical principles.

3 Data

Our analysis is based on the posts written by the users of an online knitting platform called Ravelry. It is a social networking website for people interested in knitting, weaving, crocheting, spinning and more. It is ideal for large-scale data analysis as it has more than 6 million members, with 50,000 users being added every month. It provides a rich platform for textual analysis of social interactions, as it is a host to roughly billions of posts, thousands of user groups and discussion forums from different parts of the world.

This is a community of people who have a shared interest in fiber arts. Members use this platform to create groups and forums. Some of these groups target people with specific characteristics, for example: groups for beginners, groups for people with heart conditions, groups for men who like to knit. Members discuss and share their ideas, projects and collections of yarn, fiber and things that they find interesting. People generally borrow knitting patterns from other members and adapt them for their own projects. Therefore, the social dynamics of this community affords people the opportunity to share their interests and learn from each other.

These features of the community make the platform suitable for studying social influence in interpersonal interactions. We can observe the language used in a post, the members exposed to it, and the number of members who use a project pattern (which we refer to as a knitting pattern) mentioned in the post for their own project. These form the foundation for the approach described below.

3.1 Operationalization of Influence

Ravelry allows us to maintain information about the knitting pattern used in a project and the time stamps of the posts in a thread. Using this information, we can identify the knitting pattern adopted by a user and the posts that mention the pattern. This helps us to link a post and the knitting pattern mentioned in it to the users who adopted and potentially adapted the pattern after it was posted. We study these posts in order to identify the indicative linguistic features that lead to the pattern uptake. Therefore, we operationalize both the 'users exposed' and the 'pattern uptake'.

3.1.1 Exposure

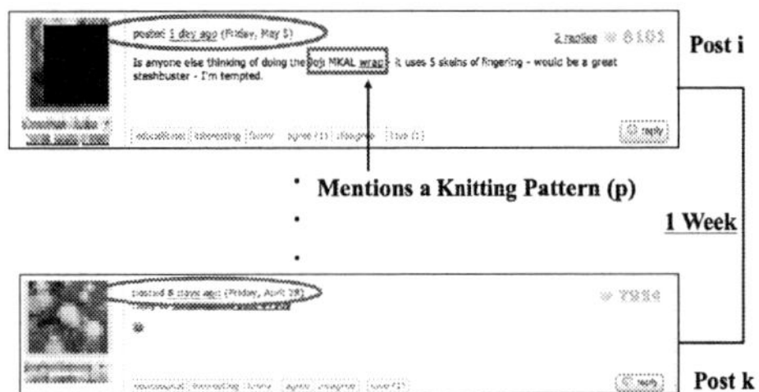

Figure 1: Operationalization of Exposure

Figure 1 shows how we operationalize exposure. The **exposure** of a post reflects the approximate number of users who read the post. There is no direct way to know who read a particular post. However, we have the information of the users who posted on the same thread and the time stamps of the posts. The traffic varies across different forums. By analyzing this traffic, we came up with the following heuristic to identify the number of people exposed to a post: we observed that people mention reading posts most frequently within a week of the post time. Posts older than a week cease to garner attention. Thus, we define exposure as:

*If a post **i** mentioned a knitting pattern **p**, then we consider all the users who posted to the thread up to one week after post **i** as exposed to post **i**.*

3.1.2 Uptake

Another heuristic that we use to label the posts is **uptake**. For each user, we check if she/he used the pattern mentioned in the post or added it to her/his knitting queue after she/he was exposed to the post. Uptake reflects the percentage of exposed users who used the knitting pattern mentioned in the post or added it to their knitting queue[2]. Uptake is defined as:

Let x *denote the number of users who were exposed to the post* i *and used the knitting pattern* p *mentioned in the post. Let the total number of users exposed to the post* i *be* n. *Then for the post* i, *percent uptake is* x/n * 100

Therefore, uptake is the percentage of users exposed to post i that took up a knitting pattern mentioned in it. In our experiments, if the percent uptake of post i is greater than 0, we label the post as *influential* otherwise we label it as non-influential. With this approach, the raw data consisted of 34.10% influential posts and 65.90% of non-influential posts. A subset of this dataset was sampled for manual annotations for our experiments, described in detail in the following sections. A total of 700 posts were selected, with 340 influential and 360 non-influential posts.

4   Annotation of Influence

In order to identify and distinguish the linguistic characteristics of influential vs non-influential posts, we look for language features motivated from the basic principles of social influence. In a platform like Ravelry, the principle of 'Social Validation' is an undercurrent of people's activities across different groups. Cialdini and Goldstein define social validation as a phenomenon in which people frequently look to others for cues on how to 'think', 'feel' and 'behave'. In our experiments, we operationalize influence assuming that people take cues from influential posts in order to think and decide on which pattern to use.

Theoretical grounding of cues. In order to model the presence of these influential cues, we must understand the novelty of the language used to present the pattern. In a post, excitement reflects the happiness experienced by the member while using a pattern. Consequently, this cue motivates another member to use that pattern. Similarly, a detailed description of a pattern by using enhancing qualifiers, makes a post more attractive and triggers 'liking' towards that pattern. Using different materials (yarn or fiber) or creating a modified version of the original pattern reflects the interest and the effort that a user puts into a pattern. A

display of creativity makes a pattern more attractive by looking 'new' and 'different' and in turn motivates others to adapt the modified pattern.

We qualitatively looked at 50 influential and 50 non-influential posts for language cues that can make a post interesting to users. Based on our analysis, we propose three features that act as markers of these cues. These features are: 'Enthusiasm', 'Qualifiers' and 'Modification'. The following sub-sections analyze each of these, provide examples, and explain how they are motivated from the basic principles of influence.

4.1   Enthusiasm

Enthusiasm is defined as a person's excitement and its intensity as displayed in a post. In influential posts, the expressed emotion is strongly positive. We focus on enthusiasm that is expressed towards a knitting pattern, project, yarn or related entities. If a user seems excited about these entities, that might entice others to be interested in the object of enthusiasm, as accordance with the social validation principle. We ignore enthusiasm expressed towards other users and entities not connected to the knitting project. In order to quantify the intensity of excitement, we look for punctuation markers (specifically exclamation marks) qualifying the statement with positive valence. Some examples of enthusiastic and non-enthusiastic posts are:

- Enthusiastic

    - *Yours **look really great!** And that reminds me that I never posted mine in this group! :) So here they are.*
    - *Cable mittens. Knit flat and seamed - **an easy way to make thumbs!** Of course you have to seam them, but you can barely see the seam on the moss stitch.*

- Non-Enthusiastic

    - *I enjoyed making this Hue Shift afghan so much that I am sure I will make another. By the way, the camera picks the red up, in real life the red does not form a cross.* → intensity of excitement is **low.**
    - *;-P sun came out today! The camera was set for flash and that was the best photo, so the cable work is very visible. The design did stand out more as more*

---

[2]Users can maintain a knitting queue, where they add their future projects and information about the materials and the pattern they plan to use. They might use the pattern without adding it to their queue

4.2 Qualifiers

Qualifiers are words or phrases that provide descriptive details that enhance the impact of the description of a pattern. Qualifiers can either highlight a pattern's quality or usability, features of the yarn or the stitches used, color effects and more. Some example phrases are: *'quick and easy to follow'*, *'perfect pattern'*, *'super-soft handspun yarn'*.

Therefore, qualifiers hint at the attractiveness and usability of the pattern or the yarn. A post that presents the pattern in a positive light with these qualifiers may exert influence to adapt them, consistent with the 'liking principle. The following example posts illustrate valid qualifiers:

- *This is the cuff of the left mitt, couldnt stop and finished clue 2 before I took a picture of both cuffs. But I like how the Zauberball comes out, they wont be identical, but I love them. Thanks, Paula, love the pattern and how you wrote it. **Its really easy going**.*

- *Ive been asked to knit fingerless gloves for my 3 nephews Christmas gifts. I did the first pair using the 75 Yard Malabrigo Mitts in two yarns, I am half done with the 2nd pair in the same pattern and have yet to start the 3rd. **That pattern seems non-gender-specific**.*

- *This is **such a nice pattern!** I knitted them last september for a swap: And I probably knit another pair for me soon :-) → (Both **enthusiastic** and has a **pattern qualifier**)*

- *Two patterns that I know of that **handle highly variegated yarns** are Aquaphobia and Harvest Dew. This one also **looks interesting**, Indiana Jones and the Socks.*

4.3 Modification

Modification captures the actual or the suggested changes made to an original pattern. Some examples of the changes that modification attempts to capture are:

- Adding or removing rows

- Changing the size or the shape of the pattern

- Using extra or lesser stitches

- Using different needles for stitching

- Adding or omitting something from the pattern

- Processing the yarn in a particular manner

This set of descriptive modifiers does not include the number of days, the effort put in the completion of the pattern or the quantity of materials required. These are not included because they vary by user but do not offer much insight into the creativity of the user.

As mentioned before, the principle of 'Social Validation' states that people often look to others in order to decide if and how to modify their behavior. Modifications exemplify an individual's creativity and interest in a pattern. By this principle, these described changes to the pattern might in turn influence other users to adopt the pattern. Some example posts that denote modification are:

- *Pattern: Maize -Yarn is Cascade 220 Heathers, color 9452, 103 yards -Any modifications to the pattern: **one extra row on the thumb for length** -This was my first mitten and I see many more in my future! The pattern was very straightforward, as it is designed for beginners.*

- *These are **my version of** the oh-so-popular Fetching. I can see why theyre so popular: well-written pattern and clever use of cables. **I cast on 40 and did an extra cable repeat at the top.**hand model but should be comfy on the 11-year-old recipient*

- *Yours look great, but if I personally were doing them, **I would modify them** to look like this: It **should be possible** to keep the colorwork regular even with decreases. I would look at the Egyptian Mittens, etc.*

- *Pattern: Norwegian Selbu Mittens -Yarn: Dalegarn Heilo - 1 skein charcoal & 3/4 skein red -Project page: Sochi Selbu -Mods: **Added some Xs for shorter floats and plain thumb tips** -Notes: Decided I prefer this stickier yarn for stranded knitting.*

5 Experiments and Results

Two annotators labeled 700 posts with the presence of enthusiasm, qualifier and modification cues. The actual class labels (**Influential or Non-Influential**) were not revealed to them for the annotation process. In order to evaluate the robustness of these annotations, we measured the inter-annotator agreement by computing Cohen's Kappa for a subset of 40 commonly annotated posts (different from the 700 posts mentioned above). We got satisfactory agreement between the annotators on the definition of our linguistic cues. The kappa values for the two annotators are shown in Table 1.

Label	Cohen's Kappa
Enthusiasm	0.7333
Qualifiers	0.9310
Modification	0.7561

Table 1: Inter Annotator Agreement Values

We performed experiments to automatically classify the posts with their influence label using our features in a machine learning model. The classifier gives an insight into the predictive power and the robustness of the linguistic features described in Section 4.

As discussed earlier, we classify the posts in two classes: '*Influential*' and '*Non-influential*'. The baseline model is a logistic regression classifier with L2 regularization that uses '**Unigram**' features only. The binary labels for 'modification', 'enthusiasm' and 'qualifiers' (**MEQ**), as identified by the annotators, are then included in addition to the unigram features. MEQ also includes four other features constructed by combining the individual binary features. In particular, this includes: 'enthusiasm and qualifier', 'enthusiasm and modification', 'enthusiasm and qualifier and modification' and 'qualifier and modification'. These combination features, or interaction terms, are important. For example, enthusiasm alone might not be sufficient to spark an interest in the user so as to influence her/him into adopting a knitting pattern. A post that emphasizes the qualities of a pattern or details the different variations possible for a pattern along with an undercurrent of enthusiasm, makes a pattern more attractive than the one with just an enthusiastic emotion.

Word-Category based features: Tan et al. (2016b)'s earlier work on persuasion used word categories (WC) as features for identifying persuasiveness in text. We explore similar categories

like 'pronoun counts', 'raw number of word occurrences', 'count of articles in the post', 'length of the post' and more (See Table 4) as features for our experiments. We used the python readability calculator to estimate these features.[3]

Sentiment based features: As mentioned in Section 2, sentiment or the way people 'feel' plays an important role in interpersonal interactions. Hence, we use sentiment features calculated by using a sentiment analyzer from Hutto and Gilbert (2014). The tool estimates four scores for each post: 'positive', 'negative', 'neutral' and 'compound'. The positive, neutral and negative score represent the proportions of the text that fall into each of these categories respectively. The compound score aggregates the overall sentiment of the post.

In order to have a fair comparison, we used a logistic regression classifier with L2 regularization and 5 fold cross-validation for all our experiments, which were performed using Lightside (Mayfield and Rosé, 2013). The results are shown in Table 2. The columns report the 'Accuracy' and 'Cohen's Kappa' values for different feature sets (Unigram, MEQ, WC and Sentiment). These experiments were performed in order to validate the contribution of our MEQ features for predicting social influence.

Model	Accuracy	Kappa
Unigram	68.71	0.3735
Unigram + MEQ	69.14	0.3825
Unigram + Sentiment	69.29	0.3850
Unigram + WC	71.43	0.4280
Unigram + WC + Sentiment	71.14	0.4223
Unigram + WC + MEQ	71.57	0.4304
Unigram + WC + Sentiment + MEQ	**71.86**	**0.4361**

Table 2: Accuracy and Kappa Results

Accuracy may not be a sufficient metric to capture specifically what the model learned about the positive (Influential) class. It is possible that the accuracy is high because the model learned to predict the negative class (Non-Influential) correctly. In order to make this distinction, we look at the confusion matrix shown in Table 3. The table shows a comparison between the true positives of

---

[3] https://pypi.python.org/pypi/readability/0.1

the baseline model and those of the best performing model along with the respective F-Scores. The true positives are the influential posts in our data labeled as defined in Section 3. The predicted positives are posts that were predicted as influential by the model. A similar definition stands for true negative and predicted negative. As shown in the table, the model trained on all the feature sets, correctly classifies more positive labels than the baseline model. Hence, we also get an improvement of 2.91 point for F-score.

	PN	PP	F	Model
TN	253	107	67.55	Unigram
TP	112	228		
TN	267	93	70.46	Unigram + WC
TP	103	237		+ Sentiment + MEQ

Table 3: Confusion Matrix for baseline and the best performing model. In the table, TN=True Negative, TP=True Positive, PN=Predicted Negative, PP=Predicted Positive and F=F-Score.

6   Discussion

The results presented above suggest that the added features play a role in achieving influence. Here we offer more insight through posthoc analysis. First we explore feature weights. Table 4 shows the feature weights for the identified significant features.

As we can see, 'Qualifier' gets a high feature weight. From our discussion in Section 4, we know that the posts with qualifier cues hint at the attractiveness and likability of the patterns by providing descriptive details about them. This suggests that the 'Liking' principle, on which the 'Qualifier' feature is based, plays a pivotal role in explaining influence in interpersonal interactions. However, 'Enthusiasm' has a lower weight than other features. In fact, 'Enthusiasm' alone might not be sufficient to predict the label of a post. However, the combinations of these features, specifically 'Enthusiasm and Modification' has a particularly high weight. This implies that, if the author of the post makes some modifications to the pattern and seems enthusiastic about it, the users exposed to the post might have a higher chance of getting interested and adapting the pattern. The principle of 'Social Validation' is therefore portrayed well by this interaction feature. The high weight is in line with our expectation that this prin-

ciple is an important undercurrent of user activities on Ravelry.

We can observe from Table 2 that the MEQ features improve the accuracy of the model. The feature weights shown in Table 4 suggests that some of these features, have high positive weights and some have higher weights than the word-category features, hinting that they might be better predictors of influence than the WC features. The word-category features capture the number of pronouns, nominalizations, articles, subordination and more. These elements are not covered by any of our MEQ features.

Feature Name	Weight
MEQ and derived features	
Qualifier	0.8277
Enthusiasm and Modification	0.7907
Modification	0.3998
Enthusiasm and Qualifier and Modification	0.3557
Qualifier and Modification	0.1082
Enthusiasm and Qualifier	0.0037
Enthusiasm	-0.1946
Word category-based features	
tobeverb	0.4921
nominalization	0.2951
complex_wrds_dc	0.1082
post length	0.0237
article	-0.2482
subordination	-0.2746
pronoun	-1.1194
Sentiment-based features	
compound	0.2886
positive	0.0912
neutral	0.0749
negative	-0.2121

Table 4: Feature weights for important features

Forward Feature Selection: In any model with a large variety and number of low level features, there may be many correlated features that share weight, and thus we cannot properly interpret the observed weights. One way of isolating the value of specific features is to do a forward feature selection and identify which features are selected for the optimal set. We ran a series of such experiments, varying the number of features to select from **900 to 200**. In all cases, the four interaction terms for our MEQ features ('enthusiasm and modification', 'qualifier and modification', 'enthusiasm and qualifier' and 'enthusiasm and qualifier and modification') along with the individual feature 'Qualifier' were selected as prominent predictors of influence. Even with the smallest resulting feature set, the classification accuracy remained at **71%** . This supports the value placed on our added features by the weight analysis above.

Error Analysis: In order to understand the limitations of the MEQ features, we performed error analysis on our model. The following example shows an influential post that was wrongly predicted as non-influential by the model:
*"This **KAL is coming at the right time wonderful!** Need to finish some WIPs: kalajoki which shall become a christmas gift puzzle socks - one down, one to go kleinkariert I and kleinkariert II. I would be glad to join you."*

The enthusiasm displayed in the post is not towards the pattern (*kalajoki*) itself. The post is enthusiastic about a KAL, which is a 'Knit Along' event occurring in the group. The users might have a greater tendency to adapt patterns during KAL and similar events. In cases like this, the measured influence of a post might be affected by other contextual factors like the occurrence of a KAL. In order to incorporate these behaviors in the classification model, a better understanding of the group dynamics is required. We leave this to subsequent work.

Following is another example of an influential post predicted as non-influential by the model:
*"This is what I choose, what do you think? In the second **picture** I put some other shades of yellow/orange; green; grey/blue"*

Even though the post is marked as influential in the data, the language of the post does not contain cues for either enthusiasm or qualifiers or modification. The attractiveness of the pattern might have been captured in the picture in the post and not in the text itself. Such noise exists in our data.

The Homophily Confound: Shalizi and Thomas (2011) identify three factors that affect the activities in a social network: 'Homophily', 'Social Influence' and 'Co-Variate Causation'. It is difficult to distinguish between them. Homophily occurs when social ties are formed among people due to similar individual traits and choices. It is difficult to identify if two people chose the same pattern because they like similar things (homophily) or because one influenced the other (social influence). We have not addressed this problem in the current setup and hope to explore it in the future.

7   Conclusion and Future Work

In this paper, we have studied social influence in an online community setting featuring interpersonal interactions. We designed an approach to operationalize influence in this setting and a task that enables us to measure the impact of textual features on influence. We presented three new features that are motivated from theoretical principles found in the literature on social influence. Adding them to a baseline model, we achieved an improvement of 3.15% in accuracy and 2.91 points in F-score with our final F-score being 70.46%.

In the future, we would like to further study influence in interpersonal interactions along three directions. Firstly, we would like to study influence in interpersonal interactions of groups that have different goals and interests. Secondly, we would like to study the ways in which the other principles of influence come into play for interpersonal interactions. This study focused on the principles of 'Social Validation' and 'Liking'. The remaining principles might give a different view of influence among people. For example, the principle of 'authority' might come into play when a moderator or an experienced person in a group recommends a pattern. Similarly, there might be an influence among people due to 'reciprocation' depending on the history of their activities in different groups. It would be interesting to explore such principles through the various activities on the Ravelry platform. Thirdly, as discussed earlier, we would like to tease apart the effects of 'Homophily' and 'Social Influence' while studying the spread of pattern usage in Ravelry.

8   Acknowledgement

This work was funded in part by NSF grant IIS 1546393, a fellowship from Bosch and DARPA grant FA8750-12-2-0342.

References

Aris Anagnostopoulos, Ravi Kumar, and Mohammad Mahdian. 2008. Influence and correlation in social networks. In *Proceedings of the 14th ACM SIGKDD international conference on Knowledge discovery and data mining.* ACM, pages 7–15.

Isabel Anger and Christian Kittl. 2011. Measuring influence on twitter. In *Proceedings of the 11th International Conference on Knowledge Management and Knowledge Technologies*. ACM, page 31.

Eytan Bakshy, Jake M Hofman, Winter A Mason, and Duncan J Watts. 2011. Everyone's an influencer: quantifying influence on twitter. In *Proceedings of the fourth ACM international conference on Web search and data mining*. ACM, pages 65–74.

Robert F Bales. 1956. Task status and likeability as a function of talking and listening in decision-making groups. *The state of the social sciences* pages 148–161.

Robert F Bales. 1973. 15 robert f. bales the equilibrium problems in small groups. *Social encounters: readings in social interaction* page 221.

Or Biran, Sara Rosenthal, Jacob Andreas, Kathleen McKeown, and Owen Rambow. 2012. Detecting influencers in written online conversations. In *Proceedings of the Second Workshop on Language in Social Media*. Association for Computational Linguistics, pages 37–45.

Meeyoung Cha, Hamed Haddadi, Fabricio Benevenuto, and P Krishna Gummadi. 2010. Measuring user influence in twitter: The million follower fallacy. *Icwsm* 10(10-17):30.

Wei Chen, Yajun Wang, and Siyu Yang. 2009. Efficient influence maximization in social networks. In *Proceedings of the 15th ACM SIGKDD international conference on Knowledge discovery and data mining*. ACM, pages 199–208.

Robert B Cialdini and Noah J Goldstein. 2002. The science and practice of persuasion. *The Cornell Hotel and Restaurant Administration Quarterly* 43(2):40–50.

Robert B Cialdini and Noah J Goldstein. 2004. Social influence: Compliance and conformity. *Annu. Rev. Psychol.* 55:591–621.

Amit Goyal, Francesco Bonchi, and Laks VS Lakshmanan. 2010. Learning influence probabilities in social networks. In *Proceedings of the third ACM international conference on Web search and data mining*. ACM, pages 241–250.

Amit Goyal, Francesco Bonchi, and Laks VS Lakshmanan. 2011. A data-based approach to social influence maximization. *Proceedings of the VLDB Endowment* 5(1):73–84.

Clayton J Hutto and Eric Gilbert. 2014. Vader: A parsimonious rule-based model for sentiment analysis of social media text. In *Eighth international AAAI conference on weblogs and social media*.

Elihu Katz and Paul Felix Lazarsfeld. 1966. *Personal Influence, The part played by people in the flow of mass communications*. Transaction Publishers.

E Mayfield and CP Rosé. 2013. Lightside: Open source machine learning for text accessible to nonexperts. invited chapter in the handbook of automated essay grading.

Sik Hung Ng, Dean Bell, and Mark Brooke. 1993. Gaining turns and achieving high influence ranking in small conversational groups. *British Journal of Social Psychology* 32(3):265–275.

Sik Hung Ng, Mark Brooke, and Michael Dunne. 1995. Interruption and influence in discussion groups. *Journal of Language and Social Psychology* 14(4):369–381.

Viet-An Nguyen, Jordan Boyd-Graber, Philip Resnik, Deborah A Cai, Jennifer E Midberry, and Yuanxin Wang. 2014. Modeling topic control to detect influence in conversations using nonparametric topic models. *Machine Learning* 95(3):381–421.

Daniele Quercia, Jonathan Ellis, Licia Capra, and Jon Crowcroft. 2011. In the mood for being influential on twitter. In *Privacy, Security, Risk and Trust (PASSAT) and 2011 IEEE Third Inernational Conference on Social Computing (SocialCom), 2011 IEEE Third International Conference on*. IEEE, pages 307–314.

Scott A Reid and Sik Hung Ng. 2000. Conversation as a resource for influence: Evidence for prototypical arguments and social identification processes. *European Journal of Social Psychology* 30(1):83–100.

Everett M Rogers. 2010. *Diffusion of innovations*. Simon and Schuster.

Sara Rosenthal and Kathleen McKeown. 2016. Social proof: The impact of author traits on influence detection. In *Proceedings of the 1st Workshop on Natural Language Processing and Computational Social Science*. pages 27–36.

Cosma Rohilla Shalizi and Andrew C Thomas. 2011. Homophily and contagion are generically confounded in observational social network studies. *Sociological methods & research* 40(2):211–239.

Xin Shuai, Ying Ding, Jerome Busemeyer, Shanshan Chen, Yuyin Sun, and Jie Tang. 2012. Modeling indirect influence on twitter. *International Journal on Semantic Web and Information Systems (IJSWIS)* 8(4):20–36.

Yanchuan Sim, Bryan R Routledge, and Noah A Smith. 2016. Friends with motives: Using text to infer influence on scotus .

Chenhao Tan, Vlad Niculae, Cristian Danescu-Niculescu-Mizil, and Lillian Lee. 2016a. Winning arguments: Interaction dynamics and persuasion strategies in good-faith online discussions. In *Proceedings of the 25th International Conference on World Wide Web*. International World Wide Web Conferences Steering Committee, pages 613–624.

Chenhao Tan, Vlad Niculae, Cristian Danescu-Niculescu-Mizil, and Lillian Lee. 2016b. Winning arguments: Interaction dynamics and persuasion strategies in good-faith online discussions. In *Proceedings of WWW*.

Jie Tang, Jimeng Sun, Chi Wang, and Zi Yang. 2009. Social influence analysis in large-scale networks. In *Proceedings of the 15th ACM SIGKDD international conference on Knowledge discovery and data mining*. ACM, pages 807–816.

Jianshu Weng, Ee-Peng Lim, Jing Jiang, and Qi He. 2010. Twitterrank: finding topic-sensitive influential twitterers. In *Proceedings of the third ACM international conference on Web search and data mining*. ACM, pages 261–270.

Non-lexical Features Encode Political Affiliation on Twitter

Rachael Tatman
Amandalynne Paullada
University of Washington
Linguistics Department
rctatman@uw.edu
paullada@uw.edu

Leo G. Stewart
University of Washington
Human Centered Design
Engineering
lgs17@uw.edu

Emma S. Spiro
University of Washington
Information School
Department of Sociology
espiro@uw.edu

Abstract

Previous work on classifying Twitter users' political alignment has mainly focused on lexical and social network features. This study provides evidence that political affiliation is also reflected in features which have been previously overlooked: users' discourse patterns (proportion of Tweets that are retweets or replies) and their rate of use of capitalization and punctuation. We find robust differences between politically left- and right-leaning communities with respect to these discourse and sub-lexical features, although they are not enough to train a high-accuracy classifier.

1 Introduction

Characterizing social media users based on their political affiliation is an ongoing challenge in Natural Language Processing and Computational Social Science (Conover et al., 2011; Cohen and Ruths, 2013; Sylwester and Purver, 2015; Wong et al., 2016). In addition, linguistic reflections of political identity are of interest to sociolinguists (Hall-Lew et al., 2010; Labov, 2011). However, the approaches of these two communities of researchers with respect to identifying political affiliation are somewhat different. Large-scale computational work has generally focused on the classification of Twitter users based on social network and lexical features. Conover et al. used unigrams (excluding punctuation) and social networks (Conover et al., 2011), while Cohen and Ruths used a large feature set including words, stems, bi- and trigrams, and hashtags (Cohen and Ruths, 2013). Sylwester and Purver, who were interested in characterizing psychological differences between Democrats and Republicans, fo-

cused on word frequency, friend-follower ratio and Linguistic Inquiry and Word Count (Pennebaker et al., 2001)–although they also excluded punctuation from their data. Another study by Wong et al. used no linguistic features at all, relying instead on social network relations with users whose political affiliation was known (Wong et al., 2016).

Much of the sociolinguistic work, on the other hand, has focused on sub-lexical features that encode political identity. Hall-Lew et al., for instance, found that American political party affiliation was strongly associated with whether a speaker produced the final syllable in "Iraq" to rhyme with "rock" or "rack" (Hall-Lew et al., 2010). Kirkham and Moore found that British politician Ed Miliband modulated his use of t-glottalling depending on his audience (Kirkham and Moore, 2016).

While the bulk of the sociolinguistic work has focused on speech, there is a growing body of evidence that, unsurprisingly, sociolinguistic variation is also reflected in text (Eisenstein, 2015; Grieve, 2016; Nguyen, 2017). Punctuation in particular has been used as a feature in a variety of tasks, including authorship identification (Chaski, 2005; Abbasi and Chen, 2005) and predicting users' gender (Bamman et al., 2012) and personality (Pennebaker et al., 2015; Golbeck et al., 2011). In addition to punctuation, there is some evidence that variation in capitalization is an important stylistic feature in informal computer-mediated communication (Ling, 2005).

What has not been investigated is whether these sub-lexical text features, like capitalization and punctuation, vary with users' political affiliation. Our central question is this: while earlier work shows that it possible to identify a user's political affiliation with high accuracy using lexical and social-network features, can we also do so using sub-lexical features and without relying on social

Proceedings of the Second Workshop on Natural Language Processing and Computational Social Science, pages 63–67,
Vancouver, Canada, August 3, 2017. ©2017 Association for Computational Linguistics

network relationships?

This approach has several advantages. The main one is the promise of a classifier that will remain accurate over time. One reason for word-based models' high accuracy is that they are capturing underlying differences in the topics each community is discussing. However, given that the topics of political discussion change frequently, these models may only be useful for a limited time frame. There is little reason, however, to suppose that non-lexical features (like patterns of use of capitalization or punctuation) would change at the same rate. In addition, if the features proposed here can successfully be applied to classifying political alignment, they may prove useful in identifying troll accounts. If a user from one political affiliation creates a fake account for the purpose of trolling users of an opposing political affiliation, they may consciously adopt vocabulary and hashtags from the community they intend to impersonate. However, it is possible that these users will not be adopt stylistic norms of capitalization and punctuation, which may aid in identifying them.

2 Data

Our data, including collection and clustering methods, are borrowed from (Stewart et al., under review). Using the Twitter Streaming API, we collected Tweets containing the terms 'shooting,' 'shooter,' 'gun shot,' or 'gun man,' as well as plural and contracted forms of each term, in order to control for topic. This collection lasted roughly nine months, from December 31, 2015 to October 5, 2016 and yielded 58,812,322 Tweets. From this larger set of Tweets, we selected all Tweets containing "#blacklivesmatter", "#bluelivesmatter" or "#alllivesmatter" (the first strongly indicative of Left-leaning politics, the latter ones more characteristic of the Right), which left us with a smaller dataset of 248,719 Tweets. Each of these Tweets contains both a shooting-related term and one of the three hashtags.gun

We next collected user data to construct a social graph. We collected only the user data for the 8,524 users who contributed at least four Tweets to the sampled dataset. For each user, we collected their followers list, capped at 100,000 followers. Followers were collected between one and three months after the end of Tweet collection: November 15, 2016 to January 17, 2017.

Using the follower data from the 8,524 users,

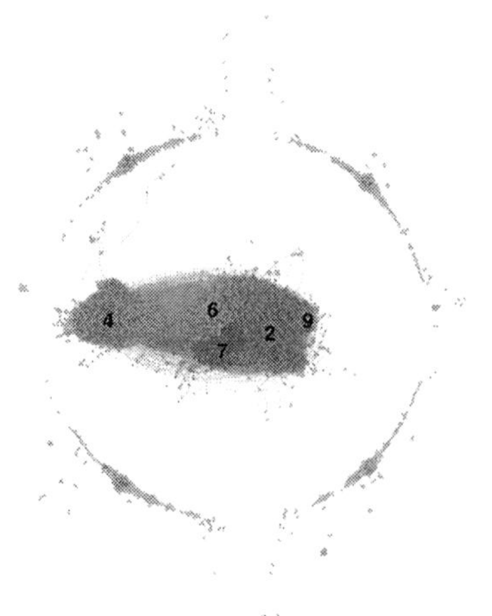

Figure 1: Shared Audience clusters.

we constructed the shared audience graph in Figure 1. In comparison to friend/follower networks, the shared audience network elicits communities of shared attention (i.e. audience), or potential influence. In this graph, each node is an account, and each edge represents the shared audience between two accounts. The shared audience metric is defined as the Jaccard similarity of followers lists (audiences) for any two accounts (see Equation 1). To prioritize the strongest connections while preserving the nuances of smaller edge weights, we select the top 20th percentile of edges by edge weight, or roughly 5 million of the 25 million original edges. Of the 5 million edges, the minimum edge weight represented an audience overlap of 1.78%.

$$jaccard(A, B) = \frac{|A \cap B|}{|A \bigcup B|} \qquad (1)$$

Our final step in constructing our graph was using Louvain clustering to elicit closely connected communities (clusters) (Blondel et al., 2011). We used Gephi (Bastian et al., 2009) to run the clustering algorithm and visualize the resulting graph. As shown in Figure 1, the clustering algorithm produced five large clusters, along with a multitude of smaller clusters and disconnected nodes.

Our analysis focuses on the five most prominent clusters. For each of these clusters, we identify them by the most commonly used hashtags in user account descriptions, shown in Table 2. Based on the frequent use of such hashtags as "#feelthebern" and "#imwithher," which refer

Cluster ID	Size	Common hashtags
4	2153	#imwithher, #feelthebern
2, 6, 7, 9	4689	#maga, #trump2016

Table 1: Clusters and commonly-used hashtags in user account descriptions from each cluster.

to support for 2016 Democratic Party presidential primary candidates Bernie Sanders and Hillary Clinton, respectively, we define cluster 4 as largely left-leaning, while clusters 2, 6, 7, and 9 are largely right-leaning, as evident by frequent use of "#trump2016" and "#maga," an acronym for Donald Trump's campaign slogan "Make America Great Again." For the binary classification task, we define cluster 4 as the Left and collapse clusters 2, 6, 7, and 9 into a composite Right category.

3 Features

Four features were calculated on a per-user basis: the proportion of Tweets that were replies, the proportion that were retweets, the average number of punctuation marks per Tweet and the average number of capital letters per Tweet.

3.1 Discourse Features

The first two are discourse features that may represent group interaction norms. A higher proportion of replies suggests that a user is engaging in a more conversations (compared to broadcasting), while a higher proportion of retweets suggests that a user is instead amplifying other users.

While there was not a significant difference between the Left and Right Twitter accounts in terms of retweets (t(3942)=-3.06, p >0.0001), there was a very robust difference in proportion of replies (t(3656)=6.45, p <0.0001). This can be seen in Figure 2. In particular, users from the Right were more likely to have no replies in the dataset than users from the Left.

3.2 Punctuation and Capitalization

Punctuation, as discussed above, is an established feature in text analysis. While most analyses look at the use of individual punctuation characters, in order to maintain parallelism with capitalization we instead used the average number of punctuation marks per Tweet for each user. This calculation was done on Tweets which had URLs and mentions (which contain the @ symbol) removed.

Capitalization was included as a feature based on empirical observations of differences between

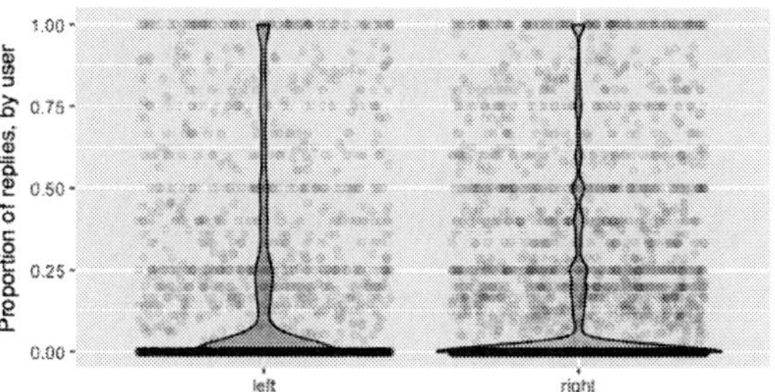

Figure 2: Proportion of Tweets that are replies, per user and per affiliation. A greater number of right-affiliated users have a smaller proportion of replies, i.e., replies make up a relatively small proportion of their Tweets.

these communities. Less capitalization is associated with an informal, casual or nonchalant writing style, but also seems to be a marker of Left-leaning identity. This is explicitly discussed in a viral Tweet (currently >120 thousand favorites) by Twitter user @PatrickCharlto5. The Tweet reads "when you accidentally type a capital letter at the beginning of a sentence" with an attached stock photo of a man with his head in his hands, with the caption "oh no my aloof and uninterested yet woke and humorous aesthetic" (Charlton, 2017). The term "woke" refers to an awareness of social justice issues that are especially prevalent in Left-leaning communities, and the Tweet directly indexes the evocation of the "woke aesthetic" via casual writing style.

Users in these two group used significantly different amounts of both punctuation (t(5006)=-6.22, p <0.0001) and capitalization (t(4465) = -16.051, p <0.0001). The distribution of users by group can be seen in Figure 3. In keeping with earlier observations, users from the Right tended to use more capitalization and more punctuation marks. In addition there was a strong positive correlation between the amount of punctuation and the amount of capitalization used per Tweet over all users (r(6831)= .33, p <0.0001). This covariance suggest that these may both reflect the same underlying stylistic differences.

Our findings have interesting implications in

that they suggest that Left-aligned Twitter users, whether consciously or not, adopt a casual writing style more than Right-aligned users do. We do not have information on age or education level, which may be confounding factors in stylistic choices online.

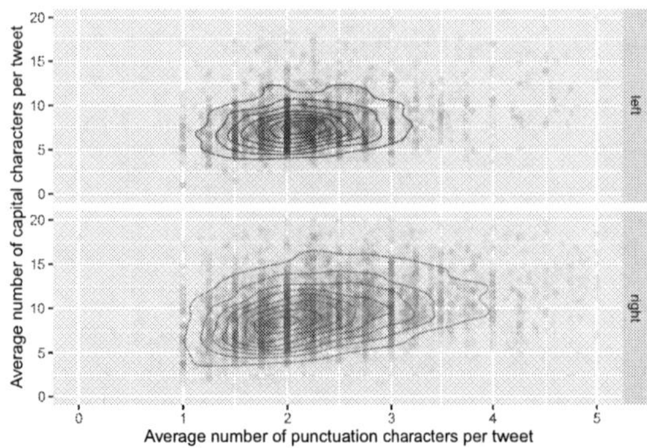

Figure 3: Use of punctuation and capitalization by affiliation. Each dot represents the average number of punctuation marks and capital letters per Tweet by an individual user. Right-affiliated users tend to use more punctuation and capitalization overall.

4   Classification

With the exception of the proportion of a user's Tweets which are retweets, all of the features discussed above are robustly different between these communities. However, it is possible that these differences are not great enough to aid in classification. In order to asses this, we constructed two classifiers were trained using the significant features discussed above.

Because the number of users from the Left and the Right are imbalanced in full data set, we trained and tested on a balanced subset of the data. We randomly sampled users from the Right to create a subset that had as many users as the Left. 90% of each subset was assigned to training set, and the remaining 10% was used as the test data for cross-validation.

Both an SVM and KNN were trained and evaluated in R (using the e1071 (Meyer et al., 2015) and Class (Venables and Ripley, 2002) packages, respectively). To select K for the KNN classifier, models were trained with K's of 1 through 200 (inclusive) and the most accurate selected, in this case 77.

Table 2: Though neither of our classifiers beat the state-of-the art, they did classify users well above chance using only three non-lexical features.

Study	Accuracy
Conover	87%
Cohen (politically active accounts)	84%
Wong (no linguistic features)	94%
KNN classifier (this study)	64%
SVM classifier (this study)	65%

As can be seen in Table 2, neither model reached the same accuracy as those used in earlier work. However, both models classified the political affiliation of accounts in the test set at well above chance. Results would likely be improved by incorporating other features known to aid in predicting political affiliation.

5   Conclusion

This study provided evidence that certain discourse and character-level features are sociolinguistically active markers that vary with users' political affiliation. This suggests several interesting areas for future work, especially in looking at the sociolinguistic role of sub-lexical text features.

We have also shown that it is possible to classify Twitter users' political affiliation well above chance without using lexical or social network features. Further work is necessary to determine whether the features discussed here are stable over time. It is possible that they may be more stable than lexical features, especially if the latter are capturing differences in what topics each community discusses. These results strongly suggest that researchers looking at political affiliation should reconsider stripping punctuation from Tweets, as they contain useful information on community norms.

Finally, it should be noted that the analysis in this paper was done on Tweets which contained hashtags. This is an important consideration, as previous work has found that Tweets which contain hashtags are less likely to include sociolinguistically-marked forms, even if the user uses them in other Tweets (Shoemark et al., 2017; Goldman, 2017). Rather than invalidating these results, however, this strengthens them: if this sociolinguistic variation survives in an environment which discourages the use of social markers, this suggests that it is very robust.

References

Ahmed Abbasi and Hsinchun Chen. 2005. Applying authorship analysis to extremist-group web forum messages. *IEEE Intelligent Systems* 20(5):67–75.

David Bamman, Jacob Eisenstein, and Tyler Schnoebelen. 2012. Gender in twitter: Styles, stances, and social networks. *CoRR abs/1210.4567* .

Mathieu Bastian, Sebastien Heymann, Mathieu Jacomy, et al. 2009. Gephi: an open source software for exploring and manipulating networks. *ICWSM* 8:361–362.

VD Blondel, JL Guillaume, R Lambiotte, and E Lefebvre. 2011. The louvain method for community detection in large networks. *J of Statistical Mechanics: Theory and Experiment* 10:P10008.

Patrick W. Charlton. 2017. "when you accidentally type a capital letter at the beginning of a sentence" Tweet ID: 846179708765130763.

Carole E Chaski. 2005. Whos at the keyboard? authorship attribution in digital evidence investigations. *International journal of digital evidence* 4(1):1–13.

Raviv Cohen and Derek Ruths. 2013. Classifying political orientation on twitter: It's not easy! In *ICWSM*.

Michael D Conover, Bruno Gonçalves, Jacob Ratkiewicz, Alessandro Flammini, and Filippo Menczer. 2011. Predicting the political alignment of twitter users. In *Privacy, Security, Risk and Trust (PASSAT) and 2011 IEEE Third Inernational Conference on Social Computing (SocialCom), 2011 IEEE Third International Conference on.* IEEE, pages 192–199.

Jacob Eisenstein. 2015. Written dialect variation in online social media. *Charles Boberg, John Nerbonne, and Dom Watt, editors, Handbook of Dialectology. Wiley* .

Jennifer Golbeck, Cristina Robles, Michon Edmondson, and Karen Turner. 2011. Predicting personality from twitter. In *Privacy, Security, Risk and Trust (PASSAT) and 2011 IEEE Third Inernational Conference on Social Computing (SocialCom), 2011 IEEE Third International Conference on.* IEEE, pages 149–156.

Nora Goldman. 2017. #yesallwomens language: construction feminist identity on twitter. Annual meeting of the Linguistics Society of America. https://www.youtube.com/watch?v=wIpUNP52qVw.

Jack Grieve. 2016. *Regional variation in written American English.* Cambridge University Press.

Lauren Hall-Lew, Elizabeth Coppock, and Rebecca L Starr. 2010. Indexing political persuasion: variation in the iraq vowels. *American Speech* 85(1):91–102.

Sam Kirkham and Emma Moore. 2016. Constructing social meaning in political discourse: Phonetic variation and verb processes in ed miliband's speeches. *Language in Society* 45(01):87–111.

William Labov. 2011. *Principles of linguistic change, cognitive and cultural factors*, volume 3. John Wiley & Sons.

Rich Ling. 2005. The sociolinguistics of sms: An analysis of sms use by a random sample of norwegians. In *Mobile communications*, Springer, pages 335–349.

David Meyer, Evgenia Dimitriadou, Kurt Hornik, Andreas Weingessel, and Friedrich Leisch. 2015. *e1071: Misc Functions of the Department of Statistics, Probability Theory Group (Formerly: E1071), TU Wien.* R package version 1.6-7. https://CRAN.R-project.org/package=e1071.

Dong-Phuong Nguyen. 2017. *Text as social and cultural data: a computational perspective on variation in text.* Ph.D. thesis, University of Twente.

James W Pennebaker, Ryan L Boyd, Kayla Jordan, and Kate Blackburn. 2015. The development and psychometric properties of liwc2015. Technical report.

James W Pennebaker, Martha E Francis, and Roger J Booth. 2001. Linguistic inquiry and word count: Liwc 2001. *Mahway: Lawrence Erlbaum Associates* 71(2001):2001.

Philippa Shoemark, Debnil Sur, Luke Shrimpton, Iain Murray, and Sharon Goldwater. 2017. Aye or naw, whit dae ye hink? scottish independence and linguistic identity on social media. In *Proceedings of the 15th Conference of the European Chapter of the Association for Computational Linguistics: Volume 1, Long Papers.* Association for Computational Linguistics, Valencia, Spain, pages 1239–1248. http://www.aclweb.org/anthology/E17-1116.

Leo G. Stewart, Ahmer Arif, A. Conrad Nied, Emma S. Spiro, and Kate Starbird. under review. From aggregation to virtual armbands: The shifting roles of hashtags in organizing political activism on twitter .

Karolina Sylwester and Matthew Purver. 2015. Twitter language use reflects psychological differences between democrats and republicans. *PloS one* 10(9):e0137422.

W. N. Venables and B. D. Ripley. 2002. *Modern Applied Statistics with S.* Springer, New York, fourth edition. ISBN 0-387-95457-0. http://www.stats.ox.ac.uk/pub/MASS4.

Felix Ming Fai Wong, Chee Wei Tan, Soumya Sen, and Mung Chiang. 2016. Quantifying political leaning from tweets, retweets, and retweeters. *IEEE Transactions on Knowledge and Data Engineering* 28(8):2158–2172.

Modelling Participation in Small Group Social Sequences with Markov Rewards Analysis

Gabriel Murray

Dept. of Computer Information Systems

University of the Fraser Valley

`gabriel.murray@ufv.ca`

Abstract

We explore a novel computational approach for analyzing member participation in small group social sequences. Using a complex state representation combining information about dialogue act types, sentiment expression, and participant roles, we explore which sequence states are associated with high levels of member participation. Using a Markov Rewards framework, we associate particular states with immediate positive and negative rewards, and employ a Value Iteration algorithm to calculate the expected value of all states. In our findings, we focus on discourse states belonging to team leaders and project managers which are either very likely or very unlikely to lead to participation from the rest of the group members.

1 Introduction

Task-oriented small groups are most effective when all group members have the opportunity to participate and be heard (Duhigg, 2016; Sunstein and Hastie, 2015). The members will have a diversity of viewpoints that can enrich the discussion and improve group problem-solving, and individual members might possess critical information that will remain hidden if the environment is not conducive to their participation (Stasser and Titus, 1985; Sunstein and Hastie, 2015; Forsyth, 2013). A group leader or project manager may be able to foster such an environment that leads to high participation levels by all team members.

In this work, we describe a novel application of Markov Rewards models to social sequence data from highly-structured small group interaction. We represent social sequence elements as complex states that include discourse information

such as dialogue act types, sentiment types, and participant roles. We associate positive and negative rewards with states, such that participation by members other than the leader has a positive reward and participation by the leader has a negative reward. We then employ a Value Iteration algorithm to calculate the expected value of each state. We particularly analyze which discourse states associated with the group leader are most likely or least likely to encourage group participation.

In Section 2, we discuss related work on applying Markov Reward models, relevant work on social sequence data and group dynamics, and various work analyzing discourse-related aspects of multi-modal interaction. In Section 3, we present our state representation, the Markov Rewards model, the Value Iteration algorithm, and the corpus of small-group interactions. We present key results and analysis in Section 4 and conclude in Section 5.

2 Related Work

In this section we survey a wide variety of research related to small group interaction, as well as Markov Rewards models.

Group Dynamics There was a great deal of research on group dynamics in the post-WWII era through to the 1970s, particularly in the fields of social psychology and organizational behaviour. For example, Steiner (1972) analyzed the effects of group factors such as group size, composition, and motivation. Forsyth (2013) summarizes much of this classic work, as well as more recent studies of group dynamics and processes. There has been a resurgence of interest on this topic in recent years, of an inter-disciplinary nature, including formal and computational models of group interaction (Pilny and Poole, 2017). Organizations such as Google (Duhigg, 2016) and Microsoft (Watts, 2016) have conducted large studies of what

Proceedings of the Second Workshop on Natural Language Processing and Computational Social Science, pages 68–72,
Vancouver, Canada, August 3, 2017. ©2017 Association for Computational Linguistics

makes some internal teams succeed and others fail. Similar empirical studies are described in books by Sunstein and Hastie (2015) and Karlgaard and Malone (2015).

Social Sequence Analysis Primarily falling within the field of sociology, *social sequence analysis* seeks to understand, model, and visualize social sequences, particularly temporal sequences, using a variety of tools (Cornwell, 2015; Bakeman and Quera, 2011). One of the most commonly used techniques is *optimal matching*, based on sequence alignment and editing procedures originally developed within bioinformatics. Social sequence analysis also often involves analysis of social network structure within sequences (Friedkin and Johnsen, 2011; Cornwell, 2015). In contrast to our current work, social sequence analysis often involves temporal sequences spanning days, weeks, or months, while we are examining microsequences spanning minutes or hours.

Multimodal Interaction In the field of *multimodal interaction*, multiple modalities of human-human interaction are investigated (Renals et al., 2012). It may be the case that the human interaction being studied takes place through multiple modalities, including face-to-face conversation, email, online chat, and notes. Or it may be the case that within a face-to-face conversation, researchers analyze many different aspects of the interaction, including speech patterns, head movements, gestures, social dynamics, and discourse structure. Multimodal interaction has also been referred to as *social signal processing* (Vinciarelli et al., 2009).

People Analytics The relatively new fields of *People Analytics* (Waber, 2013) and *Human Resource Analytics* (Edwards and Edwards, 2016) draw on some of the older fields above, in order to study aspects of human interaction and performance, particularly in the workplace. These fields examine how to improve hiring, promotion, collaboration, and group communication for businesses.

Markov Rewards Models Markov Reward models have been used to analyze many diverse phenomena, from the value of various actions in volleyball (Miskin et al., 2010) and hockey (Routley and Schulte, 2015), to a cost analysis of geriatric care (McClean et al., 1998). To our knowledge, Markov Reward models have not been used for studying social sequences in small group interaction. Markov Reward models are probably best known through Markov Decision Processes (MDPs) (Bellman, 1957), which have many applications in artificial intelligence and natural language processing.

3 Small Group Social Sequence Analysis

We focus on social interactions in small group meetings. In the following two sections, we describe the state representation used for representing these social sequences, followed by the details of the Markov Rewards model and Value Iteration algorithm.

3.1 State Representation

In our representation of social sequences in meetings, each state is a 5-tuple consisting of the following information:

- the participant's role in the group
- the dialogue act type
- the sentiment being expressed (positive, negative, both, none)
- whether the utterance involves a decision
- whether the utterance involves an action item

We are therefore analyzing sequences of complex states rather than simple one-dimensional sequences; in social sequence analysis, this is referred to as an *alphabet expansion* (Cornwell, 2015).

For our dataset (Section 3.3), the participant roles are precisely defined: Project Manager (PM), Marketing Expert (ME), User Interface Designer (UI), and Industrial Designer (ID). For our purposes here, we only care about the distinction between PM and non-PM roles. The dialogue act types are based on the AMI dialogue act annotation scheme (Renals et al., 2012), and are very briefly described in Table 1.

Example states including the following:

- $< PM - bck - pos - nodec - noact >$ (the project manager making a positive backchannel comment, unrelated to a decision or action)
- $< PM - el.ass - nosent - nodec - yesact >$ (the project manager eliciting feedback about an action item)
- $< UI - sug - nosent - yesdec - noact >$ (the UI expert making a suggestion about a decision item)

ID	description
fra	fragment
bck	backchannel
stl	stall
inf	inform
el.inf	elicit inform
sug	suggest
off	offer
el.sug	elicit offer or suggestion
ass	assessment
und	comment about understanding
el.ass	elicit assessment
el.und	elicit comment about understanding
be.pos	be positive
be.neg	be negative
oth	other

Table 1: Dialogue Act Types

3.2 Markov Rewards and Value Iteration

The Markov aspect of the Markov Rewards model is that the probability of a given state depends only on the preceding state in the sequence. The state transition probabilities are estimated directly from the transition counts in the data. In addition to the complex states described in the preceding section, there are START and STOP states representing the beginning and end of a meeting, and the STOP state is absorbing, i.e. there are no transitions out of the STOP state.

The Rewards aspect of the Markov Rewards model is that certain states are associated with immediate rewards. For this study, all of the states are associated with rewards, but some of them are negative (i.e. punishments). Since our area of interest is participation by group members other than the project manager, we associate all non-PM states with a reward of 1, and PM states with a reward of -1. In other words, it is implicit that participation by people other than the project manager is desirable.

We can then differentiate between the immediate reward of a state and the estimated value of the state. For example, a particular PM state has a negative reward because it represents a discourse utterance of the project manager, but it may have a high estimated value if that state tends to lead to contributions from other members of the group. The goal then is to learn the estimated value of being in each state. We do so using a Value Iteration algorithm.

Algorithm 1 shows the Value Iteration algorithm for our Markov Rewards model. It is very similar to the Value Iteration algorithm used with Markov Decision Processes (Bellman, 1957). The inputs are an initial reward vector r containing the immediate rewards for each state, a transition matrix M, and a discount factor γ. The algorithm outputs a vector v containing the estimated values of each state. The core of the algorithm is an update equation that is applied until convergence. In the following pseudo-code, the term v_t represents a vector of estimated state values at time step t, with the initial vector v_0 consisting of just the immediate rewards.

Algorithm 1: Value Iteration for Markov Rewards Model

Input: reward vector r, transition matrix M, discount factor γ

Output: A vector v containing the estimated values of all states

$v_0 = r'$
$t = 1$
repeat
    $v_t = r' + (M * (\gamma * v_{t-1}))$
    $t = t + 1$
until *convergence*;
return v_{t-1}

The update equation $v_t = r' + (M * (\gamma * v_{t-1}))$ essentially says that the states at step t of the algorithm have an estimated value equal to their immediate reward, plus the discounted value of the states that can be transitioned to, as calculated at the previous step $t - 1$. The discount factor γ can be set to a value between 0 and 1, and controls how much weight is given to future rewards, compared with immediate rewards. For our experiments, we set $\gamma = 0.9$. Further work will examine the impact of varying the γ value. Software for running Value Iteration and replicating these results is available at https://github.com/gmfraser.

3.3 Corpus

For this study, we use the AMI meeting corpus (Carletta et al., 2005), a corpus of scenario and non-scenario meetings. In the scenario subset of the corpus, each meeting consists of four participants who are role-playing as members of a company tasked with designing a remote control unit. The participants are assigned the roles mentioned previously: project manager (PM), user interface expert (UI), marketing expert (ME), and industrial designer (ID). While the scenario given to each team is artificial and structured, the participation and interaction of the group members is not scripted. The conversation is natural and spontaneous, and the groups can make whatever decisions they see fit. For these experiments, we rely on the AMI gold-standard annotations for dialogue act type, sentiment type, decision items, and action items (Renals et al., 2012). We report results on a set of 131 scenario meetings.

4 Results

For this paper, we focus on the estimated value of states belonging to the project manager, since we are interested more generally in how team leaders can encourage participation. Table 2 shows the key results, highlighting the top 10 and bottom 10 states according to estimated value, for states belong to the PM. The table also shows the frequency of each state within the set of meetings. The top two states both represent the PM expressing positive sentiment, in the form of a backchannel and an assessment, respectively. Specifically, the second state $< PM - ass - pos - yesdec - noact >$ involves the PM making a positive assessment about a decision item. Importantly, five states in the top 10 involve the PM explicitly trying to elicit information from the other participants. This is a less obvious finding than it may seem, for the following reason: a team leader might assume that team members will feel welcome and willing to participate in the discussion of their own volition, when in fact it may take deliberate action by the leader to elicit information from people and involve them in the discussion.

In contrast, most of the low-value states involve the PM either informing or stalling. In fact, the most frequently occurring low-value state $< PM - stl - nosent - nodec - noact >$ represents the PM stalling, and the two lowest-value states involve the PM stalling while expressing sentiment.

While we focus here on analyzing the PM states, we briefly note that of the non-PM states, all of the top 10 states in terms of value involve a non-PM group member expressing positive or negative sentiment, and the top 5 all involve stalling. The lowest-value states involve suggestions, assessments, or back-channels. Making a suggestion or assessment regarding a decision is particularly likely to bring the PM back into the

State	Value	Freq.
PM-bck-pos-nodec-noact	2.86	42
PM-ass-pos-yesdec-noact	2.75	11
PM-el.inf-nosent-yesdec-noact	2.66	23
PM-el.ass-nosent-yesdec-noact	2.64	21
PM-bck-nosent-nodec-noact	2.60	3333
PM-el.inf-nosent-nodec-noact	2.52	1527
PM-oth-pos-nodec-noact	2.47	13
PM-und-pos-nodec-noact	2.41	22
PM-el.inf-pos-nodec-noact	2.39	11
PM-el.ass-nosent-nodec-noact	2.30	832
PM-inf-pos-nodec-noact	1.72	269
PM-inf-nosent-yesdec-noact	1.68	304
PM-off-nosent-nodec-noact	1.55	488
PM-inf-nosent-nodec-yesact	1.39	220
PM-fra-neg-nodec-noact	1.38	13
PM-stl-nosent-nodec-noact	1.35	2958
PM-inf-pos-yesdec-noact	1.31	30
PM-fra-pos-nodec-noact	1.23	27
PM-stl-neg-nodec-noact	1.22	19
PM-stl-pos-nodec-noact	0.94	74

Table 2: Top 10 and Bottom 10 States, by Estimated Value (full meeting set)

discussion. At the workshop, we will present further analysis of other interesting high- and low-value states belonging to all participants. In general, we see that all participants tend to express positive or negative sentiment while stalling, as a way of engaging in floor-holding.

5 Conclusion

We have described a novel application of Markov Rewards models to understanding small group social sequence data. By associating positive and negative rewards with particular states, and then running a Value Iteration algorithm, we can determine which states are associated with a particular outcome of interest. In this paper, our outcome of interest was participation by members of the group other than the team leader. We focused on analyzing high- and low-value states belonging to the team leader, and we briefly mentioned interesting states belonging to the other group members.

There are many other possible outcomes of interest in group interaction, and Markov Rewards models should be a useful tool for analyzing social sequences in general. To encourage such research, we are making the Value Iteration software freely available.

References

R. Bakeman and V. Quera. 2011. *Sequential analysis and observational methods for the behavioral sciences*. Cambridge University Press.

R. Bellman. 1957. A markovian decision process. Technical report, DTIC Document.

J. Carletta, S. Ashby, S. Bourban, M. Flynn, M. Guillemot, T. Hain, J. Kadlec, V. Karaiskos, W. Kraaij, and M. Kronenthal et al. 2005. The ami meeting corpus: A pre-announcement. In *International Workshop on Machine Learning for Multimodal Interaction*. Springer, pages 28–39.

B. Cornwell. 2015. *Social sequence analysis: Methods and applications*, volume 37. Cambridge University Press.

C. Duhigg. 2016. What google learned from its quest to build the perfect team. *The New York Times Magazine* .

M. Edwards and K. Edwards. 2016. *Predictive HR Analytics: Mastering the HR Metric*. Kogan Page.

D. Forsyth. 2013. *Group dynamics*. Wadsworth Publishing.

N. Friedkin and E. Johnsen. 2011. *Social influence network theory: A sociological examination of small group dynamics*, volume 33. Cambridge University Press.

R. Karlgaard and M.S. Malone. 2015. Team genius.

S.I. McClean, B. McAlea, and P.H. Millard. 1998. Using a markov reward model to estimate spend-down costs for a geriatric department. *Journal of the Operational Research Society* 49(10):1021–1025.

M. Miskin, G. Fellingham, and L. Florence. 2010. Skill importance in women's volleyball. *Journal of Quantitative Analysis in Sports* 6(2):5.

A. Pilny and M. Poole. 2017. *Group Processes: Data-Driven Computational Approaches*. Springer.

S. Renals, H. Bourlard, J. Carletta, and A. Popescu-Bellis. 2012. *Multimodal Signal Processing: Human Interactions in Meetings*. Cambridge University Press.

K. Routley and O. Schulte. 2015. A markov game model for valuing player actions in ice hockey. In *Proc. of UAI*. AUAI Press, pages 782–791.

G. Stasser and W. Titus. 1985. Pooling of unshared information in group decision making: Biased information sampling during discussion. *Journal of personality and social psychology* 48(6):1467.

I.D. Steiner. 1972. *Group Process and Productivity*. Academic Press Inc.

C. Sunstein and R. Hastie. 2015. *Wiser: Getting beyond groupthink to make groups smarter*. Harvard Business Press.

A. Vinciarelli, M. Pantic, and H. Bourlard. 2009. Social signal processing: Survey of an emerging domain. *Image and vision computing* 27(12):1743–1759.

B. Waber. 2013. *People analytics: How social sensing technology will transform business and what it tells us about the future of work*. FT Press.

D. Watts. 2016. The organizational spectroscope. https://medium.com/@duncanjwatts/the-organizational-spectroscope-7f9f239a897c. (Accessed on 05/06/2017).

Code-Switching as a Social Act:
The Case of Arabic Wikipedia Talk Pages

Michael Miller Yoder, Shruti Rijhwani, Carolyn Penstein Rosé, Lori Levin
Language Technologies Institute
Carnegie Mellon University
Pittsburgh, PA
`{yoder,srijhwan,cprose,lsl}@cs.cmu.edu`

Abstract

Code-switching has been found to have social motivations in addition to syntactic constraints. In this work, we explore the social effect of code-switching in an online community. We present a task from the Arabic Wikipedia to capture language choice, in this case code-switching between Arabic and other languages, as a predictor of social influence in collaborative editing. We find that code-switching is positively associated with Wikipedia editor success, particularly borrowing technical language on pages with topics less directly related to Arabic-speaking regions.

1 Introduction

Code-switching, mixing words from multiple languages in conversation, is common in multilingual communities. This phenomenon has been studied by linguists for nearly half a century (Auer, 2013), and syntactic models of code-switching are still in development (Gardner-Chloros, 2009).

Alternating between languages can also be considered a conversational act with communicative function (Auer, 2013). Code-switching has been found to convey social and interactional meaning in a variety of contexts (Alvarez-Cáccamo, 1990; Blom and Gumperz, 1972; Bassiouney, 2006), though its role in online communities has largely been unexplored. Studying the relationship between social variables and code-switching (CS) can give insight into the role of CS as a pragmatic tool of multilingual speakers.

We offer a quantitative look at how CS functions as a sociolinguistic choice in the editing community around the Arabic Wikipedia, an online encyclopedia which anyone can edit. Our focus is on *talk pages*, where Wikipedia editors discuss article improvements, coordinate work and resolve disagreements on the content they edit (Ferschke, 2014). Relationships between linguistic and social meanings are indirect and difficult to operationalize (Nguyen et al., 2016; Ochs, 1992), but Wikipedia offers an opportunity to quantify social influence in the collaborative task of editing articles. We use code-switching features from editors' talk page contributions to predict the proportion of those users' edits that have lasting impact on the article, a measure of social influence.

We formulate three hypotheses about the social effect of CS on Arabic Wikipedia talk pages. Though other hypotheses are possible, these three are motivated by the sociolinguistic concept of *markedness* (Myers-Scotton, 1998), which attaches social meaning to talk that deviates from conversational expectations. We use markedness as a theoretical lens to assess community norms and social value placed on language choices on Arabic Wikipedia talk pages.

Hypothesis 1. Code-switching may function without clear social meaning (Auer, 2013) and simply be the accepted norm on Arabic Wikipedia talk pages. This could mean that users do not especially notice code-switching or that it is noticed but has no clear effect.

Hypothesis 2. Code-switching marks a Wikipedia user as an outsider who does not follow the Arabic conversational norm (Myers-Scotton, 1998). Code-switching has a negative effect on an editor's acceptance.

Hypothesis 3. Languages other than Arabic, such as English, may carry some sort of value in certain settings (Safi-Stagni, 1991). Code-switching could demonstrate a level of expertise or world knowledge and have a positive effect on the acceptance of an editor's contributions.

Proceedings of the Second Workshop on Natural Language Processing and Computational Social Science, pages 73–82,
Vancouver, Canada, August 3, 2017. ©2017 Association for Computational Linguistics

To determine which of these hypotheses is a more likely explanation for CS in this context, we construct a publicly released dataset that pairs discussion between Wikipedia editors with a measure of editor success in article edits.

We find a positive correlation between the presence of CS in the discussion and editor success, which supports Hypothesis 3. CS features also improve a linear regression model over a reasonable unigram baseline in predicting editor success.

An analysis of an annotated sample of our dataset suggests the possible value the Arabic Wikipedia editing community places on CS for technical language on articles unrelated to Arabic history, people, and culture.

2 Related Work

Code-switching was first linguistically studied to find systems of syntactic and morphological constraints on its use. Myers-Scotton (1995) proposed a CS framework in which grammatical structure is supplied by a dominant "matrix" language, while content morphemes can be drawn from an "embedded" language (Bassiouney, 2009). In contrast, MacSwan (2000) argues against the existence of nearly any universal syntactic constraints on CS.

Sociolinguists take interest in CS as a property of language related to social interaction. Gumperz (1982) proposes a distinction between CS based on factors internal to a conversation and on connotations a language carries across contexts.

We frame our understanding of the social effect of CS on *markedness theory*, which posits that *marked* linguistic choices deviate from understood norms for speakers in certain situations and thus carry social significance (Myers-Scotton, 1998). This emphasis on conversational norms is rooted in Grice's maxims, which give guidelines for expectations in conversation and a framework for social meaning attached to deviations from those norms (Grice, 1975). Note that we are not attempting to prove or disprove markedness theory or Grice's maxims, but instead are using them to understand meaning in interaction and to more fully explain natural language data.

We assume a community norm of Arabic on the Arabic Wikipedia and expect CS to be marked and have some sort of social effect. However, Myers-Scotton (1998) allows the possibility of contexts where CS is itself unmarked; this would also be possible in our case.

Recent computational analyses of style, metaphor, framing and politeness have investigated how language is used to achieve social goals in online communities (Danescu-Niculescu-Mizil et al., 2012, 2013; Jang et al., 2016; Tsur et al., 2015). We examine CS in a similar fashion. Interactional, discourse-level features are context-specific, and the relationship between social and linguistic features is fluid and often difficult to computationalize (Nguyen et al., 2016). Code-switching may not carry clear social meaning at all in a given context (Auer, 2013), much less a predictable signal. Our work enters this conversation by exploring the effect of code-switching on social influence in an online community.

The NLP community has largely studied code-switching apart from its social context. Much work has focused on word-level CS language identification, encouraged by shared tasks (Solorio et al., 2014; Molina et al., 2016). Others have worked to predict code-switch points from preceding text. Solorio and Liu (2008) predict code-switch points with features including the previous n-grams' identified language, POS tag, and location in constituent parses in both languages. Piergallini et al. (2016) tackle the same task in combination with language identification on a Swahili-English online forum dataset. They note the possibility of using discourse structure and social variables for predicting code-switch points.

Interest in computational models of the social and pragmatic nature of code-switching is growing. Begum et al. (2016) present an annotation scheme for the pragmatic functions of Hindi-English code-switched tweets, which includes reinforcement, sarcasm, reported speech, and changes from narration to evaluation. Rudra et al. (2016) study language preference for the expression of sentiment among Hindi-English multilinguals, finding that speakers more commonly use Hindi to express negative sentiment and English for positive sentiment on Twitter.

3 Code-Switching on Arabic Wikipedia Talk Pages

Though many language Wikipedias contain code-switching on their talk pages, we select the Arabic Wikipedia for the variation we observe and previous Arabic CS work in NLP (Solorio et al., 2014; Elfardy et al., 2014).

Talk page	Text	English translation
GNU/Linux	سلاسل المحارف and it has a multi-threaded fs.	... a string used, and it has a multi-threaded fs.
Oran, Algeria	Salam, Les missions principales du centre sont: la recherche...	Greetings, the main missions of the center are: research...
Said Aouita	hafid hassan ana fakhour الصفحة الهدف b3outa	Target page [name] I am proud to...
Lebanon	Sorry for talking english I notice you use the image...	Sorry for talking english I notice you use the image...

Table 1: Observations of non-Arabic text in Arabic Wikipedia talk pages

Terms and definitions for code-switching and code-mixing across studies vary considerably (Gardner-Chloros, 2009). Since we are interested in all deviation from the likely norm of Arabic, we accept any instances of switching between languages in a conversation as code-switching. We also include "script-switching", since we assume most editors can use Arabic characters and there may be social significance attached to writing Arabic in Latin script (something called Arabizi), especially since such language is usually dialectal (Darwish, 2014).

Table 1 presents a few motivating examples of language variety in Arabic Wikipedia talk pages. Most CS we see is Arabic-English, but there are examples of French and Arabizi, the romanized Arabic seen in the third example in Table 1.

We also note apologies for using English, including a longer exchange on the *Israel* talk page where an editor is confronted about language choice and replies in Arabizi:

> Editor 1: ...downright erasure of Jewish history in Israel. I don't have an arabic keyboard so i can't type in arabic
>
> Editor 2: you dont seem to be able to read arabic, or you havent read the article and the history section!!
>
> Editor 1: wala ya habibi? maa ta'mil assumptions, ana bahki arabi,wa baqrah arabi (trans. *Hey, don't make assumptions, I speak Arabic, and read Arabic*)

This example suggests that choice of language explicitly matters in some Wikipedia talk page contexts. Editor 1 feels compelled to explain why they are not typing in Arabic, an acknowledgment of the community norm of offering contributions in Arabic. In the second speaker's reply, not using

Arabic is leveled as grounds for not being a responsible editor. If Editor 1 is not successful, this interaction suggests Hypothesis 2, where not using Arabic negatively marks an editor as an outsider. Editor 1's response in Arabizi is another language choice with social implications, especially that it is in Levantine Arabic dialect and not in Modern Standard Arabic like the article.

Does this demonstrate enough knowledge of Arabic for status as a contributor? What social effect does writing in English on the talk page have when Arabic is an assumed norm? What effects do other multilingual choices have in other contexts? These questions motivate our study.

4 Data and Task

To capture the social effect of code-switching, we choose a task predicting social influence from CS features in discussion. In the context of the Arabic Wikipedia, we measure social success by the proportion of a Wikipedia user's edits that remain in the article's content after a discussion ends (Priedhorsky et al., 2007) and hypothesize that CS may be associated with this measure.

To set up this task, we pair discussions containing CS from Arabic to other languages with simultaneous article edits, which we use to define individual editor success. Our dataset[1] consists of 5259 instances in which an editor interacts with other editors in a talk page discussion thread and achieves some degree of influence on the associated article page. Statistics for our dataset can be seen in Table 2; a more detailed description of the dataset construction follows.

---

[1] https://github.com/
michaelmilleryoder/
wikipedia-codeswitching-data

Number of editor-thread pairs (instances)	5259
Number of code-switching instances	786
Number of discussion threads	2103
Number of talk pages	1031
Number of editors	917

Table 2: Code-switching discussion dataset

4.1 Dataset Construction

Each Wikipedia article has an associated talk page, though many are empty. We begin with all talk pages and article revisions (versions) in the Arabic Wikipedia from a 10 October 2016 data dump.

We use the Java Wikipedia Library (Ferschke et al., 2011) to remove much of the Mediawiki markup on article revisions, and segment the talk pages into posts using talk page revision history and paragraph breaks. Posts under the same heading are organized into discussion *threads*.

There must be sufficient interaction on a talk page thread to measure social effect, so we remove threads with only one participant. To identify CS, we further restrict threads to contain at least one post with at least 3 words with all Latin characters. This filtering leaves 2103 threads remaining out of the original 10,116 (20.8%). Note that the majority of text within these threads are in Arabic, but at least one post within the thread has CS.

In our dataset, we organize each instance as a specific editor's concatenated text in the entire thread (all their posts), along with the combination of all other editors' text as separate features.

4.2 Language Identification

We find a diversity of language on Arabic Wikipedia talk pages not written in the Arabic script, including English, French, Hebrew, Turkish, Chinese and even a few words written in the Tifinagh and Syriac scripts.

To initially survey the distribution of languages, we run all spans of tokens without Arabic characters (and that are not wholly punctuation) through `langid.py` (Lui and Baldwin, 2012), a language identification tool that can detect 97 languages. It is trained in a supervised fashion with Naive Bayes on byte n-grams, using cross-domain training data. `langid.py` finds 66 languages present within the dataset, but a qualitative analysis finds that named entities and noise in the dataset (special characters, usernames that passed through our pre-

processing, and Wikipedia-specific material) confuse the language identifier.

This qualitative analysis and our later annotation of a sample finds that the vast majority (estimated 94%) of CS is to English, with some scattered French, Hebrew and other languages.

4.3 Editor Success Scores

Following the example of Priedhorsky et al. (2007), we assess the impact of editors based on the longevity of the edits they make. We define a success score s for each editor in a specific discussion. This score is the proportion of their edits—words deleted and words added–that remain 1 day after the discussion ends. Note that this score only reflects changes in word frequencies, and does not take word re-ordering into account.

Formally, we consider each edit $\mathbf{e}$ as a vector of word frequency changes, both positive (additions) and negative (deletions) for each word type. For an example in English, an edit that changed one instance of *suggested* to *insinuated*, as well as adding *old* might be represented as a set {'suggested': -1, 'insinuated': +1, 'old': +1}. Let vector $\mathbf{c}$ be the changes in word frequencies from that edit to the final revision in the session. This change vector represents how many tokens that an editor deleted were put back and how many tokens the editor added were afterward deleted. Let $||\mathbf{e}||$ be the sum of the absolute values of word frequency changes of the edit and $||\mathbf{c}||$ be the sum of the absolute values of word frequency changes from the edit to the final revision. The score s of a particular Wikipedia editor u in thread t across edits $\{\mathbf{e}_1, \mathbf{e}_2, ..., \mathbf{e}_n\}$ made by that editor in that thread is:

$$s(u, t) = 1 - \frac{\sum_{i=1}^{n} ||\mathbf{c}_i||}{\sum_{i=1}^{n} ||\mathbf{e}_i||}$$

Each editor's score is the proportion of tokens they changed that remain changed, so $s \in [0, 1]$.

In a qualitative evaluation, this editor score formulation was found to accurately reflect an editor's impact on the revision of the article after the discussion.

5 Experiments and Results

Our goal is capturing the relationship between CS on talk pages and the success of editors on article pages. We consider the presence of CS in an editor's text, as well as other CS features to study the variation among types of CS (section 5.1).

We evaluate the effect of CS features on editor score in two ways. We first evaluate the association between CS and editor success with statistical measures (section 5.2). Then, we test the strength of this association by using CS features in a predictive model of editor success (section 5.3).

5.1 Features

We select code-switching features that we expect to vary in deviation from a community expectation of Arabic, a concept motivated by markedness theory (Myers-Scotton, 1998). Each datapoint separates the text contributed by one specific editor in a thread from all other text in the thread, and features (listed below) are extracted from both the editor's and all other editors' text. We examine Latin characters in particular since non-Latin and non-Arabic scripts are negligible in the corpus, and restricting to Latin characters reduces noise from nonlinguistic symbols and rare punctuation that otherwise are detected.

- **Presence of CS:** whether the text contains non-Arabic content, operationalized as three or more tokens longer than one character in all Latin characters.

- **Proportion of non-Arabic words:** the proportion of non-Arabic content, operationalized as the proportion of words in all Latin characters.

- **Proportion of code-switch points.** To capture how frequently an editor switches languages, each word boundary is counted as a potential code-switch point from Arabic to another language or vice versa. This feature is the number of actual switch points between languages, normalized by the number of word boundaries.

- **Presence of CS and quotes.** We naively capture quoting in non-Arabic languages by determining if there are more than three words in all Latin characters and two double-quotation (") marks.

- **Proportion of non-Arabic named entities.** Named entities written in scripts other than Arabic are quite frequent in our dataset and may carry less social significance than other types of CS. We operationalize this feature as the proportion of words in all Latin characters that are capitalized.

- **Apologies.** We are particularly interested in apologizing for using a language other than Arabic, as this recognizes deviation from an Arabic community norm. We naively assume that any apology is likely to be about language use, and so extract use of the word *sorry* or any version of the lemma *apolog*. However, there are too few examples of this feature even in English, the most frequent non-Arabic language used, to meaningfully compare its relation to editor score.

- **Presence of specific languages.** We extract separate features for the presence of specific languages automatically identified with `langid.py` (see section 4.2), as well as the proportion of all words that are identified as that specific language. Most likely due to noise in automatic identification and the overwhelming presence of English, these features do not improve regression performance or relate in statistically significant ways to editor success, so we do not consider them further.

We also separately consider unigrams longer than 1 letter that are completely in Arabic script or completely in Latin characters.

As nonlinguistic features, we include the number of editor turns and other turns. Both were found to have very weak negative correlation with editor success and were not considered further.

Note that named entities and full sentences in non-Arabic characters are included in our CS features. Since we want to explore as many possible effects as possible, our aim is to broadly capture any use of terms outside of an assumed Arabic norm. Thus our definition of "code-switching" is loose, including what may simply be considered borrowing words or writing a talk page post all in one language in a conversation that includes multiple languages.

5.2 Statistical Evaluation

In order to evaluate the relationship between CS and social influence, we use statistical tests of association between CS features and the editor success score. For binary features, we simply measure the difference in editor score means between instances for which a feature is TRUE and instances where a features is FALSE. For continuous features, we measure the correlation between that feature and the editor score.

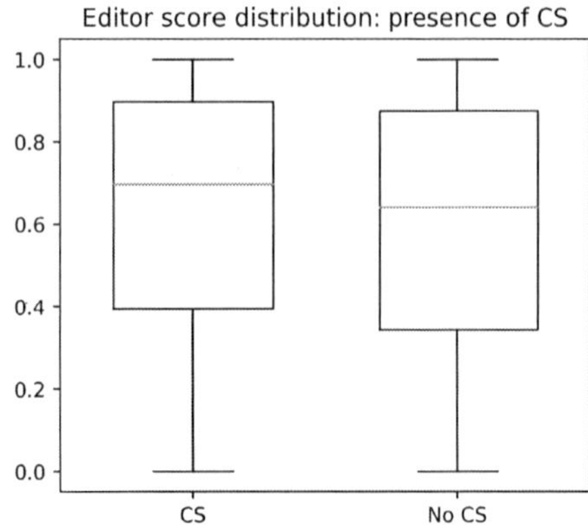

Figure 1: Editor score distributions of instances with and without CS in the editor's text. The difference between means is significant $p < 0.01$.

We find a positive association between the presence of CS and editor success. The presence of CS has a significantly positive effect on editor score, a mean score of 0.628 with CS and 0.593 without ($p < 0.01$ using student's t-test). Distributions for the presence of CS in editor text are in Figure 1. Hypothesis 1, the possibility of no social influence, is unlikely given this statistical evidence of effect on editor success, and instead, Hypothesis 3's claim of a positive social effect is supported.

The presence of CS with quotes also has a marginally significant positive effect on editor score. The mean score of instances with CS and quotes was 0.637 and 0.596 without ($p \approx 0.03$).

The strongest correlation among continuous features is the proportion of switches, which still only weakly correlates with editor success, $r = 0.058$ ($p < 0.0001$).

5.3 Predictive Modeling

We also use editor score as an outcome variable for a linear regression classifier, which we evaluate using 10-fold cross-validation in scikit-learn (Pedregosa et al., 2011). Support vector machine regression yields similar trends.

CS features are more predictive of editor scores than unigrams with feature selection and tf-idf weight (1000 features, selected by mutual information). Results for the classifier are described in Table 3, reporting root mean squared error.

Performance decreases with unigrams and CS features from the text of discussion participants other than the scored editor (*editor+other* vs.

Feature set	LinReg
Editor-only	
unigrams	0.350
Arabic unigrams	0.350
Latin unigrams	0.319*
CS	**0.315***
unigrams+CS	0.349
Editor+others	
unigrams	0.341
CS	**0.315***
unigrams+CS	0.341

Table 3: RMSE in editor success prediction. Unigrams are restricted with feature selection to 1000. Scores marked with an * are significantly different ($p < 0.01$) from editor-only unigrams. CS are code-switching features. *Editor+others* includes features from the scored editor and others in the discussion thread.

editor-only), so only the editor's code-switching has an effect.

The most informative CS feature for the linear regression classifier is the proportion of code-switch points, while the CS features are included in the top 10 most informative features for the unigrams+CS feature set.

In a further experiment, we aggressively select unigram features with tf-idf weight based on mutual information down to just 10. This restricted group of unigram features reaches the prediction performance of CS features (RMSE of 0.315). However, the unigram features are difficult to interpret; it is unclear why they index social influence (Table 4). The focus of this paper is to evaluate the relationship of CS to a measure of social influence; we leave model development toward better prediction performance to future work.

We also examine the effect of Arabic unigrams (top 1000 features selected) and Latin unigrams (no feature selection). The performance of Arabic unigrams matches that of all unigrams, but Latin unigrams perform significantly better. This reinforces language choice as relevant to social influence in this context.

6 Discussion

The social influence of CS may depend on context, and we examine different types of CS and variation in article topic as reasonable influencing factors. We randomly sample 100 instances of the

Arabic word	English gloss
عدة	several
من	from
بع	after
هذه	this
على	on it
في	in
غير	but
أو	or
أن	that
لها	to it (fem.)

Table 4: Top unigram features. Linear regression with these 10 features (after tf-idf feature selection using mutual information) reaches the performance of CS features, but these features are much less interpretable.

CS type	%	Editor success score (mean)
All	*100*	*0.631*
Named entities	36	0.539
Technical	26	0.818
Single words	9	0.714
Phrases	8	0.323
Challenges	7	0.724
Quotations	6	0.394
Translations	2	0.825
Other	6	0.722

Table 5: CS types distribution in our annotated set

data that contain non-Arabic words for manual annotation of CS type and article topic.

6.1 CS Type

The annotator (one of the authors) noted the language of CS as well as the possible reasons why CS was used in those instances, using the annotation framework by Begum et al. (2016) as a reference for structural and semantic functions of CS.

The distribution of these *CS types* are listed in Table 5. Most prominently, the dataset contains a significant percentage of instances with **named entities** written in non-Arabic script. These instances include both Western and Arabic names. For example, *Howard Stern* or *Ibn an-Nafīs*. It is interesting that several named entities are written in Latin script within a large conversation in Arabic, even though names are often freely transliterated over scripts. This could be because certain names are more familiar in their Latin form (like

Article type	Editor success score (mean)
Technical	0.796*
Non-technical	0.553
Arabic	0.537
Non-Arabic	0.747*

Table 6: Mean editor success scores across article topics. * indicates significance $p < 0.01$

CNN).

Using **English technical terms** is also commonly seen when Wikipedia articles of a technical nature are discussed (*Cytoplasm* and *vertebrates*, for instance). These are examples of topic-related CS (Barredo, 1997; Begum et al., 2016). Such code-switched technical words are likely used when there is no commonly used Arabic equivalent. We see a high mean editor success score when technical terms are code-switched. Most of the instances in which this CS type occurred were threads about articles not specific to Arabic-speaking regions and came from topics like science or world history. The strong editor success is in support of Hypothesis 3, which suggests that deflection from the norm of Arabic might be useful in particular scenarios, non-Arabic-specific technical topics in this case.

We also see instances of the **quotation function** and the **translation function** of CS (Begum et al., 2016). The former occurs primarily when the discussion involves quoting parts of the corresponding English Wikipedia page or relevant English news articles and the latter translates Arabic words and phrases to another language. In the Wikipedia context, these functions likely serve to ease explanation of article content edits, and complement the discussion which is predominantly in Arabic.

More specific to Wikipedia is the **challenge** CS type. These are instances where, within Arabic text, phrases in non-Arabic languages are used to debate or contest the content edits being discussed. For example, *there may be some errors that need to be addressed* and *the image is wrong*. Some of these instances are in the Narrative-Evaluative form of CS, which contains a language-switch between stating the fact (the suggested content edit in our case) and an opinion about the fact (Begum et al., 2016).

Apart from these types, CS with other single

Talk page	Text	English translation	Editor outcome
Endorphin	The physiological importance of the beta-endorphin ...	The physiological importance of the beta-endorphin ...	successful
Cybernetics	في ال open loop نعطي النظام القيمة...	In the open loop, we give the system the value...	successful
Egypt	وال دي ان اى هو ما لخصه الدكتور كيتا... wrote that "There is no scientific reason..."	the DNA is summed up by Dr. Keita, who wrote that "There is no scientific reason... "	unsuccessful
Yazidism	"Malak Ta'us ان تقبله وعدم has often been identified by outsiders with the Judeo-Christian figure of Satan"	not accepting that "Malak Ta'us has often been identified by outsiders with the Judeo-Christian figure of Satan"	unsuccessful

Table 7: Code-switching examples from effective and ineffective editors

non-Arabic words and phrases account for around 16% of the annotated sample. These generally consist of common English words like *had been good* and *sorry*, similar to the tag-switching structural form (Begum et al., 2016).

Although CS with English is far more prominent than other languages (94% of the instances), we also see French, Hebrew and Arabizi used in the dataset. The 'Other' instances in Table 5 refer to CS that did not have an interpretable function (Wikipedia-specific terms, for instance).

6.2 Article Topic

We used DBpedia (Lehmann et al., 2014) to get Wikipedia categories for each article. For our selected sample of 100 instances, the annotator verified these categories and judged whether the article was of a technical subject or not, as well as whether the article was centered around content from Arabic-speaking regions. Articles on general topics or topics not specifically related to Arabic history, language and culture were annotated as 'non-Arabic'.

CS on pages about non-Arabic topics is on average much more successful than on Arabic-related topics (Table 6). CS on pages with a technical subject is also more successful on average than on pages with other topics.

These findings are supported by a qualitative analysis of example Arabic-English discussion contributions with CS. Using medical terms in English on talk pages for articles on *Endorphin* and *Cancer* was associated with success, as was using English technical terms on the talk page for *Cybernetics* (see Table 7).

However, unsuccessful editors who switch to English seem to do so on pages whose subjects are more directly related to Western Asian and North African culture. For example, we find unsuccessful CS on the page about *Yazdanism*, a religion indigenous to Mesopotamia and on the *Egypt* page about the ancestry of the Egyptian population (see Table 7). Hypothesis 2's claim of CS as an 'outsider' effect may be supported in these contexts.

7 Conclusion and Future Work

We present a task and dataset to study the social effect of CS in the context of an online collaborative community, as well as an analysis of how sociolinguistic theory about deviation from conversational norms in CS can explain this data. We find that CS on Arabic Wikipedia talk pages is associated with making successful article edits, a measure of social influence. This finding supports a social interpretation of CS as a positive marker in this community, especially when the subject matter is technical or relates to non-Arabic topics.

Hypothesis 3 is most clearly supported by the positive association of CS with editor influence. Hypothesis 1, the lack of relationship between CS and social meaning, is unlikely given the effects we see on social influence. Hypothesis 2, a negative evaluation of CS as deviating from an Arabic norm, could explain the effect of CS in some contexts we observe, such as pages with topics related to Arabic culture.

In future work, norms specific to pages, users, languages and topics could be quantitatively explored and could nuance our measures of the markedness of editor contributions from those norms. Our dataset could also be used to analyze other factors contributing to editor success, such as speech acts, politeness, or conversational roles.

Further, this framework could easily be expanded to a broader multi-lingual analysis across Wikipedias of different languages, or even dialectal analysis within the Arabic Wikipedia. Different community norms about language choice on talk pages could yield different correlations with social influence.

Acknowledgments

This material is based upon work supported by the National Science Foundation Graduate Research Fellowship program under Grant No. DGE-1252522, as well as by NSF Grant No. IIS-1546393. This work was also partially supported by the Defense Advanced Research Projects Agency (DARPA) Information Innovation Office (I2O) under the Low Resource Languages for Emergent Incidents (LORELEI) program issued by DARPA/I2O under Contract No. HR0011-15-C-0114. The views expressed are those of the authors and do not reflect the official policies or positions of the National Science Foundation, Department of Defense or the U.S. Government.

References

Celso Alvarez-Cáccamo. 1990. Rethinking conversational code-switching: Codes, speech varieties, and contextualization. In *Annual Meeting of the Berkeley Linguistics Society*. volume 16, pages 3–16.

Peter Auer. 2013. *Code-Switching in Conversation: Language, Interaction and Identity*. Taylor & Francis.

Inma Munoa Barredo. 1997. Pragmatic functions of code-switching among basque-spanish bilinguals. *Retrieved on October* 26:2011.

Reem Bassiouney. 2006. *Functions of code switching in Egypt: Evidence from monologues*, volume 46. Brill.

Reem Bassiouney. 2009. *Arabic Sociolinguistics*. Edinburgh University Press.

Rafiya Begum, Kalika Bali, Monojit Choudhury, Koustav Rudra, and Niloy Ganguly. 2016. Functions of Code-Switching in Tweets: An Annotation Scheme and Some Initial Experiments. In *LREC*. i, pages 1644–1650.

Jan-Petter Blom and John J. Gumperz. 1972. Social meaning in linguistic structures: code-switching in Northern Norway. *Directions in Sociolinguistics: The Ethnography of Communication* pages 407–434.

Cristian Danescu-Niculescu-Mizil, Lillian Lee, Bo Pang, and Jon Kleinberg. 2012. Echoes of power: Language effects and power differences in social interaction. *Proceedings of the 21st international conference on World Wide Web - WWW '12* page 699. https://doi.org/10.1145/2187836.2187931.

Cristian Danescu-Niculescu-Mizil, Moritz Sudhof, Dan Jurafsky, Jure Leskovec, and Christopher Potts. 2013. A computational approach to politeness with application to social factors. *The 51st Annual Meeting of the Association for Computational Linguistics (ACL 2013)* .

Kareem Darwish. 2014. Arabizi Detection and Conversion to Arabic. In *ANLP 2014*.

Heba Elfardy, Mohamed Al-Badrashiny, and Mona Diab. 2014. Aida: Identifying code switching in informal arabic text. *EMNLP 2014* page 94.

Oliver Ferschke. 2014. *The Quality of Content in Open Online Collaboration Platforms: Approaches to NLP-supported Information Quality Management in Wikipedia*. Ph.D. thesis, Technische Universität, Darmstadt.

Oliver Ferschke, Torsten Zesch, and Iryna Gurevych. 2011. Wikipedia revision toolkit: Efficiently accessing wikipedia's edit history. In *Proceedings of the ACL-HLT 2011 System Demonstrations*. Association for Computational Linguistics, Portland, Oregon, pages 97–102.

Penelope Gardner-Chloros. 2009. *Code-switching*. Cambridge University Press.

H. Paul Grice. 1975. Logic and conversation. In Peter Cole and Jerry L. Morgan, editors, *Syntax and Semantics: Speech Acts*, Academic Press, New York, pages 41–58.

John J. Gumperz. 1982. *Discourse Strategies*. Studies in Interactional Socio. Cambridge University Press.

Hyeju Jang, Yohan Jo, Qinlan Shen, Michael Miller, Seungwhan Moon, and Carolyn Rose. 2016. Metaphor Detection with Topic Transition, Emotion and Cognition in Context. *Proceedings of the 54th Annual Meeting of the Association for Computational Linguistics (Volume 1: Long Papers)* 1:216–225.

Jens Lehmann, Robert Isele, Max Jakob, Anja Jentzsch, Dimitris Kontokostas, Pablo Mendes, Sebastian Hellmann, Mohamed Morsey, Patrick van Kleef, Sören Auer, and Chris Bizer. 2014. DBpedia - a large-scale, multilingual knowledge base extracted from wikipedia. *Semantic Web Journal* .

Marco Lui and Timothy Baldwin. 2012. langid.py: An off-the-shelf language identification tool. *Proceedings of the ACL 2012 System Demonstrations* (July):25–30.

Jeff MacSwan. 2000. The architecture of the bilingual language faculty: evidence from intrasentential code switching. *Bilingualism: Language and Cognition* 3(1):37–54. https://doi.org/10.1017/S1366728900000122.

Giovanni Molina, Rey-Villamizar, Thamar Solorio, Fahad AlGhamdi, Mahmoud Gohneim, Abdelati Hawwari, and Mona Diab. 2016. Overview for the Second Shared Task on Language Identification in Code-Switched Data. *Proceedings of The Second Workshop on Computational Approaches to Code Switching, held in conjunction with EMNLP 2016.* pages 62–72.

Carol Myers-Scotton. 1995. *Social Motivations for Codeswitching: Evidence from Africa.* Oxford studies in language contact. Clarendon Press.

Carol Myers-Scotton. 1998. *Codes and Consequences: Choosing Linguistic Varieties.* Oxford University Press.

Dong Nguyen, A. Seza Doğruöz, Carolyn P. Rosé, and Franciska de Jong. 2016. Computational sociolinguistics: A survey. *Computational Linguistics* 42(3):537–593. https://doi.org/10.1016/j.jksus.2015.08.001.

Elinor Ochs. 1992. Indexing Gender. In Alessandro Duranti and Charles Goodwin, editors, *Rethinking context: Language as an interactive phenomenon,* Cambridge University Press, chapter 14, pages 335–358.

Fabian Pedregosa, G. Varoquaux, A. Gramfort, V. Michel, B. Thirion, O. Grisel, M. Blondel, P. Prettenhofer, R. Weiss, V. Dubourg, J. Vanderplas, A. Passos, D. Cournapeau, M. Brucher, M. Perrot, and E. Duchesnay. 2011. Scikit-learn: Machine learning in Python. *Journal of Machine Learning Research* 12:2825–2830.

Mario Piergallini, Rouzbeh Shirvani, Gauri S Gautam, and Mohamed Chouikha. 2016. Word-Level Language Identification and Predicting Codeswitching Points in Swahili-English Language Data pages 21–29.

Reid Priedhorsky, Jilin Chen, Shyong Tony K Lam, Katherine Panciera, Loren Terveen, and John Riedl. 2007. Creating, destroying, and restoring value in wikipedia. *Proceedings of the 2007 international ACM conference on supporting group work - GROUP '07* page 259. https://doi.org/10.1145/1316624.1316663.

Koustav Rudra, Shruti Rijhwani, Rafiya Begum, Kalika Bali, Monojit Choudhury, and Niloy Ganguly. 2016. Understanding Language Preference for Expression of Opinion and Sentiment: What do Hindi-English Speakers do on Twitter? pages 1131–1141.

Sabah Safi-Stagni. 1991. *Agrammatism in Arabic.* Perspectives on Arabic Linguistics. John Benjamins Publishing Company.

Thamar Solorio, Elizabeth Blair, Suraj Maharjan, Steven Bethard, Mona Diab, Mahmoud Gohneim, Abdelati Hawwari, Fahad AlGhamdi, Julia Hirschberg, Alison Chang, and Pascale Fung. 2014. Overview for the First Shared Task on Language Identification in Code-Switched Data. *Proceedings of The First Workshop on Computational Approaches to Code Switching, held in conjunction with EMNLP 2014.* pages 62–72.

Thamar Solorio and Yang Liu. 2008. Learning to predict code-switch points. *EMNLP '08 Proceedings of the Conference on Empirical Methods in Natural Language Processing* pages 973–981. https://doi.org/10.16373/j.cnki.ahr.150049.

Oren Tsur, Dan Calacci, and David Lazer. 2015. A Frame of Mind: Using Statistical Models for Detection of Framing and Agenda Setting Campaigns. *ACL* pages 1629–1638.

How Does Twitter User Behavior Vary Across Demographic Groups?

Zach Wood-Doughty[*], **Michael Smith**[†], **David A. Broniatowski**[†], **Mark Dredze**[*]
[*]Center for Language and Speech Processing
Johns Hopkins University, Baltimore, MD 21218
[†]Department of Engineering Management and Systems Engineering
George Washington University, Washington, DC 20052
zach@cs.jhu.edu, mikesmith@gwu.edu, broniatowski@gwu.edu, mdredze@cs.jhu.edu

Abstract

Demographically-tagged social media messages are a common source of data for computational social science. While these messages can indicate differences in beliefs and behaviors between demographic groups, we do not have a clear understanding of how different demographic groups use platforms such as Twitter. This paper presents a preliminary analysis of how groups' differing behaviors may confound analyses of the groups themselves. We analyzed one million Twitter users by first inferring demographic attributes, and then measuring several indicators of Twitter behavior. We find differences in these indicators across demographic groups, suggesting that there may be underlying differences in how different demographic groups use Twitter.

1 Introduction

Demographics have a central role in social science research, yet Twitter and other social media platforms often do not provide traditional demographic characteristics, such as age, gender and ethnicity. Inferring demographic attributes has thus been a frequent area of research (Burger et al., 2011; Pennacchiotti and Popescu, 2011; Volkova, 2015; Rao and Yarowsky, 2010; Mislove et al., 2011), enabling large-scale analysis of demographically identified social media posts. Demographic inference has been used in many Twitter analyses, including studies of mental health (Coppersmith et al., 2015), exercise (Dos Reis and Culotta, 2015), language (Eisenstein et al., 2011; Nguyen et al., 2013) and personality (Schwartz et al., 2013).

Several studies have examined the accuracy of demographic inference and the large-scale patterns it reveals. Chen et al. (2015) and Volkova et al. (2014) examined the effect of different types of information on the accuracy of demographic predictions. Mislove et al. (2011) examined how inferred demographics compare to known demographics outside of Twitter in the United States and measured in what ways the user-base of Twitter is biased compared to the population as a whole. Sloan et al. (2013) performed a similar analysis of gender and language among Twitter users in the United Kingdom.

However, even with accurate demographic inference tools, there may be other confounding factors that make it difficult to estimate variations of beliefs and behaviors across demographic groups. Since social media analysis relies on *how* people use platforms, variations in usage behaviors by different demographic groups could introduce biases in analyses and alter conclusions. For example, if one group tends to use Twitter nicknames more frequently, a name-based demographic classifier may make more errors on members of that group. Alternatively, if we use profile pictures to infer demographics and users of one demographic are less likely to share pictures of themselves, our results may under-represent that group. Pavalanathan and Eisenstein (2015) studied these issues for geolocation algorithms, finding that classifiers which infer users' locations identify a target population that differs from the general population of Twitter. A Pew Report survey indicated that social media users' privacy settings do vary across demographics, but did not look at specific behaviors (Madden, 2012).

This paper presents a first analysis of how differences in social media behaviors between demographic groups may confound demographic inference. Our aim is to identify potential sources

Proceedings of the Second Workshop on Natural Language Processing and Computational Social Science, pages 83–89,
Vancouver, Canada, August 3, 2017. ©2017 Association for Computational Linguistics

of bias based on a large sample of Twitter users with demographic labels we infer using an ensemble of four classifiers for gender and ethnicity. We use systems that rely on several orthogonal sources of information to increase the robustness of our inference. We then measure various indicators of Twitter behaviors to identify potential differences across demographic groups. Our initial findings suggest that there may in fact be underlying differences in Twitter usage across these groups. This suggests that more work is needed to understand how these differences could impact the conclusions of Twitter analyses using inferred demographics.

2 Twitter User Data

We begin with a random sample of 5.4 million tweets taken from the 1% Twitter streaming API collected throughout the 12 months of 2016. From these tweets we sampled 1,000,000 users who had fewer than 500 followers and were not verified by Twitter, so as to exclude popular accounts, organizations, and "power users."

In May 2017, we attempted to download up to 200 of the most recent tweets of each user; this failed for the 18% of users who had made their accounts private or had deleted them altogether. For users who had tweeted fewer than 200 times, we retrieved their entire tweet history. This data reflects only those tweets that were publicly available at the time of our data collection. In total, we collected 158m tweets for 820k users, with a median of 200 tweets and a mean of 192 tweets per user that we could scrape.

3 User Behaviors

Our analyses focused on profile-based behaviors (invariant across all tweets) or those that could be estimated from (at most) 200 tweets. All behaviors appear in Table 1 in the order listed.

3.1 Profile Personalization

Many analyses of Twitter users are dependent on what information a user shares in his or her profile (Burger et al., 2011; Chen et al., 2015). We recorded whether each user included a custom profile image, URL, description, and location.

3.2 Temporal Information

To quantify each user's frequency of posting, we measured the average number of tweets per month from the time of account creation to the 2016 tweet.[1] We then computed the average of averages and the median average within each group. For the 38% of users who listed a timezone, we measured the normalized time-of-day of each tweet. Time-of-day data is useful for geolocation (Dredze et al., 2016) and understanding whether users are posting on Twitter from work or home.

3.3 Location Sharing

Several studies have examined location sharing behavior in Twitter (Mislove et al., 2011; Pavalanathan and Eisenstein, 2015; Dredze et al., 2013; Jurgens et al., 2015; Compton et al., 2014). However, these studies have not considered how this information may be correlated with demographic characteristics.

To determine the user's preference for sharing location information, we recorded whether a user had enabled geolocation sharing (a prerequisite for sharing GPS coordinates), and whether any of that user's tweets included GPS coordinates or a geotagged place. We also inferred locations for each tweet using Carmen (Dredze et al., 2013), a geolocation tool that estimates a user's location from the metadata from a single tweet. We recorded whether the Carmen tool could identify a country and/or a city from the user's profile.

3.4 User Interactions

Several previous studies have looked at how Twitter users interact with one another on the platform (Volkova and Bachrach, 2015; Bergsma et al., 2013; Volkova and Van Durme, 2015), including analyses of retweets (Luo et al., 2013; So et al., 2016; boyd et al., 2010) and replies or mentions (Honey and Herring, 2009; Hentschel et al., 2014).

For each user, we measured how many other users they mentioned across all tweets, how often they mentioned other users, how many of their tweets were retweets[2] or replies, and how often they shared images.

3.5 Devices

For each tweet, we record the contents of the "Source" field, which indicates from what type of device or platform the user posted. While there are many such platforms which represent hundreds of

---

[1]Tweet metadata includes date of account creation and total number of tweets from the account to date.

[2]We measure retweets via metadata, not the "RT" string.

different applications, we filter the results down to Android devices, iPhone devices, and desktop web clients. For each demographic group, we calculated the micro-averaged percent of tweets from each type of device and the macro-average of different types of devices used per user.

4 Demographic Classifiers

We used four separate approaches to infer the gender and ethnicity of the users in our dataset.

Demographer Demographer (Knowles et al., 2016) infers gender by first comparing a user's name against a namelist generated from the U.S. Social Security Administration, which includes the most likely gender. Second, for names not in the namelist, it uses an SVM to predict gender from character ngrams in the user's name.

Name RNN We extended Demographer by replacing the SVM with a recurrent neural network (RNN) which was trained on character sequences from Twitter names. We trained three models for predicting each of gender, 2-class ethnicity (Caucasian vs. African-American) and 3-class ethnicity (including Hispanic/Latino). As this classifiers was trained on the same data as the Demographer classifier, the two models had highly correlated predictions on users' genders.

Follower Lists Culotta et al. (2015) and Culotta et al. (2016) provide a model which uses a list of 1066 Twitter accounts which were highly correlated with demographic traits, according to Quantcast website data. The model predicts a user's gender and 4-class ethnicity (Caucasian, African-American, Hispanic/Latino, Asian) based on which, if any, of the Twitter accounts he or she follows. We gathered the entire list of followers for each of the 1066 Twitter accounts (totalling over 400 million users) to check which accounts were followed by which users. Because many users did not follow any of the accounts, this classifier did not always make a prediction.

Content Classifier Culotta et al. (2016) also provide a model that infers gender and 4-class ethnicity using the words in the user's tweet history. We ran this classifier on each of the users for which we could scrape a collection of tweets from 2017; because not all users mentioned terms within the model's vocabulary, it did not always make a prediction.

4.1 Comparing Demographic Classifiers

One issue in using this collection of classifiers is that they have different possible labels. The Follower Lists and Content Classifier methods include four categories for ethnicity, which does not match the number of categories from Demographer and Name RNN classifiers (two and three, respectively). For each classifier, White/Caucasian was the majority label in the training data and so the ambiguous instances may be classified as White. This is supported by the fact that 90% of our users were labeled as White by at least one classifier.

To account for the ethnicity label mismatch, we combine labels as follows: if the user was labeled as Asian by the Follower Lists or Content Classifier, we report the user as Asian; otherwise if the user was labeled as Hispanic/Latino by any classifier, we report that label; otherwise, if the user was labeled as Black/African-American by any classifier, we report that label; otherwise, if the user was labeled as White/Caucasian by two classifiers, we report that. This gives greater weight to ethnicity labels which could only be reported by a subset of the classifiers.[3] §5.1 discusses an alternative approach to handling this mismatch.

To reflect varying levels of agreement across the classifiers, we report separate numbers for how many classifiers agreed on gender. "M 2" means male according to two classifiers, which is a strict superset of "M 3", the users labeled as male by three classifiers. We ignored the 1.3% of users who were labeled as male by two classifiers and labeled as female by the other two classifiers.

5 Results

Table 1 shows results for gender and ethnicity, as well as the age of the user's account (discussed below). For many behaviors, there are marked differences across demographic groups. Across any two groups in the table (i.e. with at least 6.8% of the dataset per group), a macro-averaged difference of 1% between two proportions is statistically significant at the $p < 0.01$ level when using a two-tailed proportion test with

---

[3] There were 225k users twice-labeled as White/Caucasian which we reported as a different label on the basis of a single classifier. There were 107k users labeled as Black/African-American which we reported as Asian or Hispanic/Latino, and 9k users labeled as Hispanic/Latino which we reported as Asian.

a Bonferroni correction for 25 comparisons. Across the micro-averaged proportions for tweet percentages and time-of-day usage, a difference of 1% is significant using the same approach.

Gender There are several significant differences across inferred gender. Male-tagged users were significantly more likely to fill out the location and URL fields in their profiles, but were significantly less likely to enable geotagging.

There were only slight differences across time-of-day usage, though more male-tagged users had a timezone listed. Female-tagged users were more likely to use Android and iPhone devices, and less likely to use desktop web browsers or other sources.

Ethnicity Asian- and Hispanic/Latino-tagged users were far more likely to include a timezone in their profile, enable geotagging, share geotagged tweets, and include a location in their profile. Hispanic/Latino-tagged users had a higher proportion of tweets that were retweets, and were more likely to have a country identified by Carmen. White- and Black/African-American-tagged users had lower rates of almost all sharing-related behaviors, and were more likely to use iPhone devices and less likely to use Android devices or web clients.

Agreement as a Confounder Perhaps the most striking result is the difference between the gender groups with differing levels of classifier consensus ("M 2" vs. "M 3", and "F 2" vs. "F 3"). Users which had 3 classifiers in agreement for gender were significantly more likely to include a profile location or description.

This trend extends to the 2.0% of users for which all four gender classifiers agreed; the "F 4" and "M 4" users had significantly higher rates of almost every sharing behavior, including sharing one or more geotagged tweets (18.6% of users) and including a custom profile picture (99.0% of users). This indicates that agreement across classifiers is correlated with how much information a user is willing to share.

This is an important point, similar to that reported by Pavalanathan and Eisenstein (2015): propensity for sharing makes users easier to classify but presents a biased view of behavior. If correct, this may explain the differences between users labeled as either Asian or Hispanic/Latino compared to the overall usage rates. If our

classifiers only report "Asian" when specific, rare indicators are present, it may be the case that users who create a profile with those indicators also share more information than the average user.

Account Age Another confound may come from how long a user has been been on Twitter, which could influence how much information they are willing to share. 50% of the users in our dataset created their account before October 9, 2014, which we used as the cutoff between "old" and "new" users. The final columns of Table 1 compares these two groups of users; there is a clear tendency for the old users to share more information in their profiles, but also to post far less frequently. Furthermore, we measured that among "F 2" and "M 2" users, 56.6% of users were old, whereas among "F 3" and "M 3" users, 72.4% were old. Among the 2.0% of users with unanimous gender classification, 85.6% were old. Thus, a user's account age is correlated with both how likely our classifiers are to agree upon a label, and how much information that user shares.

5.1 Limitations

An important limitation of our analysis is that not all ethnicity classifiers predict the same set of labels (§4.1). Only two classifiers label users as Asian, and only three classifiers label users as Hispanic/Latino. Because these classifiers were trained on different datasets with different ethnicity labels, we also don't know how correlated their predictions would be if they had all been trained on the same dataset. New training data could highlight correlations and differences between classifiers, and provide more evidence of convergent validity.

Furthermore, we only consider a small set of racial and ethnic groups. Our methods cannot label users as Native American or Pacific Islander, and there has been little to no work in identifying these groups in Twitter. Additionally, while Asian, Caucasian and Black are considered racial groups in traditional analysis, Hispanic/Latino descent is an ethnicity. Our classifiers conflate these distinctions; this issue and its implications for demographic surveys has been discussed in public health and social science research (Van den Berghe, 1978; Comstock et al., 2004; Gonzalez-Barrera and Lopez, 2015).

Finally, we do not have clear measurements of the precision and recall of each classifier, nor do

Behavior/Data	All	Gender				Ethnicity				Account Age	
		F 2	F 3	M 2	M 3	W	B	HL	A	O	N
% users in dataset	100	27.0	6.8	31.8	7.9	43.4	28.9	15.3	12.3	50.0	50.0
% users with tweets from 2017	82.0	81.9	81.8	81.9	82.0	82.0	82.0	81.9	82.0	81.9	82.0
% users with custom profile image	95.4	96.3	96.6	95.2	97.8	93.9	95.4	97.9	98.0	97.3	93.5
% users with profile URL	20.8	21.3	26.5	23.7	29.3	16.8	20.3	26.1	30.0	25.1	16.6
% users with profile description	78.0	76.1	81.0	77.0	80.7	74.1	79.1	80.7	85.3	81.0	75.0
% users with profile location	53.6	54.9	62.6	57.3	66.1	48.0	53.5	61.7	63.3	58.6	48.7
Average monthly tweets	739	673	432	696	413	806	775	481	735	391	1086
Median average monthly tweets	205	204	203	205	206	205	205	204	204	149	297
% users with timezone data	37.8	47.9	77.9	51.3	79.3	15.4	29.7	73.8	91.1	55.0	20.6
(m) % weekday tweets before 9am	20.7	19.7	18.2	20.0	17.4	20.0	20.8	17.7	24.0	18.7	26.2
(m) % weekday tweets 9am - 5pm	25.8	26.5	27.5	26.5	28.5	26.4	25.9	27.6	23.3	26.1	24.9
(m) % weekday tweets after 5pm	28.6	28.5	28.7	28.6	28.9	28.8	28.6	28.9	28.3	30.3	24.0
(m) % weekend tweets	24.9	25.3	25.7	25.0	25.2	24.9	24.7	25.8	24.4	25.0	24.9
% users with geotagging enabled	33.1	39.1	47.5	36.0	45.2	28.2	31.0	45.4	40.0	47.2	39.1
% users with 1+ geotagged tweet	7.9	10.8	15.5	10.0	14.9	6.1	6.8	13.0	10.8	11.4	4.5
% users with Carmen country	17.2	23.8	32.2	22.5	32.8	15.1	15.8	24.7	18.8	21.0	13.5
% users with Carmen city	8.6	11.7	16.2	11.9	18.4	7.6	8.2	11.5	9.6	11.1	6.2
Number of mentioned users per user	95	106	123	105	126	85	89	119	113	102	88
(m) % tweets that mention a user	22.3	23.0	24.5	24.7	28.7	22.6	21.8	22.5	22.4	23.7	20.8
(m) % tweets that are retweets	42.6	48.3	48.8	42.7	43.2	42.3	41.6	46.7	40.0	41.2	44.2
(m) % tweets that are replies	15.3	12.4	12.1	15.5	17.1	15.5	15.2	14.0	16.4	14.6	16.1
(m) % tweets that include an image	33.9	36.4	38.3	36.4	41.7	33.2	32.9	37.1	33.6	34.9	32.6
(m) % tweets from Android sources	30.5	32.0	30.0	30.3	27.8	28.8	28.7	36.6	30.9	27.2	34.6
(m) % tweets from iPhone sources	36.9	37.9	40.7	33.5	34.0	39.5	39.7	31.2	32.1	37.7	36.0
(m) % tweets from desktop web	9.0	9.4	10.4	11.5	15.5	7.4	7.5	12.4	12.2	9.7	8.2
Number of devices used per user	1.5	1.7	2.1	1.8	2.2	1.3	1.4	2.0	2.2	1.8	1.3

Table 1: **Behavior across groups.** For gender groups, 'M' stands for Male, 'F' for Female. '2' indicates that at least three gender classifiers agreed on the label; '3' indicates that all four did. For ethnicity groups, 'W' stands for White/Caucasian, 'B' for Black/African-American, 'HL' for Hispanic/Latino, and 'A' for Asian. For age (of account) groups, 'O' stands for old (user joined before Oct. 2014), 'N' for new. (m) indicates that a percent or average was computed via micro-averaging across users' tweets; all others are macro-averaged across users. Entries that require multiple tweets per user or timezone data are computed by ignoring the users for which that data is unavailable, which may introduce bias.

we know the distribution of the users for which our ensemble does not make a prediction. While we can identify some biases (e.g. the three-class ethnicity classifier biases against labeling users as Hispanic-Latino, due to limitations with the training data), there may be other systematic errors we cannot identify. Additional bias in our measurements could be introduced from the large proportions of our users for which we could not download tweets from 2017 and did not have a timezone. Better measurements of the performance of our classifiers would allow us to combine their predictions in a principled way to vary the agreement and accuracy of our ensemble, and validate the system's robustness.

users, and use recent tools to infer their demographic labels. Our analysis highlights several behavioral differences between groups that warrant further study. As demographic inference in social media becomes common practice, it is important to validate methodologies and test whether underlying biases exist. A "black-box" predictor that assumes all input fields are equally representative of the underlying population is likely to introduce biases against groups for which that assumption is false. We hope that future work can further examine such confounds to measure their effect on conclusions drawn in the social media analysis literature.

6 Conclusion

We provide a preliminary look at possible confounds introduced by differences in how demographic groups use Twitter. We measure platform behaviors for a large set of Twitter

7 Acknowledgements

This work was supposed in part by the National Institute of General Medical Sciences under grant number 5R01GM114771.

References

Shane Bergsma, Mark Dredze, Benjamin Van Durme, Theresa Wilson, and David Yarowsky. 2013. Broadly improving user classification via communication-based name and location clustering on twitter. In *North American Chapter of the Association for Computational Linguistics (NAACL)*. pages 1010–1019.

danah boyd, Scott Golder, and Gilad Lotan. 2010. Tweet, tweet, retweet: Conversational aspects of retweeting on twitter. In *Hawaii International Conference on System Sciences (HICSS)*. IEEE, pages 1–10.

John D Burger, John Henderson, George Kim, and Guido Zarrella. 2011. Discriminating gender on twitter. In *Empirical Methods in Natural Language Processing (EMNLP)*. Association for Computational Linguistics, pages 1301–1309.

Xin Chen, Yu Wang, Eugene Agichtein, and Fusheng Wang. 2015. A comparative study of demographic attribute inference in twitter. In *International Conference on Weblogs and Social Media (ICWSM)*. pages 590–593.

Ryan Compton, David Jurgens, and David Allen. 2014. Geotagging one hundred million twitter accounts with total variation minimization. In *IEEE International Conference on Big Data*. pages 393–401.

R Dawn Comstock, Edward M Castillo, and Suzanne P Lindsay. 2004. Four-year review of the use of race and ethnicity in epidemiologic and public health research. *American journal of epidemiology* 159(6):611–619.

Glen Coppersmith, Mark Dredze, Craig Harman, and Kristy Hollingshead. 2015. From adhd to sad: analyzing the language of mental health on twitter through self-reported diagnoses. In *NAACL Workshop on Computational Linguistics and Clinical Psychology*.

Aron Culotta, Nirmal Ravi Kumar, and Jennifer Cutler. 2015. Predicting the demographics of twitter users from website traffic data. In *Conference on Artificial Intelligence (AAAI)*. pages 72–78.

Aron Culotta, Nirmal Ravi Kumar, and Jennifer Cutler. 2016. Predicting twitter user demographics using distant supervision from website traffic data. *J. Artif. Intell. Res.(JAIR)* 55:389–408.

Virgile Landeiro Dos Reis and Aron Culotta. 2015. Using matched samples to estimate the effects of exercise on mental health from twitter. In *Conference on Artificial Intelligence (AAAI)*. pages 182–188.

Mark Dredze, Miles Osborne, and Prabhanjan Kambadur. 2016. Geolocation for twitter: Timing matters. In *North American Chapter of the Association for Computational Linguistics (NAACL)*. pages 1064–1069.

Mark Dredze, Michael J Paul, Shane Bergsma, and Hieu Tran. 2013. Carmen: A twitter geolocation system with applications to public health. In *AAAI Workshop on Expanding the Boundaries of Health Informatics Using AI (HIAI)*.

Jacob Eisenstein, Noah A Smith, and Eric P Xing. 2011. Discovering sociolinguistic associations with structured sparsity. In *Association for Computational Linguistics (ACL)*. pages 1365–1374.

A Gonzalez-Barrera and MH Lopez. 2015. Is being hispanic a matter of race, ethnicity or both? *Pew Research Center* .

Martin Hentschel, Omar Alonso, Scott Counts, and Vasileios Kandylas. 2014. Finding users we trust: Scaling up verified twitter users using their communication patterns. In *International Conference on Weblogs and Social Media (ICWSM)*.

Courtenay Honey and Susan C Herring. 2009. Beyond microblogging: Conversation and collaboration via twitter. In *Hawaii International Conference on System Sciences (HICSS)*. IEEE, pages 1–10.

David Jurgens, Tyler Finethy, James McCorriston, Yi Tian Xu, and Derek Ruths. 2015. Geolocation prediction in twitter using social networks: A critical analysis and review of current practice. In *International Conference on Weblogs and Social Media (ICWSM)*. pages 188–197.

Rebecca Knowles, Josh Carroll, and Mark Dredze. 2016. Demographer: Extremely simple name demographics. In *EMNLP Workshop on Natural Language Processing and Computational Social Science*.

Zhunchen Luo, Miles Osborne, Jintao Tang, and Ting Wang. 2013. Who will retweet me?: finding retweeters in twitter. In *Conference on Research and development in information retrieval (SIGIR)*. pages 869–872.

Mary Madden. 2012. Privacy management on social media sites. *Pew Internet Report* pages 1–20.

Alan Mislove, Sune Lehmann, Yong-Yeol Ahn, Jukka-Pekka Onnela, and J Niels Rosenquist. 2011. Understanding the demographics of twitter users. In *International Conference on Weblogs and Social Media (ICWSM)*. volume 11.

Dong-Phuong Nguyen, Rilana Gravel, RB Trieschnigg, and Theo Meder. 2013. How old do you think i am? a study of language and age in twitter. In *International Conference on Weblogs and Social Media (ICWSM)*.

Umashanthi Pavalanathan and Jacob Eisenstein. 2015. Confounds and consequences in geotagged twitter data. In *Empirical Methods in Natural Language Processing (EMNLP)*.

Marco Pennacchiotti and Ana-Maria Popescu. 2011. A machine learning approach to twitter user classification. In *International Conference on Weblogs and Social Media (ICWSM)*. pages 281–288.

Delip Rao and David Yarowsky. 2010. Detecting latent user properties in social media. In *NIPS MLSN Workshop*.

H Andrew Schwartz, Johannes C Eichstaedt, Margaret L Kern, Lukasz Dziurzynski, Stephanie M Ramones, Megha Agrawal, Achal Shah, Michal Kosinski, David Stillwell, Martin EP Seligman, et al. 2013. Personality, gender, and age in the language of social media: The open-vocabulary approach. *PloS one* 8(9):e73791.

Luke Sloan, Jeffrey Morgan, William Housley, Matthew Williams, Adam Edwards, Pete Burnap, and Omer Rana. 2013. Knowing the tweeters: Deriving sociologically relevant demographics from twitter. *Sociological research online* 18(3):7.

Jiyeon So, Abby Prestin, Lyndon Lee, Yafei Wang, John Yen, and Wen-Ying Sylvia Chou. 2016. What do people like to share about obesity? a content analysis of frequent retweets about obesity on twitter. *Health communication* 31(2):193–206.

Pierre L Van den Berghe. 1978. Race and ethnicity: a sociobiological perspective. *Ethnic and racial studies* 1(4):401–411.

Svitlana Volkova. 2015. *Predicting Demographics and Affect in Social Networks*. Ph.D. thesis, Johns Hopkins University.

Svitlana Volkova and Yoram Bachrach. 2015. On predicting sociodemographic traits and emotions from communications in social networks and their implications to online self-disclosure. *Cyberpsychology, Behavior, and Social Networking* 18(12):726–736.

Svitlana Volkova, Glen Coppersmith, and Benjamin Van Durme. 2014. Inferring user political preferences from streaming communications. In *Association for Computational Linguistics (ACL)*. pages 186–196.

Svitlana Volkova and Benjamin Van Durme. 2015. Online bayesian models for personal analytics in social media. In *Conference on Artificial Intelligence (AAAI)*. pages 2325–2331.

Ideological Phrase Indicators for Classification of Political Discourse Framing on Twitter

Kristen Johnson, I-Ta Lee, Dan Goldwasser
Department of Computer Science
Purdue University, West Lafayette, IN 47907
{john1187, lee2226, dgoldwas}@purdue.edu

Abstract

Politicians carefully word their statements in order to influence how others view an issue, a political strategy called framing. Simultaneously, these frames may also reveal the beliefs or positions on an issue of the politician. Simple language features such as unigrams, bigrams, and trigrams are important indicators for identifying the general frame of a text, for both longer congressional speeches and shorter tweets of politicians. However, tweets may contain multiple unigrams across different frames which limits the effectiveness of this approach. In this paper, we present a joint model which uses both linguistic features of tweets and ideological phrase indicators extracted from a state-of-the-art embedding-based model to predict the general frame of political tweets.

1 Introduction

Social media platforms have played an increasingly important role in U.S. presidential elections, beginning in 2008. Among these, microblogs such as Twitter have a special role, as they allow politicians to react quickly to events as they unfold and to shape the discussion of current political issues according to their views.

Framing is an important tool used by politicians to bias the discussion towards their stance. Framing contextualizes the discussion by emphasizing specific aspects of the issue, which creates an association between the issue and a specific frame of reference. Research on issue framing in political discourse is rooted in social science research (Entman, 1993; Chong and Druckman, 2007) and recently has attracted growing interest in the natural language processing community (Tsur et al.,

2015; Card et al., 2015; Baumer et al., 2015) as a way to automatically analyze political discourse in congressional speeches and political news articles. Contrary to these sources, Twitter requires politicians to compress their ideas and reactions into 140 character long tweets. As a result, politicians have to cleverly choose how to frame controversial issues, as well as react to events and each other (Mejova et al., 2013; Tumasjan et al., 2010).

Framing decisions can be used to build support for political stances and they often reflect ideological differences between politicians. For example, in debates concerning the issue of abortion, the stance opposing abortion is framed as "pro-life", which reflects a moral or religious-based ideology. Correctly identifying how issues are framed can help reveal the ideological base of the speaker. However, in many cases framing abstracts this information and groups content reflecting differing ideologies together under the same frame. As a concrete example consider the following tweets:

1. *POTUS exec. order on guns is a gross overreach of power that tramples on the rights of law abiding Americans and our Constitution*

2. *With this ruling #SCOTUS has upheld a critical freedom for women to make their own decisions about their bodies*

In both tweets, the same frame (Legality, Constitutionality, & Jurisdiction) is used to discuss two different issues: guns and abortion, respectively. Despite the use of a similar frame, the two tweets reflect opposing ideologies.

A straight-forward approach for identifying these differences would be to refine the issue-independent general frames into more specific categories. However, this would limit their generalization and considerably increase the difficulty of analysis, both for human annotators and for automated techniques. Instead, we suggest to aug-

Proceedings of the Second Workshop on Natural Language Processing and Computational Social Science, pages 90–99,
Vancouver, Canada, August 3, 2017. ©2017 Association for Computational Linguistics

ment the frame analysis with additional information. Our modeling approach is based on the observation that politicians often use *slogans* in both their tweets and speeches. These are key phrases used to *indirectly* indicate the political figures' core beliefs and ideological stances. Identification of these phrases automatically decomposes the frames into more specific categories.

Consider the two tweets in the example above. In the first tweet, several phrases indicate the frame: "exec. order", "overreach of power", "rights of law abiding Americans", "our constitution". In the second tweet, the relevant phrases are "this ruling" and "upheld a critical freedom". All of these phrases indicate that the same frame is being used in both tweets. However, analyzing the specific terminology in each case and the context in which it appears helps capture the ideological similarities and differences. For example, in the context of gun-rights debates, phrases highlighting "law and order" and references to the constitution tend to reflect a conservative ideology, while phrases highlighting upholding of freedoms in the abortion debate tend to reflect a liberal ideology.

Given the rapidly changing nature of trending issues and political discourse on Twitter, our key technical challenge is to relay these ideological dimensions to an automated model, such that it will be able to easily adapt to new issues and language. Our model consists of two components combined together: frame identification and ideological-indicators identification. For the first piece we use a structured probabilistic model to capture general framing dimensions by combining content and political context analysis. For the second task, we employ a state-of-the-art textual similarity model which captures and generalizes over lexical indicators of key phrases that identify the politicians' ideology. More details of both components are described in Section 4.

In this paper we take a first step towards connecting these two dimensions of analysis: issue framing and ideology identification. We lay the foundation for more advanced research by identifying this connection, analyzing tweets authored by U.S congressional representatives, and extracting ideological phrase indicators. We build and analyze a joint model which combines the two dimensions. Our experiments in Section 5 quantitatively compare the differences in frame prediction performance when using ideological phrase indicators. We also include a qualitative analysis in Section 6 of several examples in which ideological phrase indicators can help differentiate between tweets with similar frame predictions that reflect different ideologies.

2 Related Work

Previous computational works which analyze political discourse focus on opinion mining and stance prediction from forums and tweets (Sridhar et al., 2015; Hasan and Ng, 2014; Abu-Jbara et al., 2013; Walker et al., 2012; Abbott et al., 2011; Somasundaran and Wiebe, 2010, 2009; Johnson and Goldwasser, 2016; Ebrahimi et al., 2016). A variety of social media based predictions have been studied including: prediction of political affiliation and other demographics of Twitter users (Volkova et al., 2015, 2014; Yano et al., 2013; Conover et al., 2011), profile (Li et al., 2014b) and life event extraction (Li et al., 2014a), conversation modeling (Ritter et al., 2010), methods for handling unique microblog language (Eisenstein, 2013), and the modeling of social interactions and group structure in predictions (Sridhar et al., 2015; Abu-Jbara et al., 2013; West et al., 2014; Huang et al., 2012). Works which focus on inferring signed social networks (West et al., 2014) and collective classification using PSL (Bach et al., 2015) are similar to the modeling approach of Johnson et al. (2017b), which we extend in this paper.

Several previous works have explored framing in public statements, congressional speeches, and news articles (Fulgoni et al., 2016; Tsur et al., 2015; Card et al., 2015; Baumer et al., 2015). Framing is further related to works which analyze biased language (Recasens et al., 2013; Choi et al., 2012; Greene and Resnik, 2009) and subjectivity (Wiebe et al., 2004). Important to the language analysis of our work, Tan et al. (2014) have shown how wording choices can affect message propagation on Twitter. The study of political sentiment analysis (Pla and Hurtado, 2014; Bakliwal et al., 2013), ideology measurement and prediction (Iyyer et al., 2014; Bamman and Smith, 2015; Sim et al., 2013; Djemili et al., 2014), policies (Nguyen et al., 2015), voting patterns (Gerrish and Blei, 2012), and polls based on Twitter political sentiment (Bermingham and Smeaton, 2011; O'Connor et al., 2010; Tumasjan et al., 2010) are also related to the study of framing on Twitter.

1. Economic: Economic effects of a policy
2. Capacity & Resources: Resources lack or availability
3. Morality & Ethics: Religious doctrine, righteousness, sense of responsibility
4. Fairness & Equality: Distribution of laws, punishments, resources, etc. among groups
5. Legality, Constitutionality, & Jurisdiction: Court cases and restriction and expressions of rights
6. Crime & Punishment: Crimes and consequences
7. Security & Defense: Preemptive actions to protect against threats
8. Health & Safety: Health care access and effectiveness
9. Quality of Life: Aspects of individual/community life
10. Cultural Identity: Trends, customs, and norms
11. Public Sentiment: Opinions and polling
12. Political Factors & Implications: Stances, filibusters, lobbying, references to political entities
13. Policy Description, Prescription, & Evaluation: Effectiveness of policies
14. External Regulation and Reputation: Interstate and international relationships
15. Factual: Expresses a fact, with no political spin
16. (Self) Promotion: Promotes author or another person
17. Personal Sympathy & Support: Expresses emotional response, including sympathy and solidarity

Table 1: General Frames and Their Descriptions. Detailed descriptions of the frames can be found in Boydstun et al. (2014).

Political and social science works have studied the role of Twitter and framing in molding public opinion of events and issues (Burch et al., 2015; Harlow and Johnson, 2011; Meraz and Papacharissi, 2013; Jang and Hart, 2015), as well as sentiment analysis and network agenda modeling of the 2012 U.S. presidential election (Groshek and Al-Rawi, 2013). Boydstun et al. (2014) composed a Policy Frames Codebook for use in labeling general, issue-independent frames of longer texts. These frames were extended for Twitter and studied in a computational setting by Johnson et al. (2017b,a). Our approach builds upon these findings by identifying phrases which are relevant for determining ideology and increasing prediction accuracy of frames.

3 Data and Problem Setting

Dataset: In this work, we use the Congressional Tweets Dataset of Johnson et al. (2017b,a) which consists of the tweets of members of the 114th U.S. Congress. These tweets discuss six current political issues: (1) abortion, (2) the Affordable Care Act (i.e., the ACA or Obamacare), (3) gun ownership, (4) immigration, (5) terrorism, and (6) the LGBTQ community. The dataset provides a labeled portion of 2,050 tweets, which are labeled

using 17 possible frames. A brief description of each frame is shown in Table 1.

Frame Overlap: Johnson et al. (2017b,a) found that for most tweets, one or two frames were used. Additionally, in many cases, tweets authored by Republican and Democratic politicians use similar frames, both when discussing similar and different issues. For example, consider the following two tweets concerning the shooting of the Emanuel African Methodist Episcopal Church in 2015.

1. *Our thoughts and prayers must be with 9 innocent men and women murdered in Charleston, SC. Every effort must be made to capture the killer. RIP*

2. *My thoughts are with those impacted by the #CharlestonShooting. I pray that the perpetrator is brought to justice soon.*

Both tweets frame the shooting using two frames: Frame 6 (Crime & Punishment) and Frame 17 (Personal Sympathy & Support). In Tweet (1) the politician states that the killer must be captured. Similarly, in Tweet (2) the politician hopes for the perpetrator of the crime to be brought to justice. These phrases indicate that Frame 6 is being used. Additionally, in both tweets the politicians express that their thoughts are with those affected by the crime, indicating the use of Frame 17. Despite the use of the same frames by both tweets, there are very subtle differences between the two tweets, indicated by the specific phrase choices. For example, in Tweet (1) the politician uses the phrase "men and women murdered" to specifically reference the victims, while in Tweet (2) the politician uses "those impacted", a more inclusive definition.

Phrase Identification: Using the labeled tweets of the dataset, we extracted lists of short phrases which frequently appear in each frame, for all frames. [1] All of these phrases can be further grouped into a more general phrase, which we term an *ideological phrase indicator*. For example, sub-phrases such as *rates will increase, increasing the rates this year*, and *premiums skyrocket* can be grouped into the more general ideological phrase indicator *Increase* of Frame 1 (Economic). From our observations, Democrats tend to

---

[1]Phrases are currently extracted manually by matching them to the guidelines of Boydstun et al. (2014). In future work, we aim to automate the phrase extraction.

Frame	General Ideological Phrase Indicators
Economic	Republican: Increase, Losses, Taxes, Job Effects
	Democrat: Deficit, Savings, Economy, Costs to Taxpayers
Capacity & Resources	Republican: Sources of Money, Defunding
	Democrat: Purchases, Taking Money
	Both Parties: Funding
Morality & Ethics	Republican: Morality
	Democrat: Sense of Obligation, Negative Descriptors
	Both Parties: Religion
Fairness & Equality	Republican: Race, Ethnicity
	Democrat: Women's Rights, LGBT Rights, Discrimination, Civil Rights, Demands for Equality
Legality, Constitutionality, & Jurisdiction	Republican: Branches of Government
	Democrat: Items Being Voted On, SCOTUS Cases
	Both Parties: Laws, Rights
Crime & Punishment	Both Parties: Crimes
Security & Defense	Republican: Defense, Specific Threats
	Democrat: Ensure Safety, Preventive Measures
	Both Parties: Terrorism, Protection
Health & Safety	Republican: Health Care Aspects, Threats to Safety, Health Care Effectiveness
	Democrat: Health Insurance Access, Safety, Choices
	Both Parties: Health Care Access
Quality of Life	Republican: General Quality of Life
	Democrat: Affects Families, Affects Women's Lives, Affects Everyone
Cultural Identity	Republican: Group Stereotypes
	Democrat: American, Immigrants
	Both Parties: Values
Public Sentiment	Both Parties: Americans Want, Polls
Political Factors & Implications	Both Parties: Republicans, Democrats, Congress, SCOTUS, POTUS
Policy Description, Prescription, & Evaluation	Republican: Votes on Bill Policies
	Democrat: Gun Policies, LGBT Policies, Immigration Policies
	Both Parties: ACA Policies, General Policies, Terrorism Policies
External Regulation & Reputation	Both Parties: National, International
Factual	Both Parties: Numerical Facts
(Self) Promotion	Both Parties: Media, References Self, References Others
Personal Sympathy & Support	Both Parties: Solidarity, Sympathy, Emotion

Table 2: Ideological Phrase Indicators for Each Frame. Frames are listed in the left column. General ideological phrase indicators used by each party, as well as by both parties, are listed in the right column.

use more phrase indicators (with more sub-phrases each) than Republicans for each frame. Finally, while the general phrase indicator name may be similar for both parties, the sub-phrases that are grouped under the general phrase may overlap, but are often different. For example, Frame 12 (Political Factors & Implications) has the general phrase indicator *Refers to POTUS* for both parties. However, the sub-phrases under this general phrase can differ across the parties, e.g. Republicans use phrases like "Obama admin" or "commander in chief", while Democrats use phrases like "the administration", "the president", or "thank you POTUS". Sub-phrases can also be similar across parties, e.g., both parties use "President Obama" in Frame 12. The general ideological phrase indica- tors for each frame are listed in Table 2. [2]

4 PSL Models of Language on Twitter

Weakly Supervised Models with PSL: In order to model the dependencies between politicians and the language of their tweets, we design models with PSL, a declarative modeling language (Bach et al., 2015). PSL allows the user to specify first-order logic rules using domain knowledge. Weights for these rules are learned in either a supervised or unsupervised fashion and each weight indicates the importance of its associated rule. These rules are compiled into a hinge-loss Markov random field which defines a probability distribution over continuous value assignments to random variables of the model. For more details

---

[2]Complete lists of sub-phrases are omitted due to space.

PSL MODEL RULES
UNIGRAM$_F$(T, U) $\wedge$ SIMPHRASE(T,P$_F$) $\rightarrow$ FRAME(T, F)
UNIGRAM$_F$(T, U) $\wedge$ PARTY(T, P) $\wedge$ SIMPHRASE(T,P$_F$) $\rightarrow$ FRAME(T, F)
UNIGRAM$_F$(T, U) $\wedge$ SIMUNIGRAM(T, F) $\wedge$ SIMPHRASE(T,P$_F$) $\rightarrow$ FRAME(T, F)
UNIGRAM$_F$(T, U) $\wedge$ PARTY(T, P) $\wedge$ BIGRAM$_P$(T, B) $\wedge$ SIMPHRASE(T,P$_F$) $\rightarrow$ FRAME(T, F)
UNIGRAM$_F$(T, U) $\wedge$ PARTY(T, P) $\wedge$ TRIGRAM$_P$(T, TR) $\wedge$ SIMPHRASE(T,P$_F$) $\rightarrow$ FRAME(T, F)

Table 3: Examples of PSL Model Rules. Predicates composed into rules are on the left hand side and the target predicate (prediction goal) is on the right hand side.

on PSL we refer the reader to Bach et al. (2015).

To evaluate if modeling ideological phrase indicators can increase the F_1 score of frame prediction, we use the most indicative features for predicting a tweet's frame (as determined by Johnson et al. (2017b)): unigrams, word similarity to unigrams, bigrams, and trigrams. In addition, we add tweet similarity to phrases (SIMPHRASE(T,P$_F$) described below) as a feature. These features are extracted using weakly supervised models and represented as the following predicates in PSL notation: UNIGRAM$_F$(T,U), SIMUNIGRAM(T,F), BIGRAM$_P$(T,B), TRIGRAM$_P$(T,TR). Each predicate indicates that the tweet T has that unigram U, a word similar to that unigram, a bigram B, or a trigram TR, respectively. Finally, the party of the politician who authored the tweet (PARTY(T,P)) is also used. These predicates are combined into the probabilistic rules of the PSL model as shown in Table 3.

Incorporating Phrase Similarity: Due to the dynamic nature of language and trending political issues on Twitter, it is infeasible to construct a list of all possible phrases one can expect politicians to use when framing an issue. Therefore, we use the embedding-based model of Lee et al. (2017) to determine which tweets contain phrases that are similar to our initial list of phrases. For example, given the phrase *insurance rates will increase*, we want to find all tweets which contain similar phrases, e.g., *rising insurance premiums*.

The phrase similarity model was trained on the Paraphrase Database (PPDB) (Ganitkevitch et al., 2013) and incorporates a Convolutional Neural Network (CNN) to capture sentence structures. This model generates the embeddings of our phrases and computes the cosine similarities between phrases and tweets as the scores. The input tweets and phrases are represented as the average word embeddings in the input layer, which are then projected into a convolutional layer, a max-pooling layer, and finally two fully-connected lay-

ers. The embeddings are thus represented in the final layer. The learning objective of this model is:

$$\min_{W_c, W_w} \Big(\sum_{<x_1, x_2> \in X} max(0, \delta - cos(g(x_1), g(x_2))$$
$$+ cos(g(x_1), g(t_1)))$$
$$+ max(0, \delta - cos(g(x_1), g(x_2)))$$
$$+ cos(g(x_2), g(t_2)) \Big)$$
$$+ \lambda_c ||W_c||^2 + \lambda_w ||W_{init} - W_w||^2,$$

where X is all the positive input pairs, δ is the margin, $g(\cdot)$ represents the network, λ_c and λ_w are the weights for L2-regularization, W_c is the network parameters, W_w is the word embeddings, W_{init} is the initial word embeddings, and t_1 and t_2 are negative examples that are randomly selected.

All tweet-phrase pairs with a cosine similarity over a given threshold are used as input to the PSL model via the predicate SIMPHRASE(T,P$_F$), which indicates that tweet T contains a phrase that is similar to the phrases for a certain frame (P$_F$). Table 3 presents examples of the rules used in our modeling procedure.

5 Experiments

Analysis of Supervised Experiments: Since each tweet can be classified as having more than one frame, the prediction task becomes a multi-label classification task. Therefore, we use the standard measurements for precision and recall of a multilabel task. The F_1 score is the harmonic mean of these two measures. We conducted supervised experiments using five-fold cross validation with randomly chosen splits on the labeled portion of the dataset. Table 4 shows the results of our supervised experiments. The first column lists the frame number. The second column presents the results of the baseline model, which includes all of the rules listed in Table 3 *without* the SIMPHRASE(T,P$_F$) predicate. The third

Frame No.	Baseline	Phrases
1	85.11	**87.50**
2	**82.35**	82.05
3	**88.46**	76.79
4	**82.35**	75.28
5	67.57	**71.57**
6	63.64	**70.59**
7	83.12	**89.70**
8	75.68	**89.51**
9	**76.47**	71.52
10	**88.89**	84.52
11	29.41	**29.63**
12	73.92	**81.25**
13	**65.43**	62.35
14	**85.71**	82.25
15	82.35	**83.33**
16	**82.05**	73.55
17	91.07	**91.67**
Weighted Avg.	75.95	**76.27**

Table 4: F_1 Scores of Supervised Experiments. The baseline column represents the results of the best model of Johnson et al. (2017b). The phrases column indicates the scores for the best model when combined with our proposed phrases. Items in bold are the highest score. The weighted average is the micro-weighted average of the F_1 scores.

column lists the results of our model which consists of the baseline model *with* the addition of the SIMPHRASE(T, P_F) predicate.

From these results we can see that the joint model that uses both language features (i.e., unigrams, bigrams, and trigrams) and phrase indicators (shown in Table 2) is able to improve performance in 9 out of the 17 frames. The most likely cause for the decrease in score for the other 8 frames is that it is possible that there are too many overlapping sub-phrases within the general phrases of these 8 frames. This would introduce extra noise into the probabilistic model and result in lower scores. The 9 frames which improve have either 1 or no overlapping sub-phrases across parties for each general phrase category. Further refinement of the sub-phrases is left for future work.

Ablation Case Study: To investigate the usefulness of ideological phrase indicators, we conducted an ablation study on the results of Frame 12. Frame 12 is used when a politician references other political entities (e.g., the House, Senate, former presidents, etc.) as well as political actions (e.g., filibusters or lobbying). For our dataset, we used the following general phrases for Frame 12 which include references to: Democrats, Republicans, the President (POTUS), the Supreme Court

(SCOTUS), and Congress. We ran our model through an ablation study, in which each pair of phrases is removed one at a time to study their overall effect on the final prediction. Table 5 presents the results of this experiment.

Model	F_1 Score	Change
All Phrases	81.25	—
Republicans	85.71	+ 4.46
Democrats	77.78	- 3.47
POTUS	83.33	+ 2.08
SCOTUS	85.71	+ 4.46
Congress	78.57	- 2.68

Table 5: F_1 Scores of Ablation Experiments. All Phrases represents our score for Frame 12 when using all possible phrases. The remaining rows indicate which general phrase indicators have been removed from the comprehensive model. Column 2 presents the F_1 score. Column 3 indicates the increase or decrease in score after the respective phrases are removed.

From these initial results, it appears that the way politicians refer to Democrats and Congress are the most important phrase indicators for predicting Frame 12. When these two phrase groups are removed, there is a large decrease in F_1 score. Additionally, removing references to the president has a slight increase, while removing references to Republicans and the Supreme Court has a larger increase. Therefore, references to Republicans and the Supreme Court are likely to be the least useful for predicting this frame. We leave finding the best combinations of phrases for each frame as future work, as described in Section 7.

6 Qualitative Analysis

The supervised experiments of the previous section allow us to analyze the effects of phrases as features for frame prediction. In this section, we explore the predictions of the phrase-based model to locate framing trends of a real world event. We first learned the weights of each model using the labeled data and then performed MPE inference on the *unlabeled* tweets to obtain their predicted frames. We used these predictions to analyze the political discourse on Twitter by focusing on tweets concerning the shooting of the Pulse Nightclub in Orlando, Florida (June 12, 2016). Table 6 presents the frame predictions and example tweets for this event.

Frame 17 reflects politicians tweeting that their

Date	Politician	Political Party	Tweet	Predicted Frame(s)
6/12/2016	Alex Mooney	Republican	My thoughts and prayers are with the people of #Orlando, the victims, and their families.	17
6/12/2016	Brad Ashford	Democrat	As authorities investigate the Orlando shooting, we must pray for the victims and act swiftly to keep these tragedies out of our communities.	9
6/12/2016	Lisa Murkowski	Republican	What happened in Orlando was an absolute tragic act of terrorism spawned by an ideology of hate being pushed by ISIS.	3
6/12/2016	Bob Goodlatte	Republican	The attack in #Orlando was an act of pure evil. My prayers are w/ the families of victims and the injured. We will continue seeking answers.	3, 17
6/12/2016	David Cicilline	Democrat	Voters should absolutely hold us accountable for what we're doing or not doing to address gun violence.	3
6/12/2016	Yvette Clark	Democrat	I am deeply saddened by the act of hate and terror enacted on the lives of Orlando's LGBT Community and I #StandWithOrlando	3, 17
6/15/2016	Jeanne Shaheen	Democrat	Joining @ChrisMurphyCT on the Senate floor to say #Enough and call for reforms 2 prevent gun violence.	7, 12
6/15/2016	Mark Kirk	Republican	Americans need to know Washington is listening - We must keep guns out of the hands of suspected terrorists	7
6/15/2016	Kirsten Gillibrand	Democrat	As we mourn victims of yet another tragedy, time to finally act on commonsense gun safety reforms supported by the American people.	11, 12

Table 6: Example Tweets Associated With the Orlando Pulse Nightclub Shooting on June 12, 2016.

"thoughts and prayers" are with the community, as seen in the first line of Table 6. Offers of prayers and sympathy are used by both parties as the initial response the day this (and most other) shootings occur. This can be considered both as a reflection of the politicians' immediate emotional reaction to the shooting but also to support other agendas, as Frame 17 also appears in tweets that use other frames, specifically Frames 9 and 3. Interestingly, Republicans and Democrats use these frames in nuanced ways to promote different agendas, which are identifiable by the presence (or lack thereof) of different key phrases.

Republicans used Frame 3, often in combination with Frame 17, to discuss the shooting as an act of evil or terrorism as well as to suggest links between the shooter and ISIS (examples of these tweets are shown in rows three and four of Table 6). Democrats, however, used Frame 3 to express a sense of responsibility on their part to take actions to prevent gun violence (e.g., row five of Table 6) or refer to the shooting as a hate crime or act of terror (e.g., row six of Table 6). All of these examples are expressed with Frame 3, however, the different phrases indicate differing underlying ideologies. For example, referring to the shooting as an "act of evil" indicates a religious-based ideology, which also limits possible ways to combat the problem. However, by associating the cause with hatred or terror instead, there is a subtle implication that measures can be taken to prevent future violence with similar causes. Democrats go one step further by using this frame to transition into calls for increased gun legislation, which would be a concrete step towards preventing future shootings.

On June 15th, three days after the shooting, Democrats held a filibuster to push for a vote on gun control. The top frame that day for both parties is Frame 7 (Security & Defense), however different phrases represent different ideologies in this example as well. Democrats frame the need for gun control laws as a preemptive measure that will prevent gun violence (e.g., row seven of Table 6). Republicans use Frame 7 to discuss the need to prevent threats posed by ISIS (possibly due to the shooter's association with ISIS) as shown in row eight of Table 6. Additionally, some Republicans promote bipartisan efforts to stop the sale of guns to known terrorists (row eight). While all examples use Frame 7 to support gun control, this support is limited depending on party and identifiable by different key phrases, e.g. the general goal of "reforms 2 prevent gun violence" versus the specific target to "keep guns out of the hands of suspected terrorists".

Lastly, the impacts of the shooting on the quality of life of the community (or nation as a whole) are discussed in tweets having Frame 9. For example, row two of Table 6 shows a Democrat's tweet calling for action to keep gun violence tragedies from affecting communities. For this event, Republicans are more likely to refer to the "Orlando community" while Democrats are more likely to reference the "LGBT community", indicating that national versus specific-group phrases are useful in identifying Frame 9.

7 Future Work

Currently, this work requires human knowledge and engineering to compile the sub-phrases by party. Additionally, for computational simplicity all phrases are currently added to the baseline model for evaluation. Since frames can overlap and politicians can use the talking points of other parties, we hypothesize that frame prediction can be further improved by automatically testing all possible phrases with the baseline model.

For future work, we are building an automatic search over all possible phrase indicators, designed to choose the most indicative phrases for predicting each frame. We hope this tool will be useful for scientists from other fields, allowing them to compile their expert knowledge of a domain into many rules, which can then be analyzed to indicate the most useful features for further study of a subject.

8 Conclusion

In this paper we present an analysis of the usefulness of ideological phrases as a feature for predicting the frame of a political tweet. By compiling a list of common phrases and computing their similarity to tweets, we are able to increase the F_1 scores for half of the frames over a simpler language based model. We provide an analysis of our joint model in a supervised setting and show interesting real world examples. Finally, we propose the automation of phrase searching as a future work to improve the usefulness of this technique in other scientific communities.

Acknowledgments

We thank the anonymous reviewers for their thoughtful comments and suggestions.

References

Rob Abbott, Marilyn Walker, Pranav Anand, Jean E. Fox Tree, Robeson Bowmani, and Joseph King. 2011. How can you say such things?!?: Recognizing disagreement in informal political argument. In *Proc. of the Workshop on Language in Social Media*.

Amjad Abu-Jbara, Ben King, Mona Diab, and Dragomir Radev. 2013. Identifying opinion subgroups in arabic online discussions. In *Proc. of ACL*.

Stephen H Bach, Matthias Broecheler, Bert Huang, and Lise Getoor. 2015. Hinge-loss markov random fields and probabilistic soft logic. *arXiv preprint arXiv:1505.04406* .

Akshat Bakliwal, Jennifer Foster, Jennifer van der Puil, Ron O'Brien, Lamia Tounsi, and Mark Hughes. 2013. Sentiment analysis of political tweets: Towards an accurate classifier. In *Proc. of ACL*.

David Bamman and Noah A Smith. 2015. Open extraction of fine-grained political statements. In *Proc. of EMNLP*.

Eric Baumer, Elisha Elovic, Ying Qin, Francesca Polletta, and Geri Gay. 2015. Testing and comparing computational approaches for identifying the language of framing in political news. In *Proc. of NAACL*.

Adam Bermingham and Alan F Smeaton. 2011. On using twitter to monitor political sentiment and predict election results .

Amber Boydstun, Dallas Card, Justin H. Gross, Philip Resnik, and Noah A. Smith. 2014. Tracking the development of media frames within and across policy issues.

Lauren M. Burch, Evan L. Frederick, and Ann Pegoraro. 2015. Kissing in the carnage: An examination of framing on twitter during the vancouver riots. *Journal of Broadcasting & Electronic Media* 59(3):399–415.

Dallas Card, Amber E. Boydstun, Justin H. Gross, Philip Resnik, and Noah A. Smith. 2015. The media frames corpus: Annotations of frames across issues. In *Proc. of ACL*.

Eunsol Choi, Chenhao Tan, Lillian Lee, Cristian Danescu-Niculescu-Mizil, and Jennifer Spindel. 2012. Hedge detection as a lens on framing in the gmo debates: A position paper. In *Proc. of ACL Workshops*.

Dennis Chong and James N Druckman. 2007. Framing theory. *Annu. Rev. Polit. Sci.* 10:103–126.

Michael D Conover, Bruno Gonçalves, Jacob Ratkiewicz, Alessandro Flammini, and Filippo Menczer. 2011. Predicting the political alignment of twitter users. In *Proc. of PASSAT*.

Sarah Djemili, Julien Longhi, Claudia Marinica, Dimitris Kotzinos, and Georges-Elia Sarfati. 2014. What does twitter have to say about ideology? In *NLP 4 CMC*.

Javid Ebrahimi, Dejing Dou, and Daniel Lowd. 2016. Weakly supervised tweet stance classification by relational bootstrapping. In *Proc. of EMNLP*.

Jacob Eisenstein. 2013. What to do about bad language on the internet. In *Proc. of NAACL*.

Robert M Entman. 1993. Framing: Toward clarification of a fractured paradigm. *Journal of communication* 43(4):51–58.

Dean Fulgoni, Jordan Carpenter, Lyle Ungar, and Daniel Preotiuc-Pietro. 2016. An empirical exploration of moral foundations theory in partisan news sources. In *Proc. of LREC*.

Juri Ganitkevitch, Benjamin Van Durme, and Chris Callison-Burch. 2013. The paraphrase database. In *Proc. of NAACL-HLT*.

Sean Gerrish and David M Blei. 2012. How they vote: Issue-adjusted models of legislative behavior. In *Advances in Neural Information Processing Systems*. pages 2753–2761.

Stephan Greene and Philip Resnik. 2009. More than words: Syntactic packaging and implicit sentiment. In *Proc. of NAACL*.

Jacob Groshek and Ahmed Al-Rawi. 2013. Public sentiment and critical framing in social media content during the 2012 u.s. presidential campaign. *Social Science Computer Review* 31(5):563–576.

Summer Harlow and Thomas Johnson. 2011. The arab spring— overthrowing the protest paradigm? how the new york times, global voices and twitter covered the egyptian revolution. *International Journal of Communication* 5(0).

Kazi Saidul Hasan and Vincent Ng. 2014. Why are you taking this stance? identifying and classifying reasons in ideological debates. In *Proc. of EMNLP*.

Bert Huang, Stephen H. Bach, Eric Norris, Jay Pujara, and Lise Getoor. 2012. Social group modeling with probabilistic soft logic. In *NIPS Workshops*.

Iyyer, Enns, Boyd-Graber, and Resnik. 2014. Political ideology detection using recursive neural networks. In *Proc. of ACL*.

S. Mo Jang and P. Sol Hart. 2015. Polarized frames on "climate change" and "global warming" across countries and states: Evidence from twitter big data. *Global Environmental Change* 32:11–17.

Kristen Johnson and Dan Goldwasser. 2016. All i know about politics is what i read in twitter: Weakly supervised models for extracting politicians' stances from twitter. In *Proc. of COLING*.

Kristen Johnson, Di Jin, and Dan Goldwasser. 2017a. Leveraging behavioral and social information for weakly supervised collective classification of political discourse on twitter. In *Proc. of ACL*.

Kristen Johnson, Di Jin, and Dan Goldwasser. 2017b. Modeling of political discourse framing on twitter. In *Proc. of ICWSM*.

I-Ta Lee, Mahak Goindani, Chang Li, Di Jin, Kristen Johnson, Xiao Zhang, Maria Pacheco, and Dan Goldwasser. 2017. Purduenlp at semeval-2017 task 1: Predicting semantic textual similarity with paraphrase and event embeddings. In *Proc. of SemEval*.

Jiwei Li, Alan Ritter, Claire Cardie, and Eduard H Hovy. 2014a. Major life event extraction from twitter based on congratulations/condolences speech acts. In *Proc. of EMNLP*.

Jiwei Li, Alan Ritter, and Eduard H Hovy. 2014b. Weakly supervised user profile extraction from twitter. In *Proc. of ACL*.

Mejova, Srinivasan, and Boynton. 2013. Gop primary season on twitter: popular political sentiment in social media. In *WSDM*.

Sharon Meraz and Zizi Papacharissi. 2013. Networked gatekeeping and networked framing on #egypt. *The International Journal of Press/Politics* 18(2):138–166.

Viet-An Nguyen, Jordan Boyd-Graber, Philip Resnik, and Kristina Miler. 2015. Tea party in the house: A hierarchical ideal point topic model and its application to republican legislators in the 112th congress. In *Proc. of ACL*.

Brendan O'Connor, Ramnath Balasubramanyan, Bryan R Routledge, and Noah A Smith. 2010. From tweets to polls: Linking text sentiment to public opinion time series. In *Proc. of ICWSM*.

Ferran Pla and Lluís F Hurtado. 2014. Political tendency identification in twitter using sentiment analysis techniques. In *Proc. of COLING*.

Marta Recasens, Cristian Danescu-Niculescu-Mizil, and Dan Jurafsky. 2013. Linguistic models for analyzing and detecting biased language. In *Proc. of ACL*.

Alan Ritter, Colin Cherry, and Bill Dolan. 2010. Unsupervised modeling of twitter conversations. In *Proc. of NAACL*.

Sim, Acree, Gross, and Smith. 2013. Measuring ideological proportions in political speeches. In *Proc. of EMNLP*.

Swapna Somasundaran and Janyce Wiebe. 2009. Recognizing stances in online debates. In *Proc. of ACL*.

Swapna Somasundaran and Janyce Wiebe. 2010. Recognizing stances in ideological on-line debates. In *Proc. of NAACL Workshops*.

Dhanya Sridhar, James Foulds, Bert Huang, Lise Getoor, and Marilyn Walker. 2015. Joint models of disagreement and stance in online debate. In *Proc. of ACL*.

Chenhao Tan, Lillian Lee, and Bo Pang. 2014. The effect of wording on message propagation: Topic- and author-controlled natural experiments on twitter. In *Proc. of ACL*.

Oren Tsur, Dan Calacci, and David Lazer. 2015. A frame of mind: Using statistical models for detection of framing and agenda setting campaigns. In *Proc. of ACL*.

Andranik Tumasjan, Timm Oliver Sprenger, Philipp G Sandner, and Isabell M Welpe. 2010. Predicting elections with twitter: What 140 characters reveal about political sentiment. In *Proc. of ICWSM*.

Svitlana Volkova, Yoram Bachrach, Michael Armstrong, and Vijay Sharma. 2015. Inferring latent user properties from texts published in social media. In *Proc. of AAAI*.

Svitlana Volkova, Glen Coppersmith, and Benjamin Van Durme. 2014. Inferring user political preferences from streaming communications. In *Proc. of ACL*.

Marilyn A. Walker, Pranav Anand, Robert Abbott, and Ricky Grant. 2012. Stance classification using dialogic properties of persuasion. In *Proc. of NAACL*.

Robert West, Hristo S Paskov, Jure Leskovec, and Christopher Potts. 2014. Exploiting social network structure for person-to-person sentiment analysis. *TACL* .

Janyce Wiebe, Theresa Wilson, Rebecca Bruce, Matthew Bell, and Melanie Martin. 2004. Learning subjective language. *Computational linguistics* .

Tae Yano, Dani Yogatama, and Noah A Smith. 2013. A penny for your tweets: Campaign contributions and capitol hill microblogs. In *Proc. of ICWSM*.

Author Index

Association for Computational Linguistics
209 N. Eighth Street
Stroudsburg, Pennsylvania 18360

ISBN 978-1-5108-4579-4